Judaism: A Love Story

A Theological, Ethical, and Zionistic Perspective

אור OHR
תורה TORAH
סטון STONE

מגיד
MAGGID

Rabbi Shlomo Riskin

JUDAISM
A LOVE STORY

A Theological, Ethical, and Zionistic Perspective

Ohr Torah Stone
Maggid Books

Judaism: A Love Story
A Theological, Ethical, and Zionistic Perspective

First Edition, 2025

Maggid Books
An imprint of Koren Publishers Jerusalem Ltd.

POB 8531, New Milford, CT 06776-8531, USA
& POB 4044, Jerusalem 9104001, Israel
www.korenpub.com

Image credit, chap. 8: Menora, Germany 1931,
Photo 12 / Alamy Stock Photo

The publication of this book was made possible
through the generous support of *The Jewish Book Trust.*

ISBN 978-1-59264-696-8, *hardcover*

Printed and bound in Israel

Dedicated to my beloved Vicky,
To my wonderful wife, the love of my life,
My anchor, which gives me safe harbor!
For our very special family you take prime responsibility,
While you're also chief accountant and midnight barber.
You nurture the wounded birds, you are patient with the nerds,
Your *ḥesed* just continues on and on,
But of all your good deeds, the commitment which truly leads,
Are all the hours you devote to the *maḥsan.*
You're the one who did my packing, you always provide whatever is lacking,
Whatever is accomplished would not be without you!
Your judgment is unerring, you even serve me morning herring,
And your every word is 100 percent true!
Your food is a delight, your advice is always right,
And your priorities are always set straight.
You daven with real *kavanna,* you don't put off till *mañana,*
And you're my remarkable life's partner and soul-mate.
Please grow old along with me, I hope the best is yet to be,
But even if not, we must be grateful to God Above.
We've had sixty-one years of much joy and few tears,
Filled with *nachas,* great respect, and deep love.

With much respect and admiration for

Harav Shlomo Riskin

We are honored to be Talmidim of the Great Rav Riskin,
who has inspired us throughout our lives.
From understanding our deep relationship with Eretz Yisrael
to building a Judaism that reflects compassionate justice
and moral righteousness.

May you continue לעולם *to be a source of inspiration.*

Helene and Robbie Rothenberg

Contents

Introduction

This is a book about love.

No, it is not a conventional love story, a romantic novel that tells the fictional story of two lovers and the zigzag, on-again-off-again path of their romance. This is rather a cosmic love story between God and Israel, the eternal nature of that love, and the mutual commitment that it demands but does not always receive. It tells of the havoc, separation, and exile that such infidelity engenders, and expresses the bliss of forgiveness, rapprochement, and renewal when the faithfulness on both sides is vindicated, as is happening in our generation – our return after two millennia to our eternal homeland – even as we are aware that even today this love still has ups and downs. It also points toward our challenge in present-day Israel to turn the "beginning of the sprouting of redemption" into a universal historic redemption which will encompass the entire world with God's loving peace.

But do not be put off by the mystical and utopian sounds of these words. On the most basic level, this is a book about Jewish observance and the philosophy behind that observance. It is a book that follows the rhythm of the first primordial biblical week and the cycle of the seasons of the Jewish year, the festivals and the fast days which illuminate the

Hebrew calendar with rituals and observances – how they bring poetry and pageantry into everyday family life, how they infuse human existence with meaning and significance, and how they demonstrate God's love for us and foster familial love for all humanity.

But first we must attempt to understand the nature of the world into which we were born, and – to whatever extent possible – the nature of the God who created that world. The most ancient text that deals with these issues is the Bible, given by God to Moses close to four thousand years ago according to our tradition, a book which is still a bestseller, and the foundation of Judaism, Christianity, and to a certain extent Islam. We begin our study with the biblical account of the creation of the world and, in particular, the creation by God of the human being. I believe that in order to understand Judaism, to feel its pulse as one proceeds through its ceremonies and rituals, one needs to understand what happened on that primordial "day" of the creation of the first *Homo sapiens*.

Fascinatingly, we see in our biblical sources the centrality of love in the very formation of the human being, since the first human was created in the image and from the very essence of the Divine Creator. The Hebrew word for love is *ahava*, built upon a two-letter verb form, *hav*, which means "to give" (Gen. 30:1). Hence, when it records that God created the first human being by imparting or inspiriting within him/her a portion of God's own "image" or essence,[1] the Bible is portraying God's initial human creation as an act of divine love, as an act of divine giving.

The Bible further states (Gen. 2:7): "And the Loving God formed the human being dust from the earth and exhaled into the nostrils of that earthen-clay vessel the soul-breath of life and the human became a 'living being.'" Our mystical Sages (in the Zohar and the *Tanya*; see chapter 1) emphasize that one's exhalations come from the most internal aspect of our inner beings, and the most authoritative biblical translation, *Targum Onkelos*, takes the last two words of the verse to mean רוח ממללא, translating נפש חיה as "a communicating spirit." One of the most significant ways in which humans are qualitatively different from beasts is our ability to communicate words and ideas. When God gave

1. See Genesis 1:27 and Genesis 2:17. I develop the etymology and theology of this idea in greater depth in chapter 1.

a part of His essential being to us, a portion from the Divine on High (our souls), He demonstrated His love, and when God communicated His wisdom and will as to how we ought to live our lives best, He also demonstrated His love (see chapter 1). And so, the eminent philosopher/theologian Martin Buber teaches that wherever there is positive communication between people, God is to be found, especially within loving human relationships.[2]

Moreover, it follows that all of the mitzvot, commandments, we were given by God in the Torah (the divine biblical teaching) for us to perform, express the divine love relationship between God and His most exalted creations – the Jewish people – the forerunners and heralds of all of humanity. We are to serve as God's partners in teaching the world the best way to live lives of meaning and commitment, and thereby serve as God's partners in perfecting the world under God's kingship. It is the passion aroused by this love that infuses deep meaning and motivation as we perform the rituals, celebrate the festivals, and immerse ourselves in the depths of the Torah.

Throughout my rabbinic career of nearly sixty years, I have continually been inspired by the very passion of which I speak, and especially as I see it arise in students who decide to live their lives dedicated to teaching Torah, in Jewish adults who newly begin to discover their heritage, and in Jews-by-choice, who, not born into Judaism, may have initially chosen to convert in order to embrace a Jewish partner, but after having begun to study and experience our tradition, have come to lovingly embrace Judaism wholeheartedly. This book is dedicated to all of these three groups of people, with profound admiration for their ability to feel and transmit the fire of love that lies behind all Jewish observance.

However, at the same time, I must admit that I harbor a certain sadness. I am concerned that within the circles of observant Jewry of

2. You will note that this explanation would interpret DNA also as the Divine Natural Association uniting all of humanity, both men and women, by everyone's inherent "image of God – *tzelem Elokim.*" It must be understood that God is beyond gender; the Hebrew *Elohim* seems to be a masculine form and *Shekhina* is a feminine form, but adverbs like "him" and "her" are never to be taken literally when speaking of the Divine. Our kabbalistic sources attribute both masculine and feminine aspects to the Divine, who encompasses both aspects together.

JFBs (Jews from birth), the passion of which I speak is often missing. One of the greatest dangers, our Sages warn us, is that our performance of the commandments becomes one of rote. And since we often tend to take for granted that with which we grew up, and, given the many "Jewish responsibilities" that we are expected to assume, it becomes even more difficult to avoid the danger of "rote" observance which is a brand of Judaism-all-too-easy to cast off. I can only hope that this book will enable even the more observant-background Jews to see their traditions in a new light and experience a newfound passion for Torah study and mitzva experience. After all, if we do not feel passionate about Torah, we will rarely be able to transmit our heritage to the next generation! And we must remember that our most impelling command is to hand over our tradition of freedom and equality for every individual in a world of compassionate righteousness, moral justice, and universal love to the next generation, as we learn from the *Shema*: "You shall teach Torah diligently to your children," and from Passover, the very first festival of our peoplehood: "And you shall tell it to your children" (Haggada, Ex. 13:8). It is by loving the Torah lessons of love, compassion, and righteousness that we bring meaning and, hopefully, redemption to the world.

Indeed, our commitment to transmit Jewish values and to live Jewishly is especially important for the Jews living in Israel. Truly, living the Jewish life of loving and giving, celebrating our feasts and fasts, is very much in sync with the culture and calendar of the Jewish state. But we dare never forget that the purpose of our state is to be a beacon of light for all the nations of the world, spreading the light of freedom and equality for all, illuminating the world with God's rays of peace and love. The pathways leading to such an idyllic world lie in the words of our Torah teachings, in the Torah songs we sing as we conduct our symphony of love and dance, leading us to redemption.

But do not misunderstand my intent: Judaism does not preach the necessity of "Judaism for everyone." Our prophet Micah (4:2–5), after quoting the words of Isaiah (2:3–4) – that at the time of universal redemption, when "the Torah will come forth from Zion and the word of God from Jerusalem," when humankind "will beat their swords into plowshares and their spears into pruning hooks, nation will not lift up sword against nation and humans will not learn war anymore" – posits that "each nation will walk in the name of its god and we, Israel, will walk in the name of the Lord our God" in a world society of religio-ritual pluralism and ethical universalism (the Seven Commandments of the Children of Noah).[3]

I firmly believe that Judaism is a love story, a romance between ourselves and God, ourselves and Torah, ourselves and our forebears, ourselves and our future generations, ourselves and every other Jew, ourselves and every other human on the earth. And in all of these romantic partners resides the image of the Divine, the *tzelem Elokim.* To love God and to love Torah must lead to loving humanity, as I hope you will soon learn.

Like any human romance, this special romance, between person and God, between person and tradition, takes a lifetime of effort to develop. Each side must be open to enter into the romantic experience with the other, must be willing to trust the other, and at least begin to give of him/herself to the other. And likewise, every true and loving encounter between people will always include the presence of the Other, the Divine, and will be in the spirit of our sacred Torah tradition and its universal message of love to the world. It will always be (if I could be so bold as to suggest) a *ménage à trois*!

It takes time, study, and thought to develop the passion, to feel the spirit, to hear the music of this joint symphony of love. Our symphony must begin with a conversation between the individual (or individuals) and his/her "romantic partners" – Torah, forebears, other Jews, future generations, all human beings – together with God and our tradition, and with an initial experience of tasting Sabbath peace, joy, and song.

May this book inspire you to begin to develop both the love and the wisdom that are Judaism's two great pillars. May each of us be a partner in helping to bring about that time of the complete fulfillment

3. The suggestion we are making is that the prophet Micah maintains that even in messianic times, when every nation will accept the ethical laws of the Torah, many will still retain their own religious beliefs. Micah is amending Isaiah's messianic vision by permitting theological pluralism for the gentile nations as long as there is a universal acceptance of the ethics of the Torah. While our liturgy in the concluding paragraph of the *Aleinu* prayer clearly accepts Isaiah's position, Micah's openness to religious pluralism must be noted.

of God's promise to Abraham: "Through you (Israel) shall be blessed all the families of the earth" (Gen. 12:3).

Shlomo Riskin
Efrat, Erev Shavuot 5784

Acknowledgments

First and foremost, I thank the Almighty, who gave me the privilege of planting in His vineyard.

I must thank my rabbeim, chief among them Rav Joseph B. Soloveitchik, at whose feet I sat for seven years at Yeshiva University and who formed my most fundamental direction in talmudic learning, Jewish philosophy, and the primacy of halakha in Jewish life; Rav Soloveitchik was truly *Lamdan HaDor*. I owe a great deal to Rav Moshe Feinstein, *Posek HaDor,* who unstintingly gave me several hours of his precious time on Friday mornings for questions of *pesak* during my early years in the rabbinate at the new Lincoln Square Synagogue. And certainly, I owe much of my professional and existential calling to try to reach every Jew with love and without judgment to the Lubavitcher Rebbe, Rav Menachem Mendel Schneerson, *Manhig HaDor,* whose counsel I sought at every important juncture of my life.

Yehi zikhram barukh.

My gratitude and thanks to:

Rabbi Dr. Kenneth Brander, president and *rosh hayeshiva,* Ohr Torah Stone, and Yinon Achiman, director general of Ohr Torah Stone, both of whom provided the encouragement and support for this book. Rabbi Edward Abramson, initiator and editor of the first draft of this book, a beloved student and a true friend who contributed many important insights. Rabbi Shalom Berger, final editor and invaluable *ḥavruta* with whom I spent many enjoyable hours of learning, reviewing, and editing. I credit him with bringing this book to its final draft and without him this book would have never been published. David Katz, international director, for his dedication and support. Yehuda Shtauber, educational director of OTS, for his role in bringing my books to fruition. Sima Tuchman Freedman, director of communications, for her creative contributions. Rav Shuki Reich, my longstanding personal *ḥavruta* and friend. Micky Mirvis, my executive assistant whose total dedication, commitment, wise counsel, and efficiency have enabled my multifaceted work for almost four decades. With appreciation to Helene and Robbie Rothenberg, special friends and supporters for many years.

And of course, the final product would never have been produced without the guidance and shepherding of my beloved friend Matthew Miller of Koren Publishers Jerusalem, managing editor Caryn Meltz who edited the manuscript with expertise, Tomi Mager who typeset the book, Tani Bayer who designed the cover, and Nechama Unterman and Esther Shafier who proofread the text with sharp eyes.

Chapter 1

God's Love of Humanity: Giving Meaning to Life

A WORLD OF GODLY MEANING OR A WORLD OF HAPPENSTANCE?

Judaism is essentially a template for a meaningful life meant not only for the Jews; it is rather a universal religion meant for every inhabitant of the world. Therefore, our Bible opens with God's creation of the universe, with the central figure in that universe being not the Jew, but the human being. The nature of the human being will soon become a major focus of this study, but first I must ponder the initial question of this chapter: What kind of world is it into which we were born? Is it a product of a God-Creator, Einstein's "Higher Intelligence," as it were, which itself would suggest a divine purpose to the world and to life, or is it the result of a happenstance big bang, a cosmic accident which occurred with neither rhyme nor reason? I might suggest that these two antithetical possibilities are actually verbalized by two great literary classics: the first chapter of Genesis in the Bible and the play *Macbeth* by William Shakespeare. After suffering a personal tragedy, King Macbeth cries out (act 5, scene 5): "[World, Life] is a tale told by an idiot, full of sound and fury, signifying nothing." According to this view, there is no purpose, no direction, no vector to the life of an individual. Whatever happens, happens, and there is no higher design for any event, neither in the life of a person, nor of a nation, nor of the world. "Big bang" was, in truth, an accident: "In the beginning, there was happenstance."

Very different are the opening words of the biblical Genesis, "In the beginning, God created the heavens and the earth," a veritable "headline" which dramatically transforms the "tale told by an idiot" into a premeditated world created by a Higher Intelligence, a Master of the Universe; if, indeed, there is such a Master, it stands to reason that His creation would have purpose and significance.

I experienced these two alternative worldviews many years ago in – of all places – a high school science class; specifically, in a biology laboratory. The lab instructor – who never formally told us his name but "student tradition" had for years referred to him as "The Worm" (although never to his face) – had us viewing slides of snowflakes under a microscope, taking note that each and every snowflake was hexagonal and that each flake when struck by the rays of the sun acts as a prism to refract all the colors of the rainbow – red, orange, yellow, green, blue, indigo, violet. Each flake has a slightly different configuration of those colors and so each stands alone as a unique artistic masterpiece. As I examined each snowflake in turn, and requested slide after slide to check my observations, tears coursed down my cheeks, and I uttered again and again: "How great are Thy works, O God" (Ps. 104:24). The laboratory instructor looked at me with questioning surprise: "Riskin, what are you excited about? The 'accident' of the snowflake?" I then understood the sobriquet given by the students to their lab instructor. Like a worm, he was only able to look down into the dark earth, never capable of looking up at the glorious heavens of our magnificent universe.

And so, each of us has a choice – a real choice. We can choose the "tale told by an idiot" as our guideline for life, with all that it implies: a chaotic view of existence, with no internal logic, no ultimate responsibility, no divine design for a world absent of ultimate purpose and meaning. And if, indeed, there is no ultimate significance of anything, that which is generally characterized as Greek epicureanism is the best way to live one's life: Eat, drink, and be merry, for tomorrow we die.[1] After all, in truth the world is not filled only with exquisite snowflakes; it also produces sudden, destructive earthquakes and debilitating genetic mutations. Perhaps it is the latter which most aptly characterize our condition on earth.

Undoubtedly, however, from an existential human perspective, it is not the "earthquake," but rather the "snowflake," that would be our preferred metaphor for the world. If we elect to follow the "snowflake" approach to life, with its echo of "In the beginning, God created the heavens and the earth," our lives become filled with a sense of wonder, hopefully giving way to a feeling of meaningful direction, of clear responsibility for our actions, of the presence of a Director of that great orchestral piece called world, as "The old Master Painter from the faraway hills," a song from my childhood suggests.[2] And if, indeed, this is essentially a snowflake, and not an earthquake world, there may well be ultimate meaning and special function not only for humanity, the crown of God's creation, but even for each individual person during his/her sojourn through life. Hopefully, a study of the biblical view of the existential nature of the human being from the backdrop of a God-created

1. Although this phrase is usually assumed to be a quote from the philosopher Epicurus, it is not. A similar quote is actually found in Isaiah 22:13, wherein the prophet calls the people to repentance for their wrongdoings, lest they be killed by the enemy's army; But, instead, they decide to indulge in worldly pleasures, since they assume that they will soon die anyway. The idea is the same: Since we will eventually die, and nothing in the world really carries significance, then why not just enjoy the physical pleasures of the world with abandon? "And behold, there is joy and gladness in the slaying of cattle and slaughtering of sheep, in eating meat and drinking wine, eat and drink for tomorrow we die."
2. We are, of course, not using "snowflake" in its recent slang sense, referring to groups who think of themselves as special and delicate, to whom the usual exigencies of life do not apply. We are rather thinking of the snowflake as a metaphor for the wondrous divine Creation. Indeed, one of the names of the Divine utilized in the traditional texts of our Sages, as in the last blessing before the *Amida* in our morning prayers, is *Tzur Yisrael,* literally the "Rock of Israel." Our Sages teach us: "Do not read the word *Tzur*, which means rock or mainstay, but rather read it with a slight vocal change, *Tzayar Yisrael* – merely switching the *vav* for a *yod*, thereby changing the metaphor for God from an inanimate, unfeeling object (rock) to a sentient and sensitive Artist (Painter).

world will go a long way in directing us as to how to live a life of meaning – which is, after all, the most important quest facing each of us as we stand before what appears to be our one chance at life in this world.

THE HUMAN BEING: ON THE ONE HAND A COMPLEX ANIMAL

Therefore, let us now attempt to understand from the text of the Bible the essential nature of the human being created by God. After God has created light, the seas, the world's vegetation, and the animals, the Bible states (Gen. 1:26): "And God said, 'Let us make the human being in our image, after our likeness.'" This verse cries out for interpretation. Who is "us"? Who is "our"? After all, God's unity, His Oneness, His ultimate vision of a world of compassionate righteousness and humanity redeemed is the very basis of the Bible, of Judaism, of all monotheistic faiths. The question powerfully presents itself: To whom is God speaking here?

There are many attempts at an explanation, but I am drawn to the elucidation of the Ramban (Nahmanides), Rabbi Moses ben Nahman (1194–1270), who wrote one of the deepest and most psychologically attuned of the traditional commentaries on the Torah.

The Ramban, in his commentary on Genesis 1:26, is of the opinion that God is addressing the animals and beasts that He created earlier on this same sixth day, or sixth epoch, of creation. He is saying to the animal world, "Let us – you, the earth and the physical aspects of creation which will come from the earth (like the animals), and I (who am completely Spirit) – combine our beings to create the human being." God is, so to speak, suggesting a partnership between heaven and earth, godliness and bestiality, within the very creation of the human being. On the one hand, this being will be part animal, circumscribed by a limitation of years and power, requiring nutrition, sexual reproduction, elimination of waste material. The human being will be instinctual, a complex animal valuing the singular importance of strength, power of domination, and physical adaptability reflected by Darwin's "survival of the fittest," and by the dictator's arrogant declarations that "might makes right" and "to the victor belong the spoils."

And it is indeed, this physical, earthly perspective of the essence of the human being which has dominated every totalitarian regime, the most notable being the ancient tribe of Amalek – Israel's historic archenemy, who attacked the exhausted Israelites newly freed from Egyptian slavery, slowly wandering through the desert in search of a resting place. Amalek attacked from behind, first targeting the weakest stragglers, the women and the children, the elderly and the infirm. In a similar way, based upon the entitlement of the powerful to enslave the weak, there developed the civilization of the hegemony of the most powerful conquerors, from Sparta to Macedonia (Alexander the Great), to Rome, to Babylon, to Persia, to the Ottoman Empire, to the Christian Crusaders, to British colonialists, to Nazi Germany, to Stalinist communism, to Moslem jihadists. And it is no surprise that such a civilization of survival of the fittest and the most powerful would glorify warfare: The Roman Classical work *The Aeneid* by Virgil, opens with the words "*Arma virumque cano*," "Of armaments and virility do I sing." And, tragically, such a vision has resulted in the bloody history of human warfare, bringing our present day to the brink of global destruction, with nuclear capability spreading throughout the world.

THE HUMAN BEING: ON THE OTHER HAND, ENDOWED BY AND INVESTED WITH THE IMAGE OF GOD

While the Bible recognizes the physical, even animalistic, aspect of humans, it goes on to emphasize the true essence of the human being as emanating from the Divine: "And the Lord created the human being in His image, in the image of the Lord created He him, male and female created He them" (Gen. 1:27). Who is this God in whose image the human being is created? Moses asks this question of God in the book of Exodus (33:13): "Inform me please of Your characteristics."

And, indeed, in the very next chapter (Ex. 34:6–7) God reveals His thirteen characteristics, or names, with the first name, YHVH or Yahweh, defined as "compassionate" or "unconditional love."[3] Even

3. Names in the Bible reflect characteristics, as is also true of the names of God revealed to Moses, as stated above. Referring to the first of God's revealed names,

linguistically in Hebrew, there is a striking similarity between God's Ineffable Name, spelled with the letters *yod heh vav heh,* and the word for love, *AHaVaH,* spelled *alef heh vet heh.* (Although the "v"-sound in both of these words is produced by different Hebrew letters – in God's name the *vav* and in *ahava* the *vet* – the two letters sometimes interchange, as in the case of *taava* – meaning "lust," spelled with a *vav,* and *te'avon* – meaning "appetite" [related meaning], with a *vet.*) This similarity between the Ineffable Name of God and the Hebrew word for love is a stirring affirmation that the God of the Bible is first and foremost a God of love, with all thirteen attributes expressing differing aspects of God's love. Our Sages continue to comment (Rashi on Exodus 34:6) that the reason for the repetition of the first of the names of God is to teach that God loves us unconditionally, both before we sin and even after we sin! Here we see the unconditional character of the divine love.

And so, the Ramban continues to explain, this human being will be more than part of the animal world; this being will also be part God. That is what God is saying to the beasts: This new creature will be part you, and part Me; existentially, he will contain two aspects: a bestial human, and a celestial human, and, most importantly, the celestial human will be able to rise above the bestial human, and overpower him. A bestial being – an animal – only wants to take, to receive. He is instinctual, with a need for food, and so he preys on the weaker beings, which he kills for food. Love, which, as we have seen, is a distinctly godly characteristic, is based upon the root verb which means "giving": *ahava,* the Hebrew noun "love," builds upon the root verb *hav* which means "to give."[4]

---

in Hebrew *YHVH* (*YeHoVaH*), Rashi, traditionally the primary commentator on the Torah, states that this name denotes the characteristic of compassionate love (Rashi on Exodus 34:7), which in Hebrew is *raḥamim* and akin to the unconditional and unselfish love which a mother has for the fetus in her womb, which in Hebrew is *reḥem.* Hence, the meaning of the Ineffable Name of God is definitionally "love," even if it may not be so philologically.

4. *Hav* is the imperative form of the Hebrew root *yod-heh-vav,* a less common synonym for the root *nun-tav-nun,* "to give." (The authoritative Hebrew dictionary *HaMilon HeḤadash* [The New Dictionary] by Avraham Even-Shoshan [Jerusalem: Kiryat Sefer Publishing, 1986], entry "*Hav.*") Among the many examples of this usage in the Bible is Genesis 30:1, Rachel's emotional words to her husband Jacob, "Give

But let me go even one step further. The very picture of God's creation of the first human being expresses God's deep love, and it is this divine love that He "implants" in every human being: "Then the Lord God formed the human from the dust of the earth, 'inspirited' into his nostrils the soul-breath of life; and the human became an ensouled life force" (Gen. 2:7). God took dust, representing frail and earthbound matter, and then exhaled the soul-breath of (eternal) life into the nostrils of the as-yet-not-alive earthen-clay vessel, which may have originally emerged from the dust but which was immediately gifted with the soul-breath of life.[5] This act of God breathing His divine "soul-breath" into the human earth physicality has vast implications for the human being's fundamental quality, identity, and destiny, as we shall see.

It is fascinating that the master artist and sculptor Michelangelo, in his iconic painting on the ceiling of the Sistine Chapel in Rome, depicted, in the section "Creation of Adam," the figure of God (as a white-bearded elderly human) reaching out with his finger to touch the finger of Adam, apparently in order to impart life to Adam. Although scholars insist that Michelangelo read and reread the Bible for his inspiration, and in almost every instance his biblical paintings remain completely faithful to the biblical text, in this case his painting is completely different from the text.

I believe I understand Michelangelo; it is well-nigh impossible to reproduce the act of exhaling with paint and brush on canvas. But I might suggest that since Michelangelo was a sculptor and artist, and he therefore experienced the essence of his creativity as residing in his

(*hava*, form of *hav*) me children, or else I die." The same root – *yod-heh-vet* – is the commonly used word for "give" in the cognate Aramaic language (the authoritative Aramaic dictionary *A Dictionary of the Targumim, the Talmud Babli and Yerushalmi, and the Midrashic Literature* by Marcus Jastrow, entry "*Yehav.*")

5. Take note that, in Hebrew, this verse uses a "new" word, *neshama*, which we have translated as "the soul-breath of life"; until now the biblical word for life force was *nefesh* and is used biblically for animal life. The Hebrew *nishmat ḥayim* contains the word derived from *neshama*, exclusively used for humans, generally translated as "soul," but very closely related to *neshima*, the word for "breath," and so we have translated it as "soul-breath."

fingers, he might naturally transfer the essence of God's creativity to His divine fingers as well.

The text of the biblical imagery however is very different, and I believe much more powerful and meaningful than the interpretation of Michelangelo. The Zohar, the mystical commentary on the Bible, precisely and faithfully transcribed that it was God who exhaled, as it were, into the nostrils of the "clay dummy" formed by the dust of the earth (representing the animal portion of the human being).[6] In the very first chapter of the *Tanya*, written by Rabbi Shneur Zalman of Liadi (the main work of Chabad philosophy, first published in 1797), he adds that "whoever exhales, exhales from within his most essential and innermost being." It follows, therefore, that there is an "actual portion of the Godhead from Above" within every human being, that God gives to every human a part of His own Self, as it were. And the *Tanya* adds the Hebrew word *mamash* – literally, meaning that the Godly may even enter the very physical and substantive part of the human, if the human so develops it. This is one of the most important foundational principles of Judaism, declaring that within every human being there resides an aspect of the divine essence, as it were, a portion of eternity and of divine spirituality.

There is no idea in Judaism more radical and consequential than this one. The classical biblical commentator Rashi, Rav Shlomo Yitzhaki of Worms (1040–1105), asks in his opening interpretation of the first biblical verse, "In the beginning God created the heavens and the earth": "Why did the Bible begin here with the world's creation, rather than with the first commandment given to Israel: 'Let the renewal of the moon this month of Nisan be for you as the festival of Rosh Ḥodesh, the New Moon' when you were freed from Egyptian slavery (see Exodus 12:2)?" After all, ponders Rashi, is the Bible not primarily a book of commandments even more than a book of theology or of history? Begin it with the first commandment in the book of Exodus!

My revered teacher and mentor, Rabbi Joseph B. Soloveitchik, answers Rashi's query by explaining that, within the first verse of the Bible, there can also be found the first *commandment* of the Torah. Since

6. *Midrash HaNe'elam, Zohar Ḥadash* 17c.

we are created in the essence of the Divine, so are we commanded to imitate Him as much as possible (*Imitatio Dei*): we must walk in His ways (Deut. 28:9) and attempt to replicate His deeds. And so we must learn from the first biblical verse that, just as God created a world, so must we, to the best of our ability, "create worlds" within the spheres of our influence. And perhaps we may even go a step further. If indeed we are blessed with the image of God, *tzelem Elokim*, and God created an imperfect world, must we not attempt to perfect that world, to recreate that world, in the Kingship of the Divine, to walk in God's ways by "partnering" with Him to perfect the imperfect world, to complete the incomplete world which He gave us? Our Bible deals with this as well!

THE HUMAN BEING IS TO BE GOD'S PARTNER IN ACTIVATING AND PERFECTING THE WORLD

Chapter 1 of the book of Genesis tells the story of Creation with God at the center, since He is the Creator of the world. Chapter 2 retells the story of Creation, but this time, it is the human being who is at the center of the universe; without that human being, nothing can happen.

Yes, God created a world, but one which requires human beings to activate His world: "No plant of the field was yet in the earth, and no herb of the field had yet grown, for God had not caused it to rain upon the earth, and there was not yet a human to develop the earth" (Gen. 2:5).

And so, the Bible continues, "And the Lord God took the human being and placed him in the Garden of Eden (the primordial world) 'to work it and to guard it'" – or, perhaps better translated as "to develop it and to take responsibility for it" (Gen. 2:15).[7] The world that God created was potentially perfectible, completable. But without human

7. The Hebrew is לעבדה ולשמרה. The Hebrew root *ayin-bet-dalet*, in its basic form, means to work. But the same root, in a slightly different form (*pi'el*) carries the sense of "to develop, to adapt, to re-work." The root *shin-mem-resh*, in its basic form, means to "watch" or to "guard." But it can also take on the meaning of "to take responsibility for," as in the well-known words of Cain, when asked by God about Cain's brother Abel whom he murdered. Usually translated as "Am I my brother's keeper?" (Gen. 4:9), the translation truer to the context of the verse would be "Am I responsible for my brother?"

input, it remained, at best, a work in progress, and even perhaps a negative work in progress, because from the very beginning it was a world of earthquakes alongside the snowflakes. The human being has it within his hands to turn the potential Garden of Eden into a Paradise of love and future creativity, or alternatively (God forbid) into a diabolical hell-hole of jealous hatred and wanton destruction. And indeed, the Bible itself goes on to tell us about how Adam and Eve began the process for the future continuity of life with the birth of Cain and Abel, but how the sibling rivalry between the brothers resulted in the murder of Abel and the punishment of Cain (see Genesis 4:1–15).

BUT WHY DID GOD CREATE AN IMPERFECT WORLD WITH EVIL?

The prophet Isaiah even goes so far as to seemingly attribute evil and imperfection to God Himself: "[I] form light and create darkness, make peace and create evil; I am God who does all of this" (Is. 45:7). What an amazing admission! Is God actually taking responsibility for the existence of evil in the world?!

Isaiah seems to be stating clearly what we have so far been reluctant to state unequivocally: Evil exists in the world because God created an imperfect world. And the world is imperfect because human beings, whom God created with the gift of freedom of choice, and who may well choose to act perversely, will frequently do wrong. Hence, God set the stage for humans in an imperfect world because He expects them to become His partners in perfecting themselves as well as that world. I would say that this is an epic partnership, between God and the pinnacle of His creation, the human being, who stands at the very center of the biblical view of existence. The world leaves the possibility for evil open-ended, awaiting the human being either to complete, or perfect, God's incomplete and imperfect world, or – God forbid – to destroy the beautiful but imperfect world He created.

But where do we find in the Bible that God created humans in a world with the kind of free choice which can set the stage not only for love and creativity, but also for death and destruction? And why would a God of love create a human being who could choose to act against the will of a God of love? And how can the human being even be expected to perfect God's world? Would this not be an arrogant act of hubris on the part of the human?

In order to answer those questions, we must first attempt to understand the most majestic verse in the entire Bible, the verse we have quoted previously: "And God created the human being in His image, in the image of God did He create him, male and female did He create them" (Gen. 1:27). It is crucial to understand how sharply this verse differentiated Judaism from the pagan religions that pervaded the ancient world. The Bible tells us that the human being was created in the image of God. The pagan world – the world of Mount Olympus of the Greeks – is the very opposite, a world in which the Greeks created their gods in the bestial image of humans, gods moved by the quest for physical power and domination, as in Zeus, the god of Power. These gods warred with each other, dominated and subjugated the weaker gods, and displayed greed, jealousy, and pettiness, a reflection of the basest of human frailties. The humans, within the Greek scheme of things, had no freedom of action whatsoever; everything on earth was determined by the gods on Mount Olympus, or by the Fates, the *Moerae.* And all the people could do was to propitiate – or bribe – them, by sacrificing even their children to those bestial gods. The pagan world truly lived in a happenstance world of earthquakes in which humans were virtually powerless.

Judaism turned that view on its head, dramatically reversing it with this one verse: "God created the human being in His image," thereby essentially endowing every mortal human being with a transcendent spark of the Eternal, with God's unconditional love, and thereby the divine ability to give, to help, to strive, to perfect – first himself, and then, naturally, the world around him.

But just as God is free, so is the human being free, free even to empower the bestial within himself, free to do what God would not want him to do. As Rav Ovadia Sforno (Ovadia ben Jacob Sforno, Italy 1475–1550) comments on the word *kidmutenu* ("like our image"; Gen. 1:26): "The choice of God, blessed be He, is always toward the good" (because Goodness is the very definitional essence of "God"ness), which is not at all the case with human choice which can go either way – celestial or bestial! And so, humans have even more free choice than God, who will always be consummate goodness. But is it not still difficult to contemplate why God would create such humans with the power to choose a path of destructive, horrific evil?

Indeed, Rav Chaim Vital (1542–1620), the leading student of Rabbi Isaac Luria, considered to be the father of Jewish mysticism, provides the answer, but first, in his masterful work *Etz Ḥayim,*[8] asks an earlier question: Why did God initially create human beings at all? Is not God "All in All" in Himself, as it were? Rav Chaim Vital answers clearly and to the point: God is love, and since love is expressed by giving, one cannot give in a vacuum; one must give to "other," those who are different from and other than oneself! God "had" to create *other* beings for whom to do good deeds, so that God could express His love by doing good things for *another* – *kedei leheitiv libruav.* And so, God created human beings in order to have a world peopled with others upon whom God could bestow His love and to whom He could express His loving goodness, His "givingness." Thus, the world must be peopled with others who would be free even to defy God, who were not mere puppet-extensions of God, who were "others," and might thereby do what God wouldn't want them to do, and God must love them and even empower them![9]

And therein lies the answer to our question: Human beings *must* have complete freedom of choice, even to do that which God would not want them to do. Only then would they be other than God and be able to receive God's loving goodness. And what we also learn from this is that, since loving means giving, the greatest gift of all to "other" is that of freedom, of independence, the freedom to be him/herself. If a spouse only loves his/her partner whom he/she can control; if a parent only loves the child whom he/she can control, that is not real love. It is only love of self, of beings who are extensions of self – and that is not love of "other"! It is only extended self-love! Therefore, the loving God "had to" create independent human beings with free choice so that He would

8. *Shaar HaKelalim* 1.
9. In a similar vein, Rav Moshe Chaim Luzzato (1707–1746) concurs in his work *Daat Tevunot* (*siman* 18) that God is the essence of good, and that evidence of His goodness is that He *does* good, and, in order that there be those who would be the recipients of His doing good, He created human beings, other than Himself, who would even have the power to deny God and goodness.

have objects upon whom to bestow His love, objects who were actually subjects in themselves, *other* individuals whom He could truly love, because they were not controlled by Him, because they were not merely extensions of God, as it were. And so we must likewise leave room for others, just as God left room for us, believing that the Divine within us will eventually empower us to overcome the bestial, enthrone the celestial, and perfect ourselves and our world in the image of the God of love. And God's prophets have informed us within His Bible that the Jews will eventually bring blessing to all the families of the earth, because the celestial within humanity will ultimately triumph (Gen. 12:3; Is. 2).

From this perspective, we may understand how it is that the human being serves as God's partner: It is because God invited him to be His partner, and thereby gave purpose to the life of each and every human being, gave him/her a challenge and ideal that he/she must help bring to pass. As we have seen from the Bible (Gen. 2:15): "And God placed the (first) human in the Garden of Eden (the primordial world) to develop (perfect) it and to take responsibility for it." For, you see, God created an imperfect (incomplete) world, leaving it up to those whom He created in His own image to perfect and complete. God created a world with earthquakes, not only snowflakes; with potential for destruction, but, most importantly, for redemption as well! And our prophets have foretold that it is redemption which is human destiny!

IMPERFECT HUMANS CAN PERFECT GOD'S WORLD BY LOVING

And how are humans to go about perfecting the world? By doing for others what the God of Creation did for us, that is, for Adam, the first human: by loving "other," by giving to "other," by helping and even sometimes rebuking and recreating "other" – and by so doing we are strengthening the celestial human within ourselves and thereby recreating ourselves as well!

And this analogy may be taken even one step further.

As we have stated, in Hebrew the word for "love" is *ahava*. The root of *ahava* is *hav*, to give. Because the Hebrew language is holy to the Jewish people, Hebrew etymology reflects Jewish ideals and Jewish philosophy. Thus, when we draw from its Hebrew derivation, love is an act of giving: *hav, ahava.* God gave of Himself in creating the first human being, "in the image of the Divine," inspirited by God with a portion of the Divine from Above!

This idea is exemplified and eternalized in the sexual love between a man and a woman: each *gives* of him/herself to the other, the man giving the woman his virility, his future, his seed, and the woman giving the man her body, her womb, a vital aspect of her existential being. And in this act of sexual love lies the potential for the creation of a new life-soul, a DNA, a Divine Natural Association, a combination of both parents, a child born in their image, as well as in the image of the Divine!

Hence, on the godly plane, it becomes extremely significant that God's act of creating the first human was when He gave of His own essence, the soul-breath of His eternity exhaled into the human – "Whoever exhales, exhales from within his most essential and innermost being" (*Tanya*, ibid.). In doing so, He performed a deep act of love. And in the sexual act resulting in the creation of new life, every man and woman relives most dramatically the divine creation of the first human being, when God, too, gave part of Himself (as it were) to produce new life, to create humanity. In His creation of man and woman, God expressed His eternal love for humanity, and nothing can be more empowering than the knowledge that God loves us, and is also within us. And God "inspired" within the first human man-woman a portion of His divine love and even a portion of His eternality: in the human ability to bear children and grandchildren, to come together as a family with continuity from generation to generation passing on the genetic DNA, each individual lives eternally![10] Indeed, God's gift to humans is life and love, a meaningful life of partnership with God in humanity's glorious march toward world perfection at the end of days.

10. Take note of the fourth blessing recited for a marrying a couple under the marriage canopy: "The source of blessings are You, Lord of Love our God, King of the universe, who formed humanity in His image, in the image of His likeness, and He fashioned for humanity from His very self a building for eternity. Blessed are You, Lord of Love, Creator of humanity."

And so, when we love other, when we reach out to other, when we help other and hopefully help other to help himself, we are truly loving other, we are recreating other, we are perfecting other, we are doing for other what God did for Adam and Eve. And when we truly walk in God's paths, we then love other as we love ourselves, because other is also "ourselves," because we are all siblings, all of us on earth sharing the same DNA (Divine Natural Association) since we are all children of our One Parent in Heaven and we are all responsible for each other, our sibling's keeper. It is only by universal sibling love that the world will be perfected, and humanity will be redeemed.

This is the ongoing challenge for every human being: to rise beyond the bestial to reach higher to the celestial, by loving others. All of Judaism – its ideas, its commandments, its customs – are built around this concept. The Jewish people were chosen by God to "model" that challenge, and to rise to meet it.

Understanding this view of the creation of the human being, we now also understand the ramifications of the existential choice of which we have spoken. It is still the choice between seeing the world as "snowflake" or "earthquake" – between a world of meaning or a world of happenstance. But another crucial ingredient has been added: Because of the dual nature of either bestial or celestial human being which every individual must choose for him/herself, the choice of the "snowflake" becomes more meaningful and more crucial, and more possible. From a biblical perspective, the very imperfection of the world is itself God's greatest gift, because He empowers us to perfect it, because He believes that we are capable of perfecting it.

As Victor Frankl, the founder of logotherapy, demonstrates (in his masterful work *Man's Search for Meaning),* it is neither the search for pleasure nor for power which is the most basic motivation impelling human activity, but it is rather the search for meaning, significance. Hence, God created an imperfect world to give humans the task of perfecting it, each of us in whatever way we can leave the world a little better because we were living in it; perhaps by a welcoming smile or gracious hospitality by making the stranger feel wanted and loved, or perhaps, within the familial context, the loving and nurturing of our children or the respect we accord our aged parents. On a larger canvas, it could be by making great scientific discoveries, by healing the sick, by teaching Torah or by influencing for world peace.

Hence, we see that the earthquakes are also part of the divine plan, that the very imperfection of the world is the greatest gift God could give to humans: a much-needed purpose for their lives, a significance for their being, a partnership with God. And so, we find chaos and darkness within the very creation of the world so that we may make order, so that we may bring the light.

Every human being potentially has the ability to take the imperfections of the world – the "earthquakes" – and use the power of the godliness within her or him to try to perfect some aspect of that world. And, most importantly, at the same time, the Bible is telling us that God believes the human being capable of perfecting His imperfect world, capable of being His partner on earth. After all, the human being, created in God's image, is only a little lower than God Himself. "He is only a little lower than God, and You have crowned him with glory and majesty" (Ps. 8:6). This idea provides a new meaning to what Rabbi Akiva declares: that the greatest biblical commandment is "You shall love your fellow human being like you love yourself, I am the Lord of Love" (Lev. 19:18). If the essence of God indeed is love, and the essence of love is giving to others, then it follows that every human being created in the image of God must try in some way to help other human beings. This will automatically create a more perfect world in which every human being loves and gives to others.

This is the significance of the *Aleinu* prayer which concludes each of our statutory prayers daily, as well as on the Sabbath and festivals: the messianic goal, when everyone will attempt to "perfect the world in the Kingship of the Divine," when everyone will "accept the supremacy of Your Kingship… on that day the Lord of Love (YHVH) will be King over all the earth; on that day the Lord of Love will be One and His name shall be One" (Zech. 14:9).

LOVE BRINGS REDEMPTION AND PERFECTION

The famous hasidic master Reb Zusha (1718–1800) was extremely spiritual and superbly sensitive to the depth of relationships between human beings and between human beings and God. Reb Zusha once was traveling in the midst of a snowstorm and needed to seek refuge in an inn. He was forced by the storm to stay overnight. His room was freezing, and so he sat on a chair in the heated lobby, dozing on and off, within hearing distance of the bar. Two drunken peasants sat at the bar, partaking of drink after drink: "Ivan, I love you," slurred Boris. Ivan answered, deep in his cups, "You don't love me, Boris." Boris: "I'm telling you I love you." Ivan: "You don't love me." Boris: "Damn you, Ivan, I'm telling you that I love you. How can I prove to you that I love you?" Ivan: "If you really love me, then tell me what hurts me so that you can help me feel better."

Reb Zusha often remarked that it had been worthwhile to stay in those unpleasant surroundings for the night, just to have learned the lesson of love. That real love is a mutual giving – giving to other and trying to bring healing to other, redemption to other, and, in doing so, one brings healing and redemption to oneself as well.

In a word, therefore, just as the human being is created by an act of God's love/giving, the single most important act of the human being is to give love. That is the essence of the Jewish ideal and one's purpose in life.

The great Lubavitcher (Chabad) Rebbe (Rabbi Menachem Mendel Schneerson, 1902–1994) had a long-standing custom of standing for many hours, sometimes even in inclement weather, and distributing United States dollar bills to the huge throngs who came to seek his counsel and his blessing. In one of the private visits with him (*yeḥidut*) that I was privileged to have, I asked him for the basis of this strength-wearying practice. (The "word" was that the Rebbe wanted to make the point that if the American government thought it important to inscribe the phrase "In God We Trust" on each US dollar, how much more so should we, the Jewish people, with such a long history of fealty to the Divine, internalize the message of trusting in the Almighty.) On this occasion however, the Rebbe asked me what I thought the reason might be.

I haltingly suggested that, since the image in the minds of so many is that Rebbes *take* a *pidyon* (a sum of money given by the disciple for the blessing he is receiving from the Rebbe) – perhaps the Chabad Rebbe wished to demonstrate that a Jewish spiritual leader should be giving, not taking. The Rebbe responded to my suggestion with a bright smile, the warmth of which I can still feel today. He then quoted the well-known verse "You shall love your neighbor as yourself" (Lev. 19:18), translating the Hebrew to mean that you must love your friend because he is like you; just as you naturally "give" to yourself, so must you give to others. "To love," he said, "is to give. I am trying to teach by example; if I give a dollar to someone, hopefully the recipient will likewise give to someone else, and if everyone gives to everyone, then the Messiah of Redemption will come to the world." The world will be perfected and redeemed through humanity's love of each other and giving to each other.

Of course, the truest giving is the giving of oneself, one's time, one's effort, one's advice, one's comfort, one's spiritual faith, and one's knowledge. Judaism teaches that the way to perfect the world is for each person to give within the context in which she or he lives, beginning with family, spouse, and children, then friends, then neighbors, and then as much of the world that we can reach. And just like the omnipotent Creator of the universe limited His own power by leaving room for others and empowering others to choose freely (the kabbalistic concept of *tzimtzum*), so must we be willing to limit ourselves in order to help those in need. And if we look deeply into our souls, we see that our deepest joy and satisfaction comes when we help another human being who is in need, especially if we help him to help himself.

JUDAISM'S MISSION TO THE WORLD

So, in both our relationships with other people, and our relationship with God, *giving* is the key. As we now launch into the "meat" of this book, I want to expand that notion of giving. I believe with all my heart that the very essence of Judaism is to give to the world. To be sure, Judaism has its particularistic aspects. To an extent, we are a nation and a people separate and distinct from the rest of the world because of our specific communal and dietary needs and our unique calendar of Sabbath rest and national festivities. But, somewhat paradoxically, our distinctiveness and separateness are for the sake of our expressing a unique mission to all the families of the earth!

What precisely is that mission? It is clearly delineated in two sets of verses at the very dawn of our history. In Genesis 12:2–3, God promises Abraham, "I will make of you a great nation, I will bless you and make your name great...and through you shall there be a blessing to all of the families of the earth." God's promise is essentially saying that He is making of Abraham a great nation *in order that others – the whole world – can be blessed.* With amazing brevity of expression, the Torah is saying here that the whole purpose of Jewish particularism is, in fact, universalism! And so it must be, because in truth we are all living in a global village, and thereby existentially linked to each other; we do not live in isolation! And we can hardly live in peace if the rest of the world is worrying.

But what is the substance of the blessing we are to bring to the world? Six chapters later in the book of Genesis God explains (Gen. 18:18–19): "Abraham shall surely become a great and mighty nation, and all the nations of the earth shall be blessed through him. Since I have loved him, because he is commanding his children and his household after him, to take responsibility for God's pathways, to do acts of compassionate righteousness and moral justice..."

This is the very essence of Judaism. For the world to move toward perfection, there needs to be a blueprint for living based upon love, compassion, and righteousness. The mission of the Jewish people is to take that blueprint – the way of life that is expressed in this book – internalize it and at least impart its ethical teachings and values to all the families of the earth.

But can we really teach the world? That is a very large task. I believe we can, because I believe that God has given human beings one supreme power – the power to communicate with each other. That power was invested in the human being at that being's very inception – on the biblical sixth day, or sixth epoch, of the creation of the world. God stated for all future generations to hear (Gen. 2:7): "And the Loving Lord-God formed the human from the dust of the earth, inspirited into his nostril the soul-breath of life; and the human being became an ensouled life force," which – as we noted above – was explained by the authoritative *Targum Onkelos* to mean "a communicating spirit." This ability to communicate empowers us to give to others our most profound thoughts, our deepest feelings; it is through verbal expression that we share with others our emotions of love, our teachings of wisdom; and it was through verbal expression of God's Torah teaching that God shared with Moses and Israel the divine will as to how we could best live our lives, how to perfect and redeem our world into a peaceful and productive Garden of Eden. At Sinai, for example, God communicated with all of Israel with sounds; it was only Moses who had developed his intellectual/spiritual capacities to such an extent that the Divine was able to share with him His divine wisdom, which Moses then interpreted for Israel in our Torah.[11] And so our prophets command us to be a light to all nations, the loving Lord's witnesses to the world.

And, indeed, we certainly have succeeded in imparting to a large portion of humanity the biblical Ten Commandments, teaching freedom and ethical conduct for all, and our prophetic goal of a world in which "nation shall not lift up sword against nation, and humankind will not learn war anymore" (Isaiah 2, enshrined on the Dag Hammarskjold Plaza of the United Nations building in Manhattan, New York). Unfortunately, at the time of this writing, the prophetic words inscribed thereon is only lip service, not yet meaningfully put into practice by the actions of that organization of nations. But lip service is always only a first step waiting and demanding to be activated – and it is a most crucial first step without which nothing can follow. And that is precisely why our Bible – and indeed our Jewish lifestyle – is filled with commandments, prescriptions as to what we ought to do in order to live a meaningful life; the deepest feelings of love and the wisest teachings of scholars will only be significant if they are expressed in our daily actions and relationships.

As we now prepare to study the major ideas, commandments, and customs of Judaism, we must keep in mind that everything about Judaism that we will study in the coming chapters – prayer, the dietary laws, the festivals, Jewish life-cycle observances, the centrality of the Land of Israel – all have their basis in God as a Being of love, a non-controlling love that leaves us freedom of choice. It is not a system of "all or nothing." It leaves room for individual development in stages, and is understanding of individual backsliding, especially in the commandments between the human being and God. This is a function of the divine love

11. Maimonides, *Guide for the Perplexed*, II:33; Berakhot 45a. See also *Torah Lights, Shemot, Yitro* (Maggid Books, 2005).

with which God created us, and informs the Torah he lovingly taught us. And since a portion of God-on-High is existentially within each of us, if we truly will that "portion" to gain ascent, this is our guarantee that we will eventually choose a life of love and peace. Because of the centrality of love within it, Judaism is truly a romance, a romance that can give our lives meaning, significance, and faith in a glorious future. As we study the various aspects of Jewish life and Jewish practice, I pray that we sense Judaism's romantic passion, and become inspired by the redeeming power of its love.

Chapter 2

The Complex Romance of the Prayer Experience

THE ROMANCE OF PRAYER: OUR COVENANTAL LOVE RELATIONSHIP WITH GOD

If there is a particular aspect in Judaism in which the "romance" between the Jewish people and God is played out, prayer is that aspect. Take note that we called prayer an expression of the romance between the *Jewish people* and God. Generally speaking, for example with regard to Christianity, prayer is a very personal expression of an individual, his/her needs and his/her personal relationship with the Divine. For us, however, prayer is first of all a communal experience, a stance in which the individual Jew merges with the historic community of Israel in his/her reach toward a level of intimacy with a loving God, his/her establishing a level of communication with that God, and in his/her approach to that God with gratitude for life, and for the commandments He has given us through which our lives will become more meaningful and worthwhile.

In Jewish prayer, you see, we begin to approach God with special gratitude to Him for having chosen the Jewish nation as His most beloved people. At this point it becomes necessary to add a few words of explanation, especially with regard to the idea found in this book describing Judaism as a universal religion.

The Jewish nation is a nation commanded by God to be a kingdom of priests and a holy nation (Ex. 19:6). And God even explains in the beginning of Genesis, "Abraham will surely become a great nation, since I have loved and chosen Abraham…" (Gen. 18:18–19) – note that the Hebrew word *yeda* can mean "to know" or "to love," even in the sense of a loving physical union, as in "And Adam 'knew' Eve his wife, and she conceived and bore Cain" (Gen. 4:1).[1]

This definition of Israel[2] as God's chosen people may seem a bit jarring after we have explained Judaism as a universal religion, as the Bible initially has God introducing Abraham, the first Jew and the first teacher of ethical monotheism, with the words, "I shall make you a great nation… and through you shall be blessed all the families of the earth" (Gen. 12:2–3). But please remember that William Norman Ewer (1885–1977), a British journalist, once remarked: How odd of God/To choose the Jews. (The remark went viral in the anti-Semitic atmosphere of mid-twentieth-century Great Britain.) But, the continuation of the biblical verse (Gen. 18:19) we have just quoted has, in effect, given the most proper rejoinder to Ewer's nasty remark, as God explains the reason for His choice: "I have loved and chosen him (Abraham) *because* he is teaching his children and his household (of non-Abrahamic descent) to take responsibility for the pathways of the God of Love, to do acts of compassionate righteousness and moral justice (in the world)." *God chose Abraham because Abraham chose to teach God's ways universally.* Hence, the truest response to the anti-Semitic statement "How odd of God to choose the Jews" is the pithy comeback to Ewer's barb: "It was not at all odd because the Jews first chose God." In biblical terms,

1. Later on in the Bible (see, for example, Deut. 7:6), God often speaks of the chosenness of Israel, the sanctity of Israel, and the unique treasure that is Israel, within the context of God's love for Israel because of Israel's fidelity to their unique covenantal love relationship, as will be explained further on.
2. In this chapter, and elsewhere in this book, we use "Israel" as a synonym for the Jewish people. Although, of course, the *Land* of Israel is deeply connected to the Jewish people, when we write "Israel," without specifying the Land or the State, we mean "the Jewish people."

Abraham, the first Hebrew patriarch acted and spoke on behalf of his descendants throughout history.

God is an eternal God, who entered into a covenant with Israel, first with Abraham, the first Hebrew (Jew) in the city of Hebron (Gen. 15) and then with the entire nation at the time of Moses in the Sinai desert. A covenant, in biblical language, is an eternal commitment, a contract which can never be dissolved. In the first covenant with Abraham, God committed that despite exile and persecution, the nation Israel would never be destroyed; all of our prophets maintain that, ultimately, at the end of days, we would be accepted as a light unto the nations and our concepts of moral justice and compassionate righteousness would at long last triumph in the world over the desire for animalistic power which has driven world leaders from Nebuchadnezzar to Hitler. Israel, in turn, declared at Sinai its commitment of faith to obey God's commandments of love and loving-kindness, and never to forsake their belief in the ultimate world redemption despite the shedding of blood and even martyrdom that the descendants of Abraham would have to experience: "And he (Moses) took the Book of the Covenant, and read it while the people were intently listening, and they said, 'All that God has declared, we will do, and we will internalize'" (Ex. 24:7).

It is fascinating that the prophets of Israel, especially Jeremiah and Hosea, even view the covenant between God and Israel as a "marital" covenant, replete with sacrifices and commitments which are critical aspects of an eternal love relationship; we believe that adherence to this covenant will eventually bring redemption to Israel and to the world. As the prophet Hosea says in the name of God, speaking to Israel (2:21–22): "And I will betroth you to Me forever; I will betroth you to Me in righteousness, justice, loving-kindness, and compassion. And I will betroth you to Me in faithfulness; and you shall know and love God."[3]

From this perspective, every individual Jew, standing before God in public prayer, must view him/herself as speaking to God not so much as an individual, but rather as a member of a historic community of an

3. When the Jew dons phylacteries (tefillin) each weekday morning, he wraps the leather straps around his middle finger, symbolizing the wedding ring, the sign of his marriage to God, while reciting these very verses.

eternal people with a mission to ultimately be a light unto the nations, an inspiration to all of humanity, to perfect the world under the kingship of the God of Love and thus to invite the entire world to be protected by the loving wings of the Divine Presence. And so, you see how our initial chosenness and particularism is for the sake of the universal redemption of humankind.

COMMUNAL PRAYER: THE INDIVIDUAL JEW MERGES WITH THE HISTORIC COMMUNITY OF ISRAEL

As we have seen, Jewish prayer is essentially a communal collective experience, rather than a purely personal one. And although there is room for personal prayer, as we shall see in a later section of this chapter, communal prayer is paramount. Indeed, the prayer leader (cantor) represents eternal historic Israel, and our public prayers – morning, afternoon, and evening, Sabbath and festivals – are exclusively uttered in the plural form; we ask not only for basic human needs – like wisdom, good health, prosperity – but also for national needs to fulfill our mission, such as a righteous judicial system, the restoration of the Land of Israel and the sacred city of Jerusalem, and the universal needs of compassionate righteousness and world peace.

The truth is that our mission, to teach the world about ethics and values, to display by example compassionate righteousness and moral justice, can only be achieved as a nation, never solely through one's individual efforts. And so, each time we pray, we are reemphasizing our indelible relationship to our nationhood; we unite with the historic community of Jewish peoplehood.

From this perspective, we can also understand the ease with which the individual Jew can feel at one with the march of Jewish history. Almost as soon as a Jew is born and enters the circumcision-covenant of Israel with the shedding of blood, the primal and profound connection of every Jew to Abraham – the first Jew and the first to be circumcised – is indelibly expressed. From his very birth, the Jew (or, more correctly, his parents) are testifying to the Jewish necessity of shedding blood from the very organ of propagation, bearing witness to the fact that Jewish continuity throughout the generations has often demanded the shedding of blood.[4] Time after time, we uncompromisingly upheld our view of morality in the face of massive rejection of that view by tyrannical rulers throughout history, expressed horrifically by the violence they perpetrated against us to maintain their position that "might makes right."

From the triumphant cry of the Passover Haggada that everyone must feel existentially free of any type of enslavement by any human totalitarian power, as if he or she had been personally taken out of Egypt, to the teaching of our Sages that every Jewish soul was present at Mount Sinai, to the biblical figures who are special guests in the sukka and who accompany every one of our Sukkot meals, as we will learn later, we are inextricably bound to our forebears, men and women who are the very fabric, the pulse, the heart, and the soul of Judaism eternal. And since our Bible is a dialogue between God and the Jewish nation entire, each Jew of every generation is likewise part of that same dialogue. Every member of historic Israel has therefore been addressed and touched by the eternal God. This is the real definition of Jewish history, the essence of the peoplehood of Israel. The important historical events when the Jewish people felt touched by the hand of God must likewise touch each Jew as s/he reexperiences those events as we celebrate our feast days and mourn on our fast days.

From this perspective, the individual who merges in prayer with the prayers of Jews throughout our history learns from these prayers the lessons of each festival and fast day and the real meaning of each of our holy days. (This is especially true of Rosh HaShana and Yom Kippur prayers, as we shall see in later chapters.)

We also learn from our prayers what it is that God wants us to pray for, and how He sees, as it were, the period leading to our eventual redemption. And so, we pray for the ingathering of the exiles, and our eventual freedom in our own Jewish State of Israel. Undoubtedly, the declaration of Jewish independence in Israel led by David Ben-Gurion

4. Women are clearly included in this concept, even though they do not undergo circumcision. The Talmud in Avoda Zara 27a teaches that a woman is considered (naturally) circumcised (and therefore included in the covenant of circumcision). I believe that this means that since women shed blood and place their lives at risk with every childbirth, they thereby naturally express the necessity of shedding blood for Jewish continuity.

in 1948 and followed by the successful War of Independence, the Six-Day War, and the Yom Kippur War, all of which established and maintained our return to the Jewish state, were nothing short of miraculous.

But I would submit that the true miracle and wonder is that after two thousand years of captivity we still remembered the idea of the Jewish state, what it meant to us, and believed that, one day, we would return to it and the world would be redeemed by it. In the history of the world, there is no nation which has been separated from its original homeland for even two *hundred* years, that ever thought to return to it and reestablish it as a nation-state. Undoubtedly, it was these prayers of historic Israel for two millennia which kept alive in the Jewish consciousness love for Zion and hope to return to Zion. Tied to this amazing miracle that has advanced our hope for redemption is our ongoing prayer that all of the wicked of the earth turn toward our God of love and compassion in a redeemed world.

IN THE HISTORIC DIALOGUE WHICH IS PRAYER, WHERE IS GOD'S RESPONSE?

At this point in our study, we are positioning prayer as a dialogue between the Jew and God. However, the cynical observer may logically say, "What kind of dialogue is it if we make the requests, but we never hear God's responses? Of what value is a one-way dialogue?" A rather sarcastic friend of mine, who considers himself an atheist, visits Israel often, but never visits the Western Wall. He argues that that is the problem of prayer altogether: We are hitting our heads against the wall. We are only talking to a wall that never answers back.

And that is precisely why biblical readings are such an intrinsic part of Jewish prayer. It is important to note that there are biblical and prophetic readings on every Sabbath, and every festival, as well as Mondays and Thursdays, so that, by the end of the year, any Jew who attended regular prayer services has heard clearly the Five Books of Moses, and many, many chapters of the prophetic readings and the hagiographic writings. Within the prayer book itself, there are likewise key portions from the Bible every day, most notably the three paragraphs of the *Shema*, each morning and each evening. Because, you see, in our prayers to God, we tell Him what we wish from Him, and in the biblical readings, He clearly tells us what He wishes from us. Moreover, the prophets picture the beginnings of the redemption, and tell us in God's name that if we remain faithful to Him in our observance, He will be faithful to us in returning us to Israel, in bringing the exiles from the uttermost ends of the heavens, back to Israel, and if God only *promised* these happenings for the last two thousand years, we are the generation that has actually seen the beginning of the fulfillment of those promises. The prophet Jeremiah, living through the destruction of the First Temple in Jerusalem, foresaw the future of that sacred city: "Again shall be heard in this place… the voice of joy and the voice of gladness, the voice of the bridegroom and the voice of the bride, the voice of those that say 'Praise the Lord of Hosts, for the Lord is good'" (33:10–11). And indeed, this miracle is happening for all to see today, by visiting Israel and Jerusalem.

In 1997, when I was happily settled as chief rabbi of Efrat, a young man came to see me on a Friday afternoon, not long before the Sabbath was to begin. I usually don't see people at that hour; I think of this time as my "private time" with God. But he was insistent. He said that he needed to talk, and that he had a problem and a question. I said, "OK, what is your problem and what is your question?" He replied, "I want to convert to Judaism."

But then he added, "I am the great-grandson of Rabbi Israel Zolli." That got my attention. Rabbi Israel Zolli was the chief rabbi of Rome, who – shockingly – converted to Christianity at the height of the Holocaust. He converted together with his wife and daughter, and was given a job in the Vatican Library. This young man who stood before me wanted to convert "back" to Judaism. He understood that this would mean keeping the commandments, and he assured me that even during the period of his grandfather's apostacy he had done so. I arranged for his conversion.

About two years later, he came back to see me, along with his fiancée. He asked me to perform their wedding. I agreed. But then he added, "But, I want my wedding to be held in the Great Synagogue of Rome." I agreed, and the wedding – a small one – was held in that synagogue. All went according to procedure, but as I completed intoning the final blessing, the one based upon the verse above – "There will yet be heard in the streets of Jerusalem the rejoicing voices of the bride and groom" – this bridegroom screamed out: "Grandfather!! Did you hear?? There will yet be heard the sound of brides and grooms rejoicing in Jerusalem! Grandfather, you didn't believe God's promise! And therefore, you turned away from your faith. Grandfather, I want to bring you *tikkun* (repair)! Wherever you are, I want you to repent. Because, despite everything, and despite the Holocaust, God is true to His promise. God will redeem – indeed, He has already begun the process! Grandfather, I want to be your redemption!"

This young bridegroom understood, more deeply than is imaginable, the promises God made to historic Israel which are beginning to be fulfilled in our day. As we pray and merge with historic Israel, we hear God's promises to us, and we hear what He expects of us in order to bring the world to complete redemption.

PERSONAL PRAYER AND A PERSONAL GOD

And so, God certainly spoke to us throughout Jewish history and through those special moments in Jewish history when we have felt especially close to Him. Hence, we have tried to internalize the events in our own prayer and festival experiences. But, in addition to the individual as part of historic Israel, the individual still remains an individual, with his/her personal disappointments and triumphs, joyous celebrations and tragic times of mourning. In addition to the God of Jewish history, is there room for a personal God and His relationship with the personal individual? There is a beautiful story which sheds light on this question.

The story is told of the renowned German Jewish philosopher Hermann Cohen, who drew closer to religious Judaism in his later years. Cohen meets an old-fashioned rabbi on a train, and they sit down together. The philosopher says to the rabbi, "Rabbi, I have developed a whole new philosophical approach to God and to prayer. Can I explain it to you, so that you can give me your comments on it?" "Certainly," says the rabbi, "Go ahead."

The philosopher launches into a very lengthy and complex philosophical discourse about the existence of God and a description of His essence. The rabbi listens carefully. When the philosopher finally concludes, he asks the rabbi, "So, Rabbi, do you have any questions?" "Just one question," responds the rabbi. "*Vu iz mein tateh in himmel* – Where, in all of this philosophy, is my Father in Heaven?"

Essentially, the rabbi wanted to know what happened to the personal God – a loving, caring God. He needed to know that the compassionate God, the forgiving God, God the *mameh/tateh in himmel,* did not get lost in the midst of the theological discourses.

Indeed, Judaism most certainly leaves room for personal prayer. Our central *Amida* prayer opens by addressing God in exactly that way: "Blessed are You, our God and the God of our ancestors, the God of Abraham, the God of Isaac, and the God of Jacob." We invoke these "first Jews" as we begin our prayer specifically because each of these iconic figures had a personal relationship with God, a relationship which they defined, explained, and exemplified in the book of Genesis, the first book of the Torah. This invocation, coming as it does as a prelude to our prayer, encourages each of us to develop her or his unique relationship with God. This is certainly possible and desirable within the silent *Amida.*

In fact, Jewish law states that an individual with a personal request is encouraged to insert that request within any of those more formal requests in the *Amida* prayer; and if one's individual request does not match the subject matter of any of the specific requests, he or she may include it in the final request blessing – the *Shema Koleinu* – which is a generally worded petition for God to accept all of our prayers. We may pray in any language we wish; there is a paragraph immediately following the *Amida* in which we can include any personal supplications – even lengthy ones – and another prayer following called *Taḥanun* (Supplications) in which each of us individually looks deeply within him/herself to share any "final" personal thoughts with God. Both concepts of prayer – the communal and the personal – are expressed in the daily formal liturgy. The *Amida* – our central prayer – is first recited silently, and here we can articulate our deepest personal needs, and engage in a personal dialogue between ourselves and God. Following this silent prayer, the prayer leader repeats the *Amida,* this time uttering it as a communal prayer: historic Israel in dialogue with the Creator.

And so, we open our morning prayers with a very personal statement:

> My God! The soul You placed within me is pure. You created it, You formed it, You breathed it into me.

This prayer suggests a very intimate and personal relationship between every human being and the Almighty. Indeed, the first "One" we address each morning upon awakening is God!

But where may we find God? Our morning Psalms suggest that we find God in the beauty and majesty of the universe: "Blessed is He who spoke and the world came into being!" We will expand on this idea later on in this chapter.

I believe, however, that we can find God not only by looking out, but also by looking in. Indeed, this is the suggestion of the prayer itself: My God! The soul You placed within me is pure. You created it, You formed it, You breathed it into me.

Within each of us is found an element of God's essence – the *tzelem Elokim*. The soul that God breathed into us – as He did to Adam, the first human being, "*vayipaḥ be'apav nishmat ḥayyim*" (Gen 2:7) – is what enables us to dialogue with Him. Where may we look to find God? Where can He be found? Deep within ourselves. It is that essential aspect of God within us that cries out for expression and urges us to seek Him out, to dialogue with Him. Indeed, the God within us is urging us to look for Him because He loves us, and the lover always seeks His beloved.

Hence, it must be clearly understood that we most certainly believe in a personal God with whom we can engage in dialogue.

REPETITION IN PRAYER

Many chafe at the repetition each day of the same prayers. I believe that this repetition is critical. Most of us take life and health for granted. In Jewish tradition the individual rises every morning and thanks God for giving him/her new life, for enabling her/him to rise with the dawn, then recites the series of blessings with which the morning service begins, thanking God for the most basic necessities of life and the most elementary movements of a living being: opening one's eyes, the ability to stand upright, walking on the ground, having clothing and shoes to wear, etc. These blessings hopefully remind us to appreciate life every day and our ability to function properly every day. They remind us to use each day as an opportunity to utilize our physical beings to good purpose, and, on a daily basis, to acknowledge the miracle of our lives, to develop a relationship with God based on thankfulness and appreciation of the gifts of life.

Another prayer is repeated at the conclusion of every single one of our statutory prayers: the *Aleinu* prayer, which serves as a crescendo to all our requests. In the *Aleinu,* we describe our futuristic vision of world redemption: "That all of the inhabitants of the world shall know... and shall accept upon themselves the responsibility of your Kingship – that sovereignty is Yours, and that You shall reign forever, as it is written in Your Torah (Ex. 15), 'The Lord of Love shall reign forever.' And it is also said (Zech. 14), 'God will be Sovereign over all the earth. On that day will God be One and His name One.'" This pinnacle of each prayer service extends the prayer-dialogue even beyond the Jewish people, and embraces the entire world, a fulfillment of the Jewish mission of a world perfected in peace and love.

DOES GOD ANSWER? THE GOD WITHIN AND THE GOD WITHOUT

Nevertheless, how can this be a dialogue with God if we never receive an answer from Him? We have already provided a suggested answer to the prayer of the individual who is praying as part of communal Israel: God speaks to us in the biblical readings that are included in our prayer service. But what about each of our individual petitions for which we often crave a more direct answer? From a certain perspective, perhaps it is superfluous for God to answer our prayers. After all, in the conclusion to the request section of the *Amida,* we declare, "Blessed are You, God, who *hears* prayer," without saying, "Blessed are you, God, who *answers* prayer." If, indeed, God is all-knowing, and since we ourselves often do not know what is best for us, we must rely upon God to answer us by the very events which occur to us in life. We must be prepared for "no" as an answer to a specific request. No less a figure than Moses received such a negative reply, after he pleaded with God to allow him to enter the Promised Land.

On a deeper level, however, we have already explained that there is a portion of God from on high within every human being, who is, after all, created in the image of the Divine and endowed with the eternal soul-breath of the Divine within his/her very being. Judaism does not necessarily believe in a universe which is directed in every way by God, to the extent that nothing happens in the world unless God wishes it to be. That God does control every event is one school of thought within the Talmud, but that is not the exclusive view. In fact, the majority view is expressed in the Talmud by the dual dicta of "The world follows its natural course [without divine intervention]" (Avoda Zara 54b) and "There is no reward in this world for [the performance of] commandments" (Kiddushin 39b). These statements teach us that God created the human being with freedom of choice to act positively or negatively and the human responsibility to live a moral and sacred life. Despite the fact that this is not a perfect world, the individual must try as best as s/he can to act in the image of God and to utilize and express the God within him/herself to help him/her overcome negative animalistic desires, and to reach out in love to every human being.

I deeply believe that there is a God within and a God without. Of course, it is the same God, but we perceive Him differently in various situations. The God without is the God of the universe, the God of history, the God who promised us redemption. Sometimes it is difficult to feel that the God without listens and answers; He may seem distant, dealing as He does with great cosmic and historical matters.

But there is also a God within, and that is where prayer and action come together. We will soon discuss the creation of the human being, who has a great deal in common with the animal world, but who also is uniquely created in God's image and holds within him/herself the soul-breath of God. When I am praying to the God within, I am addressing the godliness within me; I am talking to the best within me. In effect, I am praying to the God within to give me the strength and the will to make a difference, to change the situation, to cross the Reed Sea.

The Hebrew word "to pray" is *lehitpalel*. It is in the reflexive form, which is not reflected by the English "to pray." Rabbi Samson Raphael Hirsch famously says that it means "to judge oneself" (from the root *p-l-l*, "to judge"). When one prays, one judges one's actions and one's life in the presence of God. I would suggest that the reflexive can also imply that one is praying to the God within oneself. When we address that God, we are also addressing ourselves, moving ourselves into action to help as much as we can to bring about the result for which we pray. When we pray to the God within, we are reaffirming our partnership with God, acting with Him to perfect the world. And therefore, when we pray for messianic times, for example, it is our actions – our moving to the Land of Israel, our defending the country – which are necessary for redemption to be realized. For generations the Jewish people believed that we had no choice but to wait passively for the arrival of the Messiah. This was a mistake. We need to partner with God to create a world to which the Messiah will be drawn.

I would like to share a personal anecdote. When I first came to Israel as a young man, I studied in Yeshivat Kerem BeYavneh. While I had little spending money, I was drawn to a certain *seforim* store – a bookstore selling religious books – whose proprietor, Reb Shmuel, took a liking to me, and I to him. Whenever I came by, he would greet me with a grunt, from which I could determine whether he had any new books that would be of interest to me. He grunted rather than spoke to me because he often accepted on himself a *taanit dibbur* – a "fast day" when he refrained from speech. Reb Shmuel believed that most people sin with the words they speak rather than the actions they perform. Hence, whenever I heard a grunt from him, I understood that this was his way of atoning for the sins of the generation. We had an agreement that he would sell me books on credit and I would send him payment once I returned home to America. On one occasion, just before I was to leave, I visited his store and he gave me a hearty greeting, speaking to me freely and at length. When I asked him why he was so garrulous on this particular day he told me that he was in good spirits because the Messiah was in Jerusalem!

As a young man, I was very impressionable, and I was hopeful that he had heard news that in some way would point to a more imminent redemption. I made sure to listen to the hourly news broadcasts, waiting to hear the broadcasters announce an event heralding the arrival of the Messiah. But there were no such reports on the radio. Early the next morning, just before my flight back to America, I knocked on Reb

Shmuel's door, which he answered in his nightclothes. Concerned, he asked me why I had come to his house so early. I explained that I wanted more information about the Messiah's arrival, since there had been no announcement about it on the news.

Reb Shmuel looked at me and said, "You are making a mistake. You think that we are waiting for the Messiah. Truly, the Messiah is waiting for us." I learned an important lesson from Reb Shmuel; it is up to us, as God's partners, to help prepare the world for the arrival of the Messiah. At that moment I made a vow that as soon as I was able, I would move to Israel.

In a similar vein, in the last mishna of chapter 4 of Tractate Pesaḥim, the Mishna mentions that the biblical King Hezekiah hid away the Book of Healings (traditionally attributed to King Solomon). This book apparently contained formulas for the curing of various diseases. Why would the righteous Hezekiah suppress this valuable information? Rashi and others say that the monarch Hezekiah did this in order that people would rely upon God to heal them from illness, and not rely upon medical strategies mentioned in this Book of Healings. This line of thinking holds that this approach would strengthen the people's faith in God and His healing powers. It would seem from Rashi that it is necessary for us to depend upon God, and not to depend upon God would constitute a lack of faith. However, in his commentary on the Mishna, the Rambam, who was a physician in addition to being a great Torah scholar, vociferously disagrees with Rashi's position, and, on the contrary, praises the author of the Book of Healings which urged its readers to take action against disease, and would never have suggested that it be hidden away, unless its remedies were totally false and dependent upon idolatrous rites.[5] I believe that the Rambam's view here points to

5. Maimonides's commentary reads:

> I heard and also it was explained to me that [King] Solomon composed a book of healing and Hezekiah saw that the people did not trust in God in their illness but rather on this book of remedies, he stood up and hid it.... And according to their confused and stupid imagination, if a person is hungry and turns to the bread and eats it and it cures him from that great pain of hunger, shall we say that he has removed his trust from God? But they are fools, for just as I give thanks to God at the time that I eat that He provided me with food to remove my hunger and to

another aspect of prayer to the God within; we pray to the God within us in order to spark ourselves and our fellow humans to action; in this case, the advancement of medical science to relieve suffering and bring about healing. Sometimes, our prayers are answered through the accomplishments of human beings.

HOW CAN ONE BEGIN TO PRAY WHEN UNSURE ABOUT FAITH IN GOD?

The reader may well be asking at this point, "But how can I begin to pray if I don't even know if I have faith in a divine being altogether?" Admittedly, the Rambam presents knowledge of God (and/or belief in God) as the primary commandment, writing:

> The foundation of all foundations and the pillar of wisdom is to know that there is a Primary Being who brought into being all existence. All the beings of the heavens, the earth, and what is between them came into existence only from the truth of His being.[6]

Nevertheless, the Torah cannot possibly demand that an individual begin his/her search into Judaism with absolute certainty of God's existence. Such knowledge or belief can only come after one comes to interact with God and His commandments. Judaism wants us to first "experience God" and through that experience come to know Him. As the psalmist says (34:9) – "Taste and see how good the Lord is." The first step is for the individual to "taste," to "try out" God's commandments. To experience, for example, the familial warmth of the Shabbat

keep me alive and preserve me, so too, we should thank Him that He furnished a medicine that cures my illness. And I would not have to contradict this terrible explanation were it not for its popularity.

6. *Mishneh Torah, Hilkhot Yeshodei HaTorah,* chapter 1. Basing himself on the opening verse of the Ten Commandments – "I am the Lord your God" – the Rambam writes, "To acknowledge this truth is a positive commandment." He refers to this commandment as "this doctrine which is the great principle on which everything depends."

lights and the inner peace of Sabbath togetherness every week, inviting the less fortunate to join our Shabbat table. The psalmist assures us that experiencing the moral and ethical imperatives commanded by God will bring us to understand His greatness.

On the basis of what we have just said, the first step in Judaism must be the performance of the commandments, rather than to seek the nature of the theology to which we subscribe. For Judaism, it is *faithfulness* to the biblical commandments of love and loving-kindness which is cardinal, and not the theological system of belief.[7]

And indeed, the *Midrash Rabba* on the book of Lamentations, Introduction 2, quotes the verse in the book of Jeremiah 16:11, "They (the Jewish people) forgot Me (God) and they did not observe My Torah." The Midrash then makes an amendment to this statement, speaking in God's name: "Would that they would have forgotten Me, but kept My Torah." I would have preferred, God is saying, that people who are not sure about their faith in Me would have continued to observe My commandments, including those of morality and ethics, together with the Sabbath, festivals, and so forth. This is a resounding statement that our tradition holds positive action to be more significant than theological faith. After all, our mission is to perfect the world through our actions, which is why Judaism is a religion of commandments rather than a religion of catechisms of faith. What the God of the covenant wants is our faithfulness to His commandments even more than our theological faith in His divine being.

Faith – if it is truly to be effective – must be the product of a lifelong search rather than a preordained conclusion. Relationships develop and mature over time. The only way for someone to have a relationship with God is by engaging in dialogue with Him. Ultimately, faith will come from faithfulness.

7. The source for the translation of *emuna* as "faithfulness" or "steadfastness," rather than as "faith," is Exodus 17:12. The Bible there recounts the battle with Amalek, Israel's archenemy. During the battle, Moses raised his hands to heaven (in order, explains the Mishna, to direct the people's attention to God, that He make them victorious). Moses's hands became "heavy," as time passed, so Aaron and Hur supported his hands, which allowed them (his hands), the verse says, to be "*emuna*" – "steadfast" – until sunset, when the battle was won.

DAILY MORNING PRAYER: THE BLESSINGS BEFORE AND AFTER THE SHEMA

Having accepted the fact that it is much easier to command righteous action and well-nigh impossible to command religious faith, it is the prayer book that provides a pathway to help us feel God's presence and even enable us to comfortably address the Divine. This is made very clear through the structure of both our morning and evening prayers, every day of the year. So, let us attempt to analyze our daily morning prayers, understanding that most of the prayer book was composed by the Sages of the Great Assembly.[8]

The central part of daily morning prayer – on weekdays, Shabbat, and festivals – consists of the most central declaration of the faith of historic Israel, *Shema Yisrael A-donai Elokeinu A-donai Eḥad,* "Hear O (historic) Israel, the Lord our God the Lord is One." This was the clarion call throughout the ages by which the Jew expressed his/her faithfulness to God, even when s/he was forced to give up his/her life because of that faithfulness. During the Crusades, the Jews intoned the *Shema* instead of kissing the Christian cross which would have enabled them to live; and during the Holocaust, the Jews walked into the gas chambers of Auschwitz and Treblinka with the words of the *Shema* on their lips. The exact meaning of the words of the *Shema* testified to their undying faith in God's covenant. Hear, O (historic) Israel, the Lord (YHVH) is our God now, but will eventually become the Lord of the entire world (Rashi on Deuteronomy 6:4). The three paragraphs of the *Shema* are God's words to us in His eternal dialogue. He wants us to commit ourselves completely to godliness within this world. He

8. The "Sages of the Great Assembly," who functioned between approximately 410 BCE and 310 BCE, are generally understood to have been a group of 120 great Jewish scholars, including several of the last prophets of the Jewish people, who lived just before the cessation of prophecy. Extremely sensitive to the needs of a nation just thrown into exile, they enacted some of the most important post-biblical institutions and laws that secured the religious function of Judaism throughout the coming millennia. In essence, following the massive trauma of the destruction of the First Temple, they successfully recast Judaism from a Temple-centered into a synagogue-centered religion.

tells us how living in accordance with the commandments will perfect, and so redeem, the entire world.

But how can we get to the point that we feel as if we are standing before the *Shekhina* – the Divine Presence – and become inspired by His words? Even before the individual mouths God's words of the *Shema*, and His message to us, the prayer book relates – in the first of the two blessings before the *Shema* – the blessing of nature. God reveals Himself, as it were, through the awesome grandeur of the heavenly bodies, the magnificent hues and colors of sunrise and sunset, of flowers and foliage. Hopefully, the magnificence and the majesty of nature round about will inspire us to come closer to the Creator of such creations, to the awe-inspiring "Old Master Painter from the Faraway Hills" (as noted above, a song from my childhood). Let us listen to the words of Psalm 19 that expresses the truth that God speaks to the entire world through the glories of nature: "Day moving inexorably into next day is itself eloquent speech; night inexorably leading into next night is in itself profound knowledge." By immersing ourselves in God's universe, we actually hear God's words. In effect, the prayer book is taking our hand and saying, "You want to enter a rendezvous with God, and you are desperately searching for something which will make you feel close to that God. Just look all around you at the grandeur of nature!" Hence, the prayer book is teaching us its first lesson before the *Shema*: As we thank God for sunrise, we catch an initial glimpse of the one God of the universe, whom we are seeking to approach.

In a similar fashion, the second blessing, in which we thank God for His life-enhancing and love-inspiring commandments, will hopefully also serve to bring us a step closer to the God whose love and wisdom are so beautifully expressed by the commandments of the Torah. When we realize that the secret of Jewish eternality and the manner by which we will rise above the animal and redeem the world are the commandments given us by God, we only wish to come even closer to the One who gave us that Torah.

While the magnificence of nature and the deep wisdom of the Torah may lead us and inspire us to recognize that there must a God responsible for these two gifts, it is only after we have accepted God's being and His teachings that we can begin to see how history has confirmed all of the divine biblical prophecies. Hence, the third blessing – after the *Shema* – evokes the God of history and stresses our eternality: "Our eternal king, the shield of our salvation through all generations." Despite exiles and persecutions, our faithful God has proven Himself to have maintained His eternal covenant with us as His eternal nation. This was recognized even by Leo Tolstoy, the great Russian non-Jewish novelist, who marveled at our eternality and exclaimed, "The Jew is the symbol of eternity.... He is the one who for so long had guarded the prophetic message and transmitted it to all mankind. A people such as this can never disappear. The Jew is eternal. He is the embodiment of eternity" (from "What Is the Jew?" 1908).

Every other nation in the world rose and fell, with the present inhabitants of their original homeland having no cultural connection with the original denizens of those countries. Present-day Romans (Italians) are not direct products of the Ancient Roman culture; present day Persians (Iranians) have no cultural tie with the Persians of the ancient world. In accordance with the covenant, Israel has remained faithful to the God who promised us eternality, and God has remained faithful to His promise never to allow us to be destroyed.

We see here, too, that our covenant with God is based upon our faithfulness to His commandments rather than our theological belief in His divine being, and the real meaning of the Hebrew "*emuna*" is "faithfulness to correct action," rather than faith as a theological belief. This may explain how some Jews during and after the Holocaust remained steadfast to the commandments, while at the same time questioning their faith in God. After four thousand years of cultural connection, and two thousand years of exile, we have even returned to our original homestead, the Land of Israel.

And so, we conclude this third blessing with our prayer to God for ultimate redemption: "Rock of Israel, arise together with the help of Israel, and redeem Your nation Judah and Israel.[9] Our Redeemer, the

9. Note that the wording is בעזרת ישראל, rather than לעזרת ישראל. That is, we are not calling for God to redeem us on His own, but for a partnership between God and Israel working toward redemption.

Lord of Hosts is His name, the Holy One of Israel. Blessed are You, O Lord, who has redeemed Israel."

And so, the blessings of nature, Torah, and history take us by the hand and make us long for coming ever closer to the God of our eternal covenant. We hear God's voice and are desirous of coming ever closer to Him through the power and the beauty of nature all around us, through the moral and ethical vision of the biblical commandments He has bequeathed to us, and through the promises we have kept to each other for thousands of years during which we remained steadfast to God's laws and God remained steadfast to the protection of His eternal nation.

An even greater miracle than that of our return to our homeland after two thousand years of wandering is that we still wanted and dreamed of the Jewish state, which never would have happened without our merging in prayer with historic Israel.

CONTEMPORARY JEWISH PRAYER

Contemporary Judaism has within it many denominations or "streams": *ḥaredi* (ultra-Orthodox), Modern Orthodox, Conservative, Reform, Reconstructionist, secular, trans-denominational, and post-denominational. This book focuses on what would be called traditional, Modern Orthodox, or classical Judaism.

It is obvious that we believe that the best way of living Judaism is through the lens of our halakhic four-thousand-year-long tradition. I would also suggest that it is very important to learn and begin to practice halakhic (Orthodox) Judaism in order to understand it within the light of its four-thousand-year-long connection. After such study and period of practice, how much of the tradition the individual Jew decides to practice is, of course, entirely up to him or her.

The various denominations or streams vary greatly in their approach to prayer, using differing texts for the prayer book, different modes of seating (separation of sexes versus "family seating"), and even whether – for secular Jews – prayer is appropriate at all. We regard the seating arrangement for Orthodox prayer as the most conducive to the kind of focus that "successful" prayer requires. The separation of sexes for seating in the synagogue allows for greater concentration on prayer – which is not meant to be a social or even a family experience, but rather an encounter with the Divine. And the traditional prayer book – which needs to be studied – contains within it the most basic philosophy and theology of Judaism, aiding the individual in his or her search for God and spirituality.

That said, we strongly deny that Judaism is an all-or-nothing experience. We fully respect whatever amount of the tradition an individual Jew may wish to maintain, and we believe, as does the prayer book, that God hears everyone's prayer no matter what the context.[10]

10. Many versions of the traditional prayer book, in the final request blessing, rather than saying "for You hear the prayers of Your people Israel," say instead, "for You hear the prayers of every mouth" – a clear statement of God's universal acceptance of all prayer.

Chapter 3

Forbidden Actions: The Roots of Jewish Morality

THE FORBIDDEN FRUIT AND MORAL KNOWLEDGE

Everyone knows the story of Adam and Eve in the Garden of Eden, and of the "forbidden fruit" they were told by God not to eat. This is not just a fanciful story that stands by itself as a fable from the mists of time; it is rather God's message of morality for every human being.

God gave only one commandment to Adam and Eve: not to eat of the Tree of Knowledge of Good and Evil in the center of the Garden of Eden. God made it clear that they were permitted to partake of the fruit of every other tree in the garden, but the fruit of the Tree of Knowledge of Good and Evil was absolutely forbidden.

But why is the eating of this fruit the primordial sin? Certainly Judaism is not telling us that acquiring knowledge is forbidden! Judaism – the Bible in so many of its books – prizes knowledge! We are encouraged to acquire scientific knowledge, knowledge of the development of civilizations, cultural knowledge. So, if this fruit would bring Adam and Eve knowledge, why did God forbid it?

Let us open the Bible to see if we understand the answer to this question. Eve looks at the forbidden fruit and takes note (Gen. 3:6) that the fruit is nutritious ("good to eat") – apparently without calories or cholesterol – has a very aesthetic presentation ("a delight to the eyes"), and full of the kind of protein that aids cognition ("lovely for understanding"). What Eve has conveniently forgotten is just one quality of the fruit: God said not to eat it. God says it is not good. In fact, it's bad. The human being has freedom of choice, and is encouraged to study and learn and understand philosophical and theological truths, scientific processes, and human behavior. But the human being must depend upon a higher truth for his/her definition of good and evil. God decides what is right and what is wrong.

Like Eve in the garden, everyone tries to justify his or her actions, no matter how far-fetched or illogical that justification may be. Ernest Jones was a student, colleague, and official biographer of Sigmund Freud. In his 1908 article "Rationalization in Every-Day Life," Jones wrote, "Everyone feels that as a rational creature he must be able to give a connected, logical, and continuous account of himself, his conduct, and opinions; and all his mental processes are unconsciously manipulated and revised to that end."

Early in my rabbinic career, the mother of a Jewish, religiously observant family came to me with the suspicion that her husband, who traveled regularly for business, was having an extramarital affair. This woman had hired a private detective, who confirmed her suspicions; he was having a longstanding affair with a non-Jewish woman. Afraid to confront her husband, the woman asked me to do so, and I did. When I asked him how a committed Jew, who should revere the sanctity of marriage, could conduct himself in this way, he "explained" to me:

> You see, Rabbi, our marriage has never been very good, and my wife is a very delicate person. I always believed that if I told her I wanted to divorce her, she would be devastated and great harm would come to her. So, I feel that I am actually doing a good deed by remaining married and carrying on an affair. What's more, the woman with whom I am now involved was a hopeless drug addict. As we continued to see each other on my travels, she was inspired to better herself, which she did. So there, too, I felt I was truly doing a good deed. So, in sum, I helped both my wife and my lover.

I could not believe my ears. This man had violated his marriage bond, cheated on his wife with no regrets, and he recounted his actions to me as two great good deeds that he had valiantly performed! I learned then how powerful are self-justification and rationalization. Freud and Jones were most certainly correct.

Among the various messages of this biblical episode – and the one that is particularly pertinent for us at this point in our study – is that, for the knowledge of what is right and what is wrong, we must depend on God, His universal laws, His absolute morality. If God decided that eating the fruit of this particular tree was prohibited, immoral, evil – then so it was, even if Adam and Eve could not understand why.

At this early point in its narration, the Torah makes clear that we do not believe in "situational ethics," a system in which desire pushes aside all ethical and moral decisions. When it comes to deciding what is intrinsically good and what is inherently evil – for that we must rely on God's judgment and His definitions. The failure of Adam and Eve to understand this led to their expulsion from the Garden of Eden.

Our Sages teach us that the only character in this Adam and Eve story who spoke the truth was the serpent – who beguiled Eve into eating the fruit by telling her (Gen. 3:5) "... on the day you eat the from it [the forbidden fruit] your eyes will be opened and you will be like God, knowing good and evil." This was true – but in a negative sense. By eating the forbidden fruit, Adam and Eve arrogated to themselves the role of God – defining what is right and what is wrong. Judaism firmly teaches that the ability to define right and wrong is in God's province alone.

THE KOSHER LAWS: AN EXTENSION OF THE FORBIDDEN FRUIT

There is a great deal more to be learned from the story of Adam and Eve in the Garden of Eden, but, for now, it is important to draw a line between this primordial prohibition of eating the fruit from this special tree to the later food-related prohibitions in the Torah. Initially, only the eating of fruits and vegetables was permitted; the consumption of meat was not. (More on this a bit later in this chapter.) But later, perhaps as a concession to human desire, meat was permitted, but with many important guidelines that limit meat consumption.

This whole area, which is referred to in Hebrew as *kashrut*, can be summarized as follows: the prohibition of eating milk (or milk products) and meat (or meat products) together; regarding four-footed animals: the permission to eat the meat only of those animals who both chew their cuds (have two stomachs) and have split hooves; for fish: eating only those with both fins and scales; for birds and fowl: eating the meat of only those delineated by the Torah and by Jewish tradition. Permitted animals and fowl require a special type of ritual slaughtering by individuals trained for this purpose.

It is difficult to fathom, by reading the relevant biblical verses, why certain foods are permitted and others are not. However, we can rely on the prototype of these prohibitions, the interdiction of eating the fruit of the special tree of knowledge in the Garden of Eden: God decides, often beyond our ability to understand, why certain things are morally correct, or morally incorrect – whether they are right or wrong.

The fact that we cannot understand each detail of such prohibitions does not mean that we cannot glean strong lessons for life from the overall concept of permitted and forbidden foods. I would like to tell a personal story – one that happened a long time ago – to illustrate this point.

When I was ten or eleven years old, a "kosher-style" Chinese restaurant opened in New York. This was long before the plethora of multi-ethnic, reliably kosher restaurants; this restaurant had no rabbinical supervision and was not really kosher. But my parents, who were not strictly observant, wanted to take me to this restaurant.

So, I called my wonderful, religious grandmother, who was such an inspiration to me, to ask her what to do. She said, "There is no such thing as 'kosher-style.' It's either kosher or it isn't. *Mein kind*," she added, "if you want to be big and strong, eat only kosher." I was always short and a little chubby, and, boy, did I want to be big and strong, and so, after that conversation, I only ate kosher.

Fast forward to a number of years later. I was a student at Yeshiva University, and I was on the debate team. We debated teams from other colleges in our area. One Sunday, we traveled to West Point, the home of the famous United States Military Academy, to debate their team. Prior to the debate, we toured their magnificent campus, and watched their football team win a game.

Before the debate, they served dinner. The West Point cadets got steak with all the trimmings; our kosher fare consisted of plates with a whole tomato, a whole cucumber, a whole head of lettuce. Then, just before the debate, as was the custom, we shook hands with the opposing team. All three of our team members – most certainly including me – were short and not so physically strong. Well, when I approached my first cadet for the handshake, I didn't believe that my head actually even reached his navel! And the handshake – I could feel the bones in my hand being crushed.

At that moment, I thought to myself, "Grandma, you lied! These guys don't eat kosher, and they're big and strong. I've been eating kosher since birth, and I'm not even close to being big and strong."

Of course, I understood, on a much deeper level, that one can also be "morally big and strong," and that it is also "big and strong" to be able to say "no" to mouth-watering steak, and be satisfied with a head of lettuce. Simply put, I could not eat the steak, because God said "no."

By the way, we won the debate!

Its humor aside, this episode gave me a deep understanding of *kashrut* – and of many other prohibitions in the Torah. When one learns to depend upon God for definitions of right and wrong, and, therefore, to exercise control and discipline in one's actions, then the individual, hopefully, emerges morally stronger and ethically more clear-headed. It is not automatic; there must be a clear desire to "make this work." But it all goes back to the lesson – at least to one of the lessons – of the "forbidden fruit" in the Garden of Eden. At that early point, the Torah set the stage for the free choice given to human beings in arguably the most important areas of their lives – the realms of self-control, discipline, and moral clarity. Food is universal; every living being eats – it is every creature's most basic desire. When I eat only the foods that God has permitted, I am allowing – as we discussed previously – the godly part of me to take precedence over the animalistic aspect of my being. Animals eat whatever is put before them; human beings have a choice. Eating in accordance with God's will grants me the ability to express the image of God in which I am created, even in the arena of partaking of food. My diet, in effect, contributes to the godliness which I would hope must determine every aspect of my life. And by observing these limitations, I bring compassion into every area of my life.

LEARNING THROUGH EATING: DEVELOPING COMPASSION, DISCIPLINE, AND SANCTITY

Kashrut stands today as one of the central observances of Judaism. Food gives us nutrition and pleasure; this is a universal experience. But the distinctive Jewish "take" on food is that it is also a means toward discipline and holiness. This set of laws is observed mainly in the home – the so-called "kosher kitchen" – because, in Judaism, emphasis is more on the home, and less on the synagogue. In order to feel God's presence in the home, the home must become a sacred sanctuary, a family temple. Virtually every activity that takes place in the home is sanctified through specific commandments – food and its consumption being perhaps at the top of the list.

There is another crucial element at play when we speak of food consumption – specifically the eating of meat. That element is compassion. We have spoken about God's qualities of love, compassion, and forgiveness, and that His revelation to us of those qualities is so that we can emulate them. Just as He is compassionate, so must we be compassionate. But how does meat consumption fit in with this? We are, after all, killing an animal in order to satisfy our desire for its flesh. Indeed, many people have chosen to be vegetarians or vegans precisely because they abhor the taking of animal life for our gustatory pleasure.

As we have mentioned, in the world's original, primordial state, God permitted human beings to eat just fruits and vegetables. Only after Noah's flood did God begin to allow the consumption of meat; it became obvious to Him, so to speak, that human beings had a desire for the consumption of flesh; they weren't yet ready to reach the spiritual heights of refraining from meat. It would seem that God "recognized" the potential for violence within human beings, and thought it better that that unfortunate tendency not be directed toward fellow humans, but rather toward the animal world as a means of obtaining food.[1] That said, it may well be that the message of the Torah is that no sort of killing is good, and, therefore, to be a vegetarian or a vegan is really preferable.

The great Rabbi Abraham Isaac Hakohen Kook (1865–1935), the first Ashkenazi chief rabbi of British Mandatory Palestine, suggests that in the eventual rebuilding of the Third Temple in Jerusalem, animal sacrifices would no longer be offered.[2] His sense was that, in that future time, humankind will have evolved to the point where the killing of animals, certainly in the service of God, would not be acceptable. In support of this view, he would quote the verse from Isaiah 11:9 which prophesies a future time: "They shall not harm nor destroy in all My holy mountain; for the earth shall be full of the knowledge of the Lord, as the waters cover the sea." Rabbi Kook felt that this verse strongly militated against the killing of animals – certainly for sacrifices to God. It may even be that, at that future time, the world will return to its pristine state of before Noah's flood; perhaps, then, we will all be vegans!

But for now, an important balance is at work here. On the one hand, the permissibility of eating meat seems to go against the imperative to show compassion to all creatures. On the other, God placed the earth and its creatures under human control when He stated in Genesis 1:28, "And God blessed them [the humans He had just created]; and God said unto them: 'Be fruitful, and multiply, and replenish the earth, and subdue it; and have dominion over the fish of the sea, and over the fowl of the air, and over every living thing that creeps upon the earth.'" So, in which direction do we go – toward compassion, thus refraining from meat consumption, or toward what seems to be God's permission to us to control animals as we see fit?

First of all, we have a choice. If we do not wish to eat meat, we may refrain. But the larger question still remains. The Torah seems,

1. See Shabbat 156a, where Rav Ashi suggests that someone who is born under the sign of Mars, and is therefore a potential killer, should become a bloodletter or a circumciser.
2. Rav Kook writes: "In the future, the abundance of knowledge will spread to and penetrate even animals… and the sacrifices, which will then be from grain, will be as pleasing to God as in days of old in yesteryear [when there were animal sacrifices]" (*Olat Re'aya*, vol. 1 [Jerusalem, 1983], 292).

as it often does, to strike a middle ground. Eating meat is permissible – but only under certain conditions which underline the need for compassion, even for those who will consume meat. The method of slaughter in Jewish law is the least painful and least prolonged for the animal.[3] Meat must be soaked and salted to remove blood, because, as the Torah states, "For the soul of [the animal's] flesh is in the blood" (Lev. 17:11). The bottom line is that, even for those who eat meat, the *kashrut* laws cause us to be far more mindful even as we consume animal flesh: meat from only certain animals, those animals slaughtered properly, the blood removed.

As mentioned, we are not permitted to eat milk (or milk products) and meat (or meat products) together. This is based upon the verse that appears three times in the Torah, "You shall not boil a kid (goat) in the milk of its mother." The Rabbis explain that the prohibition includes not cooking any type of meat and milk together, not eating that combination, and not deriving financial benefit from that combination. True, you may eat the meat. But to go so far as cooking and eating the very life-giving substance – mother's milk – together with the animal itself – that, already, is lacking sensitivity and compassion. The laws of meat and milk even extend to the amount of time one must wait after eating meat or meat products before eating dairy. (There are various customs as to the amount of time.) Once again, sensitivity and compassion are demanded.

All of these rules and regulations can seem onerous – an entire checklist that I need to review before I consume a piece of meat. To address that point – that to have so many laws surrounding the simple act of eating can seem burdensome – a beautiful parable is instructive.

At the time of Creation, the birds were created. And the bird came to God with a complaint. "It's not fair. You have given us these little, short legs. When our predators come after us, we cannot run away

3. The eminent American academic and animal behaviorist Dr. Temple Grandin has written extensively about how *sheḥita* – Jewish ritual slaughter – is the most humane form of slaughtering animals for consumption. See her website, https://www.grandin.com/ritual/rules.shechita.proper.cut.html, where she writes: "There are five rules that Jewish law requires for a correct cut. I have observed that if the rules are disobeyed the animal will struggle. If these rules are obeyed the animal has little reaction."

quickly, and we are caught and devoured. Please help us!" So God fashioned wings for the bird, and placed them upon its back. The next day, the bird returned to God even more distraught. "It was bad enough before, Almighty. When they came after us, we could at least try to run away. Sometimes we could even do so. But now, you have given us these heavy appendages on our backs, and we have no chance to escape those who would devour us." God smiled, and showed the bird how to use the wings to fly high above the predators, to escape them. So it is with the commandments. Sometimes they feel like heavy appendages – you must do this, you cannot do that. But then, when we use those appendages as wings, we can soar very high – approaching God Himself.

Yes, the various regulations regarding food consumption are numerous. But, taken as a whole, they raise the mundane act of eating to a spiritual activity, an activity that allows us to constantly rediscover the image of God in which we are created, and to assert the God-side of our makeup, and keep in check the animalistic tendencies that are part of our makeup.

Those all-important qualities of self-control, discipline, moral clarity, and compassion are taught, through the family structure, in the Jewish home. It is crucial that *kashrut* should not be seen as only a list of dos and don'ts, or even as only searching for the "kosher symbol" on the product package, but as a means of developing a closeness with the Divine, and meeting the challenge of accepting God's definitions of right and wrong in one's life. The story of Adam and Eve in the Garden of Eden stands as a crucial underpinning for our understanding of this educational process; they failed to conform to God's one "*kashrut*" commandment – not to eat of the fruit of that special tree. We are given a chance to right their wrong.

ADAM, EVE, CAIN, ABEL: MISSED OPPORTUNITIES FOR ACCEPTING RESPONSIBILITY

Going a bit more deeply into the Garden of Eden story, we can ask the question: Exactly what aspect of the actions of Adam and Eve brought about their punishment of banishment from the garden? Was it the sin itself – going against God's command not to eat of that fruit? I believe that, more than the act itself, the aftermath of the sin was even more problematic.

When Adam was asked by God about what he did, the first human replied, "The woman whom You gave me to be with me gave me of the fruit, and I ate" (Gen. 3:12). And then Eve says, "The serpent beguiled me, and I ate." We have already discussed the prodigious human ability to rationalize and justify one's actions, and to avoid accepting blame at all costs. Adam and Eve – who are really Everyman and Everywoman – blamed their sin on some extrinsic factor, and not on themselves. This is the true prototype of sin: the human being's inability to take responsibility. I would suggest that it was this failure that brought down upon them the expulsion from the Garden of Eden. After all, if their original "assignment" in the garden was to "develop it and to take responsibility for it" (my translation of Genesis 2:15), then by attempting to shirk that responsibility – which surely included following God's one commandment relating to the garden – they forfeited their right to reside there.

A similar problem is found in chapter 4 of Genesis, in the story of the murder by Cain of Abel. When God asks Cain where his brother Abel is, he replies, "I don't know. Am I my brother's keeper?" Why did God need to ask Cain the whereabouts of his brother? God knew what had happened. Rashi suggests that God was giving Cain the opportunity – a belated one, admittedly – to take responsibility for his actions and say, "I killed him; I sinned; I'm ashamed and sorry." But Cain failed to assume responsibility, and, instead, tried to deny the very notion of responsibility: "Am I my brother's keeper?"

Again, this story, coming as it does so early in the Torah, sets the stage for all of the Torah's commandments to follow. If we are to fulfill our task as Jews, then we must continually assume responsibility for our actions; that idea could even be seen as the very definition of mitzva, which we usually translate as "commandment," but which is inextricably bound up with the idea of responsibility – to God, to our people, to all human beings in the world. One of the eternal messages of the Cain and Abel story is about responsibility of siblings one for the other, and, by extension, responsibility of all of us for each other. The rationalization of "Am I my brother's keeper?" is never in place, because the answer is "yes," because we are all created in God's image, we all have part of God within us. We must love each other, we must give to each other, and, of course, we must not harm each other or take from each other.

There is another early Torah episode that speaks deeply about responsibility, and that is the story of Noah and the Flood. The Noah saga contains, as did the story of Adam and Eve and that of Cain and Abel, the elements of sin, potential repentance, and forgiveness. The major theme throughout these incidents is that God waits, with reasonable patience, for human beings to repent. Adam and Eve (initially, at least) do not repent; rather, they place blame on others. Cain does not repent; he tries to deny responsibility for his own brother.

God gave Noah 120 years to build his ark. Rashi suggests that this lengthy period afforded Noah the opportunity, when asked by his generation why he was building a giant boat, to tell them of God's plan to destroy the world by a flood unless they repent and change their evil ways. Once again, the Noah generation had the opportunity to accept responsibility, but failed to do so, resulting in their destruction.

Each of these biblical episodes ended in disaster: Adam and Eve are expelled from the Garden of Eden, Abel is dead and Cain is condemned to wander the earth, Noah and his family are saved, but the entire population of the world is destroyed. So, what hope is there for the world? What do the outcomes of these episodes portend? Can people truly take responsibility for each other – or even for themselves?

The great biblical commentator Rabbi Samson Raphael Hirsch (1808–1888) strikes an optimistic note.

After the flood's waters had abated and Noah and his family had left the ark, God made a covenant with Noah, promising never again to destroy the earth by water. The eternal symbol of the covenant is to be the rainbow. In his commentary on Genesis (9:15), Rabbi Hirsch explains the symbolism of the rainbow:

> In spite of all differences in the degree of human development, God would never again decree the downfall of the whole human race, but that its future education to its godly purpose was to be founded just on these differences and varieties of humanity. For is the rainbow anything but the one pure complete ray of light,

> broken up into seven degrees of seven colors...and from the one to the other, are they not all rays of light, and, combined all together, do they not form the one complete pure white ray?... God unites them all together in one common bond of peace, all refracted rays of the one spirit of God. Even the lowest, darkest one, most distant from the light, is still a "son of the light."

Rabbi Hirsch's point about unity in diversity is buttressed by one final episode in the Bible that is recounted right after the story of Noah and the Flood. The Bible tells us that "the whole earth was of one language and of one speech." This would seem to describe an almost utopian situation – the world is unified by one single language. However, apparently that extreme degree of unity presented a problem. Because everything was uniform, there were no differences of opinion, only one single message. This situation led to the evil of materialistic totalitarianism, the notion that everyone must be the same. God's response to the building of the Tower of Babel was to disperse the people and thereby bring diversity to the human race. The message is clear: Unity is very good, but uniformity is not.

These early stories of Genesis teach us so much. The Garden of Eden, beautiful and idyllic as it was, is not a realistic setting for human beings to carry on their lives. Sin and its repair are major factors of human moral existence, with human beings charged to perfect an imperfect world, not the dream world of Eden. We need to be schooled to accept responsibility for our actions, for that shouldering of accountability is the vehicle for world perfection. God continues to send messages encouraging the human being to engage in self-perfection and world perfection, but people often seem immune to these messages: Cain, the generation of Noah. The greatest counterforce to this assumption of responsibility is arrogance; the after-Flood promise of no destruction is sealed by the rainbow of diversity – a message ignored by the one-dimensional generation of the Tower of Babel.

Flowing through these stories is one uniting thread: the understanding of God as the arbiter of moral knowledge, and the rejection of a relativistic notion of morality. The forbidden fruit must not be eaten; murder is wrong; corruption and violence are morally reprehensible;

diversity is productive. What we are allowed to eat and what we are prohibited from eating produces a godly discipline within us, and helps us take responsibility for our actions and for those around us. God commands, and His commandments are absolute, but, if we but take responsibility, God is compassionate, loving, and forgiving. We will see this in more detail later in this book, when we discuss the one day of the year which brings automatic forgiveness as an expression of God's love – the day of Yom Kippur, the Day of Forgiveness.

THE JEWISH PEOPLE: DISTINCT AND SEPARATE, YET TOGETHER WITH ALL

There is an important final word about *kashrut* that applies to many other Jewish observances as well, but is perhaps most prominent in the area of our dietary limitations.

For human beings, eating is a social experience. Dining together promotes conviviality, friendship, sometimes even love. But several times the Torah speaks of the Jewish people as being *separate* from the other nations. Some degree of separation – and this is a delicate balance – is necessary in order for us to retain our special mission in the world; assimilation does not allow us to perform our assigned task. And so, the kosher laws – and some of our other practices – are seen as a way of producing, subtly perhaps, that certain level of separation from the rest of the world. If it is more difficult to dine with someone, it is less likely that courtship and marriage will follow.

Another story from my debate team days. We traveled to Washington, D.C. to debate the team at Howard College (now Howard University), an African-American college. This was in the late 1950s, when segregation was the order of the day, and apparently the Howard team had previously only debated with other African-American colleges. At the conclusion of the debate, we did what we always did – shook hands with our opponents. We were shocked to see the entire Howard College audience rise to their feet and give us a prolonged standing ovation. Thank God, things have changed so much in our own day. But I remember thinking then – against so much of what white America was thinking – how important it was the we were there to demonstrate the unshakeable Jewish belief that every human being – regardless of race, creed, or color – is created in God's image and therefore must be treated as an exact equal.

As Jews, our assignment is a joyful one, but a difficult one: to develop within our individual selves and our nation the moral clarity and compassion that we need in order to teach the world about these qualities so that the world can ultimately reach a state of perfection. As teachers-by-example to the world, we cannot retreat to an ivory tower of separateness; teachers must interact with their students, and certainly not remain aloof from them. However, we are also a unique people, nurturing our peoplehood in order to enrich our lives, to develop our intimacy with God, and to carry out our mission.

The Garden of Eden and its mysterious Tree of Knowledge make their presence felt as we try to navigate our way through life as citizens of the world, as well as committed Jews. Instinctively and intuitively, we want to know, and we want to understand. Even as we study and observe the commandments we have been given, we hearken back to that one directive that our ancestors Adam and Eve were given. That imperative stands as the prototype, certainly of our commandments relating to eating, but also to every mitzva in the Torah.

God commands because He loves. Many of His commandments we can understand in great depth; some, we cannot. We often see ourselves as a separate people, but we also feel universal, as a profoundly integral part of humanity. In the midst of these paradoxes, we accede to discipline, accept responsibility, strive for holiness. We struggle for meaning, even in our most mundane activities, such as eating. The fruit of that primordial tree, my head of lettuce at West Point, the lunch I will be eating today – all of these help me feel, in different ways, closer to God, to the Jewish people, and to my assignment to teach the world about compassionate righteousness and moral justice.

Chapter 4

Shabbat: A Sanctuary in Time

THE ULTIMATE EXISTENTIAL QUESTION – AND THE ROUTE TO ITS ANSWER

The deepest question a person can pose to herself or himself, the most existential question of all, is "Who am I?" This is not a question that can be answered by merely stating one's name, one's address, one's nationality, or one's profession. One cannot even properly reply to this self-query by listing aspects of one's personality or character traits: I am friendly, I am curious, I am fearful, I am honest. We cannot even answer this question by touting our Facebook page, because everyone knows that our Facebook page is very much "doctored up" to show only that part of our personality that we want our other "Facebook friends" to see. To arrive at anything approaching a truthful answer to this question requires time, thought, effort, painful introspection, and self-analysis. Perhaps this is why few people are honest enough and courageous enough to risk asking themselves the question, much less trying to answer it.

The Bible, on the other hand, refuses to leave this question unanswered. As we have discussed, God created the human being in all of that being's complexity. So let us turn to the two biblical chapters of

Creation for at least the beginnings of an answer to our question. While the process of self-discovery may often be uncomfortable, the path that Judaism suggests will not only be positive, but often joyful.

TWO CREATION STORIES, TWO PROTOTYPES OF THE HUMAN BEING

On the basis of what we have been taught by my teacher and mentor Rabbi Joseph B. Soloveitchik in his masterful work *The Lonely Man of Faith*, the first two chapters of the book of Genesis present two different prototypes of the human being. The first – to whom Rabbi Soloveitchik refers as "Adam I" – is the "Creative Human Being," formed as part of the physical natural world, but as the apex of that natural world; he is endowed not only with the animalistic drives and limitations of all of the other creatures that walk the earth, but also with the image of the transcendent God: "And the Lord created the human being in His image, in the image of God created He him, male and female created He them" (Gen. 1:27). It is important to note that Adam I is already gifted with the transcendent image of God. However, that gift must wait for its full development and activation until Adam I is joined with Adam II, as we shall see. We have been biblically commanded to walk in God's ways (Deut. 28:9), and just as God created worlds, so must we – in His image.

And so, Creative Human Being is commanded to populate the world, to rule over it, and to eventually bring humanity under the aegis of the image of the Divine (when he is joined with Adam II, as we shall see). "And God blessed them [the first humans] and God said to them: 'Be fruitful and multiply, replenish the earth, and subdue it. Have dominion over the fish of the sea, and over the birds of the air, and over every living thing that moves on the earth'" (Gen. 1:28). This Adam I is to be the conqueror of the lesser creations and the partner with God in *recreating* the incomplete world in which he was placed; indeed, he is also charged with recreating *himself* by "subduing" and refining his own animalistic characteristics.

Moreover, the Midrash on the words "Male and female created He them" maintains that initially God created one being who was a man-woman complex (Genesis Rabba 8:1) and who was to be God's junior co-creator with a mandate to conquer the world. This primordial being, the original Adam I, is completely self-sufficient. He uses his female counterpart merely as an adjunct with whom to propagate the world, and his progeny are merely convenient extensions of himself through the generations to be used as tools to help activate his master plan to eventually subdue the world.

The second chapter of Genesis retells the story of the creation of the human being, but this being seems starkly different. It is about "Adam II" that God says, "It is not good for the human being to be alone" (Gen. 2:18), because this human being is far from being self-sufficient, and deeply feels existential aloneness and social loneliness. He/She feels the angst of solitude, craves an existential partner with whom to communicate, with whom to create, whom to love and by whom to be loved, and especially with whom to produce continuing generations to pursue the mandate of perfecting the world under the kingship of the eternal God of Love. This human being is called "Redemptive Human" by Rav Soloveitchik because this Adam II is very cognizant of what he/she lacks, and is desperately searching for his/her redemption – through a soulmate companion, through familial continuity, through like-spirited others united in community, and through an intimate relationship with especially the "God within," that portion of God on High which the God Above lovingly "inspired" within each and every human being. For Adam II, woman is not a mere adjunct, but a real partner, and the progeny – likewise created in God's image, and with freedom of choice – will either enhance world development or impede it.

Redemptive Human is especially anxious to listen to, internalize, and even develop the sacred voice of the God within himself; this God within is the entranceway to our connection to the inspirited voice within every other human with whom one may wish to partner in some way. Tragically, however, it is often the cacophonous voices roundabout, initiated by those who wish to dominate by brute force, that will drown out the divine "still small inner voice" of love and commitment and continuity, of peace and harmony and forgiveness.

And although on the international level it is the warmongers who shut down the divine voice of the peace seekers, on the personal level it is most often Creative Human who drowns out the voice of God, even from within himself. He is constantly on the go, always a few minutes late for the coming plane trip, full of ideas for the next world ready to be conquered – and he has no time to contemplate about what he really requires, what he truly wants to accomplish, and who he actually is. He is so addicted to acquisitions that he has neither the mind nor the patience for human relationships, for family development, for a loving commitment. It is indeed Creative Person who leaves no room for Redemptive Person, who turns off and tunes out the still small voice with sarcastic superiority and supercilious scientism.

The reader has certainly realized by now that we are not discussing two different human types – although the contrasting typologies are certainly to be found in every community. The more likely situation is the struggle between both typologies, Creative Person and Redemptive Person, within the very same individual. A healthy mix between the two would certainly be the goal, but what is the way to get there? Can there be real synthesis between Creative Human and the still small voice of the Divine which would sanctify creativity with godliness and perfect humanity by suffusing sibling love throughout the world?

SHABBAT ENABLES REDEMPTIVE HUMAN TO JOIN WITH CREATIVE HUMAN IN ONE BEING

It is fascinating to note that before the Bible begins its second chapter, in which it describes Redemptive Human, it provides an amazing segue between the description of Creative Human in chapter 1 of Genesis and Redemptive Human in chapter 2 of Genesis:

> Now the heavens and the earth were completed and all their hosts. And God completed on the seventh day His physically creative work that He performed, and He ceased on the seventh day from all His physically created work that He had made.

Yes, the segue between Creative Adam I and Redemptive Adam II, between Active Human and Contemplative Human, is the Shabbat. It is the Shabbat which will enable Creative Human to begin to internalize the values and lifestyle that will empower him to become a Redemptive

Human as well, to truly partner with God to perfect and redeem the world in the kingship of the Divine.

This magnificent idea and ideal of the Sabbath may be seen in an important textual comment by our most classical biblical interpreter, Rashi. Rashi notes an internal contradiction in the second of the three Sabbath verses cited above: On the one hand, the text states that God *completed* (*vayekhal*) His creative activity on the seventh day, when He made His final creative act, to be able to declare, "He did it all." (The word "*vayekhal*" is related to the word "*kol*" – "all" or "everything.") Yet, the very same verse continues, "And He *ceased* (*vayishbot*) on the seventh day from all the physically creative activity which He had performed." What happened on the Sabbath? Did He complete – and thus add all the final touches to – the world, or had He already ceased His creative activity before the advent of the Sabbath, when it was still the end of the sixth day? How is it possible that He both created and ceased from creation on the same Sabbath day?

SHABBAT: THE DAY OF SACRED AND LOVING COMMUNICATION

Rashi magnificently explains that with the coming of the Sabbath there was still one critical act of creation missing, perhaps the most important creation of all: *menuḥa,* the uniquely spiritual creativity of contemplation, of introspection, of communication with the closest people to us whom we often take for granted, like our family and our community, and, most important of all, of communication with the God within and the search for the God without. The Sabbath is a unique day created by God in which the human being must leave the transient world of acquisition of things, and devote him/herself to the eternal world of deeply felt relationships; must leave the arena of constantly upgrading and developing physical amenities in order to enter the arena in which one upgrades and develops oneself, one's friendships, one's dedication to sharing and helping those in need. As the Bible says in chapter 2 of Genesis, "And the Lord God of Love formed the human being of dust from the earth and breathed into his nostrils the soul-breath (*neshama*) of life, and the human being became a 'living, loving' soul," translated by the *Targum* as *ruaḥ memallela,* "a communicating spirit."

Creative Human uses his mind for new inventions and novel scientific and technological creations. Redemptive Human uses his soul for spiritual and godly creative insight in order to better understand himself, and the God within himself. Creative Human utilizes all of his cognitive power in order to change the physical reality around him and subdue and conquer it under his dominion. Redemptive Human utilizes his godly spiritual powers in order to reach out in love, complete/perfect himself, his family, and every "other" with whom he comes into contact. If we can learn on the Sabbath to recognize and commune with the God within, it will open our eyes and hearts to understand that if we are all children of God, blessed with the God who is within each of us, then we are all siblings of each other, sharing the same Divine Natural Association (DNA), and we are all united together in depth and in quality despite any superficial differences between us, whether they be in material means, skin color, or social status. As the Bible teaches, you must love your fellow human like you love yourself, because the fellow is existentially part of you, and you are existentially part of him/her, and both of you are part of the Divine.

The aspect of the human being presented in chapter 1 of Genesis, as we explained, is Creative Human. This human is deeply involved in the world, and sees himself or herself as the master of it. This is the persona that dominates in most of us. We are very involved in physical creativity, doing business, accumulating money and objects of material value, earning a livelihood; but often, in the hectic pursuit of livelihood we lose our lives, our true existential selves, the "personal" person, who has the divinely endowed ability of forging close relationships, forming enduring friendships, learning to give and receive love, and recognizing familial continuity as bestowing eternal life upon the progeny from generation to generation. As an anonymous poet once wrote, "I searched for myself but could not find me. I searched for my God but could not find Thee. I reached out in love to 'other,' and I found all three."

SHABBAT AS THE PATHWAY TOWARD REDEMPTIVE HUMAN

And so, along comes the institution of Shabbat in between the story of the Creative Human Being and the Redemptive or "Personal" Human Being. Shabbat creates the bridge which enables Creative Human to meet and merge together with Redemptive Human. Shabbat tells us that there is a time to cease being creative, and begin being reflective, to cease physically creating in order to appreciate what has already been activated, and most importantly, to concentrate on the spiritual creativity of loving human relationships, of in-depth human communication. And it is necessary to begin with those relationships closest to home: oneself, one's God, one's spouse, one's children, one's community.

The Bible specifically states: "A person may not leave his 'place' on the seventh day" (Ex. 16:29). The Sages of the Talmud interpreted these words to mean that on the Sabbath one may not go beyond two thousand cubits (a little over half a mile) of the city limits; at the very least, the verse is telling us that the Sabbath was given to enable deep communication with those who are in closest proximity to us.[1]

Love requires, first and foremost, communication, but a sacred communication which is a human function that emerges from the soul-breath of the Divine within each of the communicators. An exchange of ideas and thoughts and feelings, and the ability of one individual to truly understand the other in the fullness of his/her being – soul-talk – emphasizes both the commonality of every human as well as the uniqueness of each individual. And it is precisely such soul-felt communication that is so necessary for the human being to express the image of God within him, so necessary for him to express his truest and deepest self. This is what the Bible means when it says, "It is not good for the human being to be alone" (Gen. 2:18). One of the worst punishments the human being can experience is that of solitary confinement.

1. The part of the verse in question reads, "A person may not go out of his place on the seventh day." The talmudic Sages provide an entirely different interpretation by changing the vocalization of the word *yetzeh* (to leave) to *yotzi* (to take out) which they take to mean that one may not carry objects on Shabbat from the private domain to the public domain and from the public domain to the private domain. Jewish law accepts both interpretations, but for our purposes, we prefer the plain meaning of the text which, at the very least, is encouraging us to spend the Sabbath day close to home.

SHABBAT PROVIDES THE OPPORTUNITY FOR SACRED COMMUNICATION

The rituals throughout Shabbat emphasize this soul-talk. Just before sunset on Friday, the woman of the house kindles the Sabbath candles, hopefully infusing light and love throughout the house. This is the time when the wife-mother spontaneously petitions God concerning every member of the household. She generally lights one candle for each close family member – the two parents and each of the children. There are many homes in which one extra candle is added for the guests who may be present on any given Shabbat. We then welcome God's emissaries – or "angels" – of peace around the Shabbat table who, according to Jewish lore, accompany every Jew to his/her Friday evening dinner table; these invisible emissaries actually embody the Divine Presence within the Jewish home. We greet them with the blessing of peace – *Shalom aleikhem,* "Peace unto you" – because they hopefully will help the family experience the wholeness (the real meaning of the word *shalom,* from the root *shalem)* and sense of fulfillment which are the greatest gifts of Shabbat.

We then chant *Eishet ḥayil,* the paean of praise of the husband to his wife, but which is mystically considered to be a hymn of praise to the feminine aspect of the Divine, the *Shekhina.* The sexual union between husband and wife, which is very much encouraged by Jewish law, and especially on Friday night, reflects the spiritual union between God and His nation Israel, as well as the act of spiritual communication inherent in the sexual love between husband and wife.

Parents traditionally bless their children on Friday evening with the Priestly Benediction: "May God bless you and keep you. May God cause His face to shine upon you and show you favor. May God lift up His face to you, and grant you peace."

Just before beginning the meal we recite the Kiddush, the special blessing of sanctification over wine. The text of this blessing is a reminder of God's creation of the world and a reminder of the exodus from Egypt, that God created us with love and expects everyone to be free, inviolate, and involved in loving relationships. This is precisely the message that we are mandated by God to share with the world.

The book of Psalms (104:15) tells us that wine brings joy (*simḥa)* to the heart of the individual. The Hebrew word *simḥa* is usually used for a profound feeling of happiness and fulfillment, as on the occasion of a wedding or a circumcision ceremony, or the naming of a baby daughter. *Simḥa* is very different from the "good times" associated with overindulgent drunkenness and wild abandonment of clear thinking and individual responsibility. I learned a lesson of what sacred happiness is all about from a teacher of mine, Rabbi Moshe Aharon Poleyeff, who, at the end of his life, lost his eyesight but knew many of the tractates of the Talmud by heart. It was the custom at Yeshiva University for students to visit their Talmud instructors on the day of Purim, a day associated with drinking a bit more wine than usual. Rabbi Poleyeff said to us, "Let me teach you the proper and necessary attitude toward the drinking of any inebriating beverage. If you feel happy and fulfilled within yourself, and close to the God within yourself, then the drinking to express that joy and happiness is sacred drinking. But if you are empty inside, and you are looking to the wine to insert within you that happiness, then that drinking will only lead to drunkenness." That is why Sabbath wine in the fullness of the family or friendship context becomes an act of sacred communication.

A similar message is delivered by a classical Jewish source, the Midrash (*Tanḥuma* on *Parashat Noaḥ*, 13), commenting on the vineyard that Noah planted after leaving the ark. The Midrash states that Satan asks to be Noah's partner in the planting of the vineyard. As the Midrash recounts, Satan slaughters a lamb, a lion, a monkey, and a pig over his planting. And the Midrash goes on to explain that one drink of wine will make the individual "meek" as a lamb; two drinks make one feel mighty as a lion; three will cause one to be actively gamboling like a monkey, "hopping about, dancing, giggling, and uttering obscenities in public"; and the fourth drink makes one wallow disgustingly in waste like a pig.

Both my teacher's message and the stark symbolism of the Midrash carry with them the profundity of our use of wine for the blessing of the sanctification of Shabbat: Utilize the physical joys of eating and drinking which our material world supplies, but make certain that they will lead to spiritual elevation rather than drunken inebriation. Hence, the Jew raises the Kiddush cup and chants the words "Blessed are You, God, who sanctifies Shabbat," assuming responsibility for spending the day in the atmosphere of joyousness and familial love, and expressing the truth that every aspect of the physical world, even an intoxicating beverage like wine, can bring in its wake sacred communication.

Therefore, the meal is punctuated with special Shabbat Songs or *zemirot*, turning the physical act of eating into the framework of sanctity and spirituality. Music is the language of the soul, words of poetry which allow the spirit to soar; Shabbat, after all, is a day much more of poetry than of prose. Everyone around the table is encouraged to give a Torah message, usually based upon the portion of the week read in the synagogue that Shabbat. At my own table I encourage each person to tell about something special that happened to him/her that week, or simply express a thought or a question which has been bothering her/him – ethically, spiritually, politically, humanistically – and in this way the entire meal becomes an act of sacred communication, climaxing in the Grace After Meals, in which we give God His due. This is also true of the Sabbath-afternoon meal, and it is to be hoped that this unique "table-culture" of soul-talk and soul-song will even extend, at least in part, to family meals as often as possible throughout the week.

Even the closing of the Shabbat day contains a unique form of sacred communication. Shabbat ends with Havdala, the Separation Ceremony, recited over a cup of wine, a double-wicked candle, and fragrant spices (to symbolically revive the soul from its loss of Shabbat sanctity). We began the Sabbath with candelabrum lights and a cup of Kiddush wine. There is also a custom to inhale fragrant spices at the beginning of the Sabbath, representing the unique spiritual fragrance of the Sabbath Day.[2] As such, we end Shabbat much in the way that we began Shabbat. It is as if Shabbat is a never-ending day, presaging a redeemed world that is called "A day that is completely Shabbat" (*Pirkei DeRabbi Eliezer*, 19).

The following is the text of the Havdala blessing:

2. The Talmud in Shabbat 33b tells the story that R. Shimon bar Yoḥai and his son, after having spent thirteen years hiding in a cave in order to study Torah and escape the Roman persecution, emerged on a Friday just before Shabbat. They saw an old man holding two bundles of myrtle and running at twilight. "What are these for?" they asked him. "They are in honor of the Sabbath," he replied. "But one should suffice you." "One is for 'Remember' and one is for 'Observe'" [both the positive and the negative commandments of Shabbat], he replied. Said he (R. Shimon bar Yoḥai), "See how precious are the commandments to Israel."

> Blessed are You, Lord our God, Sovereign of the Universe, who separates holy from profane, between light and darkness, between Israel and the nations, between the seventh day and the six days of physical creativity. Blessed are You, God, who separates between the holy and the profane.

Havdala, as the climax of Shabbat, like Shabbat itself, is a glimpse of the World to Come, the world of redemption, without any of the dualities of this world. For Havdala, we take the two lights with which we began Shabbat, and we merge them into one (the double-wicked candle). In doing so, we imagine the time when darkness will be emblazoned with light, when the profane will be transformed and elevated into the sacred, and when the gentile nations will be at one with Israel. We follow Havdala with a song about Elijah the Prophet because he is the prophet who will announce the ultimate redemption. As the prophet Malachi (3:23) prophesied: "Behold, I will send you Elijah the prophet before the coming of the great and awesome day of the Lord."

SANCTITY OF TIME: A SPECIFICALLY JEWISH CONCEPT

The verse near the very beginning of the book of Genesis which discusses the Sabbath begins with the words "And God blessed the seventh day and sanctified it" (Gen. 2:3). The authoritative Hebrew dictionary *HaMilon HeḤadash* by Avraham Even-Shoshan (Jerusalem: Kiryat Sefer Publishing, 1986) cites this verse as an example of the meaning of the Hebrew verb *vayekadesh,* usually translated as "[God] sanctified." Even-Shoshan explains the etymology as "separated from the profane (or secular)." According to this etymology, the verse means that God *separated* Shabbat from the other days of the week; therefore, the Hebrew word *kadosh,* usually translated as "holy," etymologically carries with it the notion of "separate" or "other." When the verse tells us that God "sanctified" the day of Shabbat, it is really informing us that God made the day "separate" or "other" or "qualitatively different" from all the other days of the week – actually, from all other time.

It is very interesting that the first example of any form of the word *kadosh* – sanctified – in the Torah is in this verse we have just quoted, which is about the sanctification of time, not place: "And God sanctified the *seventh day.*" Most religions contain the idea of special or sacred places, spaces, or sacred objects that take up space. These include temples, shrines, holy objects.[3] Judaism contains this notion as well: the Holy Temple that once stood in Holy City of Jerusalem, the Holy Land of Israel, the space of a synagogue – a house of prayer – or a *beit midrash* – a house of Torah study – the Holy Bible, the Holy Torah Scroll. All of these places or objects are to be found in space. They are all "separate" and "apart" from usual secular spaces and objects. They usually require special cleanliness or purification on the part of those who enter their portals or touch the sacred objects.

However, it is Judaism that uniquely developed the "sanctity of time." The great theologian Rabbi Abraham Joshua Heschel, in his seminal book *The Sabbath: Its Meaning for Modern Man* (1951), states that "Judaism is a religion of time aiming at the sanctification of time." Heschel points out, "We know what to do with space but do not know what to do about time."

If we think about this, we realize how true this is in our own lives. We know how to use space: our homes, our workplaces, our spaces for recreation. After all, space and objects in space seem to belong to us, are under our mastery. However, we seem to be under the mastery of time.

Rabbi Shmuel Salant (1816–1909), who was the chief rabbi of Jerusalem, had a sundial clock erected in the area of the Jerusalem open marketplace (the *shuk*). When you looked at the clock, you could actually see the ebbing of the day, from sunrise, going down to sunset and then darkness. In place of the usual numbers on a clock, on this sundial clock there were the twelve Hebrew letters of the phrase from Psalms 144:4 ימיו כצל עובר, "His days are like a passing shadow." Obviously, the message of the clock is that time controls us, and, whether

3. The philosopher Rudolf Otto (1869–1937), in *The Idea of the Holy*, writes at length about the meaning of the word "holy" (he coins the term "numinous") and gives many examples of how the concept is expressed in what he calls "art," which for him includes architecture and music (see his chapter IX, section 3). Since he is a Christian, not a Jewish, theologian, he speaks about the sanctity of place, even sound (music), but not time. He speaks of the fear, and often dread, of God. We are emphasizing, to a much greater extent, God's love.

we like it or not, every human being is born, develops, and eventually dies, generally too early for himself and his loved ones, but completely out of his control.

At my graduation from elementary school at age twelve, the speaker was Rabbi Alexander Linchner from Yeshiva Torah VaDaas, the founder of Boys' Town of Jerusalem, the famous orphanage and educational institution. He looked at us, some sixteen graduates, and presented to us a parable from the great rabbi, the *Ḥafetz Ḥayim*. He told us that the younger generation might not be sensitive to the parable, but that the older generation would fully understand it. He said to us,

> I envy you, because death is very far from your minds. You see a long life in front of you, and you certainly feel eternal. The Ḥafetz Ḥayim said that life is like a postcard. You begin to write on the postcard. You don't have much to say, and the space on the postcard seems plentiful, so you write large, with much space between the words, and especially between the lines. As you come to the middle of the postcard, you realize that you had more to say than you thought. So, you start writing in small letters, words running into words, lines running into lines. All too often, you conclude the postcard without having written your most important message. Sometimes, there is not even room for your name.

I have never forgotten Rabbi Linchner's talk, and on my office desk I have a replica of Rabbi Salant's sundial clock. I generally feel as if I am waging a war against time: there is so much to do and never enough time to do it in. I am constantly aware of the fact that ultimately we seem to be conquered by time.

I recall the first time that I had a study appointment with a very special individual who eventually became a beloved friend, a most diligent Torah student, and a respected benefactor, Sanford Zalman Bernstein. I arrived twenty minutes late for the appointment. His secretary gave me a look that suggested that no one ever comes late for Mr. Bernstein, and handed me a green telephone. (Everything in Mr. Bernstein's financial office was green, the color of American dollars.)

"Rabbi," said the voice on the other end of the line in a rather gruff manner, "time is money. You made me wait for you twenty minutes; you will now wait for me twenty minutes."

"I apologize for being late," I sheepishly replied. "I came by bicycle and the traffic was unbearable. But time is much more precious than money. Time is life. So let us now make the most of the time that is before us, and begin our Torah appointment."

I have always been taken aback by the expression "to kill time," usually meaning to waste time because you have nothing meaningful to do with the time that is before you. Life is measured in time, and if you waste the time at your disposal, you are not killing time as much as you are killing yourself – literally committing suicide. We live within time, and time continues beyond our own life span; indeed, time is eternal. Objects in space, physical objects, even the most magnificent of buildings, even human beings, eventually decay and pass from the world. It seems almost as if time is mocking us. In the dimension of space, we do not control time; time controls us.

However, ideas and ideals, words and thoughts – which exist in the dimension of time – may very well live forever. Hence, Rabbi Heschel sees Shabbat, which is a veritable oasis of spirituality in time, as teaching us how to control and eternalize special words and acts by sanctifying them, and thereby eternalizing them. According to our Jewish tradition, God's divine words were communicated to us some four thousand years ago at the Horeb mountain in the Desert of Sinai in the presence of all of Israel, newly freed slaves from Egypt. The Divine communicated Ten Words or Ten Commandments which are the foundation stone for the message of Israel to the world: Every human being created in God's image must be free, inviolate, moral, and compassionate. The culture of the Egyptian pyramids, massive structures in space, barely exists today, whereas the Ten Commandments, the sacred communication from God to Israel, still remain the basis of human and national morality for every civilized nation, and represent the only hope for a redemption of humankind in a future world of peace. The pyramids exist in space and are finite. The divine word still resounds in time – past, present, and future time – in eternal time.

The sacred communication on Shabbat of which we have been speaking likewise occurs in the dimension of time, not space. Great words and spiritually significant events are timeless, eternal; thus, our love relationships live on in and through our progeny from generation to generation. Great lessons we have learned from our teachers are likewise transmitted from generation to generation.

Shabbat, which we have seen as a day of sacred communication, a day of loving relationships, family, friends, and community, a day of soul-talk, soul-song, and soul-study, that is the day that has been called "an oasis in time," a time-out from the dimension of the finite, and a time-in to experience the infinite. And it is important to note that, after God created a magnificent if incomplete world of natural phenomena – both inanimate and animate – as well as humans, the first of His creations that He terms "sacred" is just that oasis in time, the Sabbath. The fact that Shabbat is above and beyond ordinary time is reflected by the fact that it begins with sunset on Friday and concludes with the coming out of the stars on Saturday night – a later time, making it a very extraordinary twenty-five-hour day. God, Shabbat, and Israel must live in eternity.

SHABBAT IS TRUE LIFE, NOT MERELY EXISTENCE

It is clear from what we have said that the sanctity of time is of much greater import than the sanctity of space. This is captured in a very interesting way in terms of Jewish law. The holiest object within our tradition is the Sanctuary, which housed the two tablets of stone containing God's revelation to Moses at Sinai. Just where the Bible describes the Sanctuary and all of its appurtenances, it calls out: "But My Sabbaths shall you keep!" (Ex. 31:13). Our Sages explain that this means that all of the thirty-nine physically creative activities that were involved in the construction of the Sanctuary are those very activities that are forbidden on the Sabbath day. Our tradition makes it very clear that physical creative activity, even for the construction of our most important physical object, the Sanctuary, has become subservient to the sanctity of time, the Shabbat.

The Mishna – the compendium of the Jewish Oral Law – takes these thirty-nine categories of physical creative activity that are prohibited to us on Shabbat and places them in a fascinating order. These categories of forbidden activity fall into four groupings: bread production, clothing production, leather production, and building production. These groupings can be seen as providing the basic needs that all humans require for their existence: food, clothing, and shelter. Of course, these acts are perfectly legitimate for six days of the week; we must perform them in order to exist physically and nutritionally. But on Shabbat we refrain from them, because, as we have explained, Shabbat is the day given over to spiritual creativity, not physical creative activity, the day of sacred communication.

That is why we must prepare all the physical necessities that we will require during the Sabbath – our meals, the clothing we will be wearing – before Shabbat begins; the money that we generally use in order to acquire physical objects is forbidden for us to touch on the seventh day. All of this is in order that Shabbat may be devoted exclusively to the sanctity of time, and to sacred communication.

God Himself supplied us with food in the desert, the special manna, which fell from the heavens each day (except Shabbat) for the Israelites to eat. The purpose of this heavenly food is expressed by the Torah in Deuteronomy 8:3: "Not by bread alone does the human being live (Hebrew: *yiḥyeh),* but rather by that which issues from the mouth of God does the human being live (Hebrew: *yiḥyeh*)." The *Targum* (the Aramaic translation/commentary on the Torah) uses two completely different words to translate the same Hebrew word *yiḥyeh,* rendering the verse to read "Not by bread alone does the human being *exist* (Aramaic: *mitkayem*), but rather by that which issues from the mouth of God does the human being *live* (Aramaic: *ḥayeh*)." Physical objects, even physical necessities, produce only existence. That which issues from the mouth of God – His laws, His parables, His teachings – bring true life.

SHABBAT: PLUG OUT IN ORDER TO PLUG IN

As we have said, Shabbat is a day dedicated to spiritual creative activity, to *life* in its very deepest sense, rather than mere physical *existence.* I investigated a number of languages, and found that Hebrew is the only language in which the word for life – *ḥayim* – is in the plural. The two outer letters are *ḥet* and *mem,* which spell the Hebrew word *ḥom,* warmth, or love. At the center of the word *ḥayim,* the letter *yod* appears twice, representing God's name. Life is a plural noun because we are never alone; every one of us lives together with the God within us (*tzelem Elokim,* the image of God). Living with God means living with eternity, with soul-spirit; it means living with sacred communication, which we attempt to bring to all of our relationships, first on Shabbat, and then throughout the week.

This profound idea was brought home to me through an incident connected to the conversion of a young woman, a very sensitive and intelligent professional dancer. After her year-long study, I brought her before the Conversion Court, where she was asked by one of the judges, "Why have you decided to convert to Judaism?" At first, she replied, "Because I fell in love with my Jewish fiancé and wish to marry him." But then she continued, "But now, after a year of study, I would say that the real reason is that I have also fallen in love with Judaism." "What is it about Judaism that you especially love?" asked the judge. The answer came immediately: "Shabbat. I don't think I could live without Shabbat." "What is it about Shabbat that makes you love it so?" She replied, with intensity and feeling,

> That there are no telephones on Shabbat. Every day of the week, most of us are concerned with acquiring objects, both as part of our work world and as part of our play world. But Shabbat is a day of acquiring relationships. Objects readily go astray, and very often break down, the more they are used. Relationships, especially if they are worked on, only become stronger. Nowadays, however, because we are living in a society of technology, even when two people are eating together, they are not looking at each other or even talking to each other. Each is usually intently involved with the cell phone in front of him/her and checking messages, or else talking with someone about business or some other function of their lives. The greatest blessing for me on Shabbat is that there are no telephones.

This convert truly understood the Shabbat message of sacred communication, a message that, unfortunately, is sadly lacking in our technology-driven world. I observed this woeful deficiency while having dinner with my wife at a restaurant, when I noticed, a few tables away from us, a couple at whose engagement party I had spoken only a few weeks before. I took note that they were both speaking on their cell phones while they were eating. I actually "clocked" the duration of this – twenty minutes. Finally, I went over to their table and said, with tongue in cheek, "Excuse me, but I assume that you were speaking to each other on your cell phones." Somewhat embarrassed, the new couple admitted that, even when they are together, they are focused on the "object" – the cell phone – and not upon each other. I reflected to myself, yet again, how desperately we need Shabbat, a day when the focus is never on "objects," but on our loved ones, on our spiritual selves, on our loving God, on achieving true sacred communication.

Our world of technology is a wondrous one. All of our modes of communication enable us to be in constant contact with many, many people. But, at the same time, there must be limits; we cannot substitute technology for in-depth human relationships. Facebook "friends" are rarely our real friends. We need to plug out of technology in order to plug in to humanity, at least one day a week.

Shabbat is the day when our existence truly becomes life – with God at the center, and loving relationships with other people as its goal. In Heschel's words, Shabbat is truly "a palace in time," indeed, a sacred Sanctuary in time.

Chapter 5

Rosh HaShana: A New Year with the Shofar's Wails

SACRED COMMUNICATION WITH THE ADDED ELEMENT OF THE SOUND OF THE SHOFAR (RAM'S HORN)

Our study of Shabbat in the previous chapter taught us that the very definition of Shabbat's sanctity is that it is a day of sacred communication. In a very strong sense, that is true about all our major festivals: they are a kind of "Shabbat," because sacred communication – with oneself, one's family, one's God – pervades their character.[1] However, each holiday adds its own special facet, its own distinctive "brand" of that special level and type of communication.

1. The Ramban notes on Leviticus 23:24 that the word *Shabbaton* – a "Sabbath-like" day – is used by the Torah regarding many of the festivals, and, by inference, applies to all of the festivals, as well as Shabbat. He explains that, in addition to the negative commandment of not performing *melakha* – the specific categories of physical creative activity that are prohibited on Shabbat and festivals – there is a special *positive* commandment denoted by the word *Shabbaton,* which emphasizes a special, distinctive, and unique atmosphere of tranquility which must pervade these holy days.

With regard to Rosh HaShana, its special character is the idea of *teshuva,* repentance. To best understand the concept of *teshuva,* and therefore to comprehend in depth the message and character of Rosh HaShana, we turn to the biblical verse in Leviticus 23:24: "Speak to the children of Israel and say, 'In the seventh month,[2] on the first day of that month, it shall be to you a Sabbath-like day (Hebrew: *Shabbaton),* a remembrance of the staccato sound of the shofar, a day of sacred assembly.'"

The reader will note that heretofore we have not adopted the conventional meaning of Rosh HaShana as New Year's Day, according to the literal meaning of the Hebrew words *Rosh HaShana,* "The beginning of the year." However, it is so explained by our Sages (in the first mishna of Tractate Rosh HaShana) who apparently see an inextricable link between the New Year and the staccato sound of the ram's horn, which is the one commandment of Rosh HaShana mentioned in the Bible, and is, as we shall see, the call to *teshuva.*

THE TERUA SOUNDS OF THE SHOFAR: LOOK INTO YOURSELF AND LEARN TO WEEP

Rosh HaShana is a festival that is shrouded in mystery.

The Bible refers to it as *Yom Terua,* "The day when the horn is sounded." The Sages of the Talmud agree that the *terua* sound which is to be extracted from the ram's horn is to be a staccato-broken sound. There is a difference of opinion on whether that sound should be like nine sobs – echoing the weeping cries of a person in distress – or three wailing sighs, echoing the sounds of an individual bemoaning lost opportunities.[3] We blow both of those sounds on the shofar on Rosh HaShana.

In most cultures, the marking of the New Year reminds one of the passage of time, as well as the passage of individuals under the

2. The Torah counts the months beginning with the month of Nisan, the month in which the festival of Passover, the birth of the Jewish nation, falls. Tishrei, the month of Rosh HaShana, is therefore the seventh month. The Sages, however, count the years beginning with the month of Tishrei. See chapter 11 for a full discussion of the Hebrew calendar.
3. The discussion is to be found in Rosh HaShana 33b.

inexorable and inscrutable mastery of time over them. As individuals realize the brevity and uncertainty of their mortal lives, they react with the response which sums up their world view: eat, drink, and be merry, for tomorrow we die. And so, from a secular perspective, the New Year is an occasion for unbridled raucousness and excessive drinking – witness the scene of the New Year's celebration in Times Square, New York.

From a Jewish perspective, however, the view is radically different. Our approach to marking the New Year, with its glimpse into the inevitable passage of time, must remind the sensitive individual of the necessity for stocktaking and personal self-examination. After all, life is a gift, and so we must employ our Rosh HaShana realization of the precariousness of life to begin to ponder whether we are making proper use of that gift. We must properly sanctify and utilize the time that is in our grasp to improve our lives by coming closer to the God within ourselves and to the God within every other human being. This may all be summed up by the statement of the Sages: "Repent one day before you die" (Mishna Avot 2:10). And so, our tradition holds that the broken cry of the shofar represents the self-examination and introspection that begins the process that we call *teshuva*, repentance.

For most human beings, such a reconsideration of one's life can only begin with a cry, a tear, a sob, and a sigh, an honest recognition that we are, after all, mortal, physical, and even part-bestial, and that we are in need of further developing our godliness and our responsibility to make a difference in ourselves and in the world. An individual who is self-assured and self-satisfied can never repent and is incapable of weeping due to the inadequacies of his character, which he rarely stops long enough to recognize. With this mandate of soul searching and soul uplifting before God, the festival of Rosh HaShana develops the ideal of sacred communication – now expressing the deepest recesses of the individual's soul – to new heights of love of God and love of human beings.

THE TEKIA SOUND OF THE SHOFAR: JOY AND OPTIMISM

This deep introspection sounds daunting, and, to a certain extent, it is. However, there is another sound that we blow on the shofar, called the *tekia*. The *tekia* sound, which surrounds the *terua* blast, is a straight sound, clear and unbroken. While the cry of the *terua* reminds us of how much in need of repair each of us is, the *tekia* is the triumphant and optimistic promise by God that each of us may succeed in self-improvement and self-development.

And it is not only ourselves who are in need of improvement on Rosh HaShana; our imperfect world also requires "fixing," as we have already explained. The *tekia* sound gives us optimism on this front as well. As we say again and again in our Rosh HaShana prayers, the day of Rosh HaShana is the anniversary of the birth of the world. Hence, the shofar does not only sigh and sob; it also shouts – joyously, exultantly, triumphantly! This is the firm and upbeat *tekia* sound – and each weeping *terua* sound is preceded and followed by the exultant *tekia* sound, a ratio of 2:1 in favor of joy and optimism. And indeed, if each of us is improving him/herself, the collective improvement equals the improvement of the world: *tikkun olam*.

And so, in the Rosh HaShana liturgy, we shout with joy in our recognition of God as Creator, Owner, and "King" of a world of wondrous beauty replete with dazzling colors and exquisite variety, a world of the uninterrupted rhythms of sunrise and sunset, of summer, fall, winter, and spring, a universe containing galaxies of stars in the heavens above and variegated fish and flora in the seas below. We are moved to tears – as I was, in that biology lab long ago – when we investigate snowflakes under a microscope. One might ask, "Where is the place of the mortal human being in light of what appears to be the infinite expanse of the heavens and the seas?" Why, he/she is the astronomer, the scuba diver, the one with the ability to see, to contemplate, to calculate, to correlate, to create, and to recreate. The human being is, after all, God's partner in perfecting His world, and the *tekia* promises that that perfection of humanity will eventually come to be.

THE SHOFAR: RECREATING OURSELVES AND THE WORLD

In order to better understand the deep connection between the sound of the shofar, Rosh HaShana, and repentance, it is important to note that the first and second days of the Hebrew month of Tishrei commemorate the creation of the very first human being. Let us reexamine how God created that first human being: "And the Lord God created the human from dust of the earth, and He exhaled into his nostrils the soul-breath of life; and the human became a living soul" (Gen. 2:7).[4] We have already seen that perhaps the central commandment of the Torah is for us humans created in the image of God to become God's partners in recreating ourselves and eventually recreating and perfecting the world. Hence, on Rosh HaShana each formed human being (nowadays, the appointed representative of all of the people in the synagogue on Rosh HaShana) takes a ram's horn, the beauty and strength of the animal – but, at the end of the day, only a bestial and limited animal, in a certain sense similar to the dust of the earth – lifts up the ram's horn and exhales into it from his most internal, existential being, from his soul-breath of life initially breathed into him/her by God. It is now our *tzelem Elokim* – the image of God in which we are created – which empowers us to bring forth from the animalistic part of ourselves the eternal sounds of the whisper we have already heard from the God within: on the one hand, our own inadequacies (*terua*) which are crying out for improvement, but also our divine empowerment to recreate ourselves and to help recreate the world (*tekia*). The shofar sound is, indeed, the sound of the God within, with whom we dialogue during this period of repentance.

This idea is actually built into the very biblical verse that commands the sounding of the shofar on Rosh HaShana: "Speak to the children of Israel and say: 'In the seventh month, on the first day of that month, it shall be to you a Sabbath-like day, a *remembrance* of the staccato sound of the shofar, a day of sacred assembly'" (Lev. 23:24). Note that the day is called a *remembrance* of the staccato sound; when we sound it (or hear it) from the shofar, we remember the primordial day – the very first Rosh HaShana day – when God took the animal aspect of the human ("dust of the earth") and infused within it His own divine essence, at once enabling the human being to recognize his own inadequacies, but also at the same time empowering him to raise his celestial self over his bestial self, by which he can perfect himself and perfect the world. Our blowing of the shofar is a recreating of God's initial act of

4. *Nefesh ḥaya,* usually translated as "a living soul," is translated by *Targum Onkelos* as *ruaḥ memallela,* "a communicating spirit."

the first creation of the human being on Rosh HaShana. It is that primordial divine exhalation that is the soul-breath which is the very image of God within each of us that we are remembering on Rosh HaShana, and that we now repeat with our blowing of the shofar. That is why the Bible refers to Rosh HaShana as the *remembrance* of the divine primordial shofar sound at the time of His creation of the first human being.

So, on the festival of Rosh HaShana the dramatic sounding of the shofar proclaims two marvelous life-changing opportunities: to recreate ourselves, and to help recreate the world in the image of the Divine.

ARE WE TRULY FREE TO MAKE SUCH AN INTERNAL CHANGE IN PERSONALITY?

However, many deterministic philosophies as well as human excuses for the retention of weaknesses, and even addictions, maintain that the individual is not truly free, that he is enslaved to his nature and nurture. Sigmund Freud and Ingmar Bergman[5] have taught that children are doomed to repeat the mistakes of their parents, that we are the sum total of the genes with which we were born as well as events that have happened to us, and the actions to which we have been subjected by others.

Here again comes the shofar with a message that is very different from determinism, but is rather the message of the existential freedom within every individual which emanates from the image of God within him/her. Our Bible ordains that the shofar is not only to be sounded on Rosh HaShana, but, during biblical times, also at the beginning of every fiftieth year, called the "Jubilee Year" in the Bible, because "jubilee" (*yovel*) is another biblical word for shofar (according to Rashi on Leviticus 25:10). The Jubilee Year marks a foreshadowing of the Redemption, with humanity and world perfected at the End of Days. On this fiftieth year, all slaves were freed, and all debts were canceled, and families were resettled together on the lands which were originally tribally distributed. "And you shall sanctify the fiftieth year, and proclaim freedom throughout

5. Ingmar Bergman (1918–2007) was an influential film director and screenwriter, many of whose films were inspired by Freud's theories.

all the land to all its inhabitants;[6] it shall be a Jubilee for you, and you shall return every person to his possession, and every person to his family" (Lev. 25:10). The Bible is clearly telling us that the human being is indeed free to change, that the human being is far more than the sum total of his nature and nurture, that Freud and Bergman notwithstanding, the human being is free to recreate himself, to help recreate the world, and will eventually become God's partner in perfecting us into a world of peace under the majesty of God. This, too, is the message of the shofar that emerges from the God within each of us.

Undoubtedly, this is very difficult, and requires looking deeply into ourselves and into the nature of our relationships with family and with friends. But this is really the commandment of *teshuva,* of repentance. This concept of recreation is not left by Jewish tradition in some abstract form, but rather incorporated into specific imperatives that aid the individual in her/his *teshuva.* For example, the Rambam states:

> Among the paths to *teshuva* are the following: The penitent should frequently cry out to God with supplication, should give charity according to his ability, should keep far away from the matter in which he sinned, should change his name, as if to say, "I am another; I am not the same person who committed those deeds," and he should change all of his actions for the good, and for the straight path. (*Hilkhot Teshuva* 2:4)

The Rambam beautifully presents the existential difference between the individual before his or her *teshuva,* and what that person becomes, having done *teshuva*:

> Great is repentance, because it brings the individual close to God's Presence.... Repentance brings close those who are distant. Just last evening, he was disliked before God...and today he is beloved and precious, close and a friend... (*Hilkhot Teshuva* 7:6)

6. This phrase is inscribed on the Liberty Bell, the symbol of American freedom.

...and even, perhaps, a "partner." The process of *teshuva* involves recognizing that one has erred, feeling genuinely sorry for the error, and resolving not to make the same mistake again. And, perhaps even more importantly, the *teshuva* process also includes asking for forgiveness for having done wrong – from God, but especially from any individuals whom we have wronged: parents, children, one's spouse, one's friends. And it is crucial to remember that, at least in the case of God, His divine hand is always outstretched to those who seek His forgiveness; He is ready to receive our repentance with joy.

Even though our goals for doing *teshuva* seem prodigious, the Torah enables us to repent in stages. According to the great sage and Torah commentator the Ramban (Nahmanides,1194–1270), the Bible is speaking of the commandment of *teshuva* when it proclaims, "For this commandment which I command you today is not too wondrous for you, nor is it far off. It is not in heaven..., nor is it across the sea..., but rather the matter is very close to you, in your mouth and in your heart, to perform it" (Deut. 30:11–14).

So, is *teshuva* hard or easy? The process of *teshuva* may very well be difficult and demanding. It is not easy for an individual to admit that he has sinned, and especially difficult to say "I'm sorry" to someone else. Furthermore, to recreate one's personality is a lifelong task. But how to begin to do this is not that difficult, and is probably best explained by the famous statement from the Kotzker Rebbe (1787–1859) in his interpretation of the verse in Psalms 103:12: "As far as east is from west, God has distanced our sins from us." The Rebbe asked his students, "How far is east from west?" The Hasidim piped up with a variety of linear measurements: ten thousand miles, four million miles. The Rebbe said: "No. Not all those huge distances. The distance between east and west, between wickedness and righteousness, is only *eine kleine drai* – one small turn." It is only a change in direction – one small turn. It is that switch in direction that we are expected to take on Rosh HaShana.

THE GREATEST ROSH HASHANA IN HISTORY

The joy of the *teshuva* of Rosh HaShana is expressed in perhaps the most critical Rosh HaShana in history. Following the exile to Babylonia (present-day Iraq) after the destruction of the First Temple in Jerusalem in 586 BCE, the great leader and prophet Ezra led the return of the Jews from Babylonia back to the Land of Israel, to join there with the community of Jews who had remained in Israel after the Temple's destruction.

What Ezra found was extremely disheartening: the Jews of Judea had intermarried with local pagans, adopted many of their customs, and had all but abandoned Jewish observance. At a dramatic assembly held on the day of Rosh HaShana, Ezra, with his prophetic mantle and charismatic personality, read and taught the Torah inspiringly to the people, gently exhorting them to repent of their errors and to return to Jewish observance, and especially teaching them about the great opportunity that *teshuva* affords. Chastened, the people began to weep, and to sink into depression as they reflected on their misdeeds. In a transformational moment, Ezra clarified to them the true nature of Rosh HaShana: optimism. "This day is holy to the Lord your God; do not mourn, or weep – for all the people wept when they heard the words of the Torah. Then he said to them 'Go your way, eat sumptuously, and drink sweet beverages, and send portions to those for whom nothing is prepared, for this day is holy unto our Lord, for the joy of the Lord is your strength'" (Neh. 8:9–10).

Ezra transmitted to his people assembled, and to Jews for all generations, the optimistic joy of repentance, the exaltation which comes from our realization that we have the power to change ourselves. Ezra helped his community – and us – to understand that on Rosh HaShana we celebrate our joy with food and drink, confident and joyful that our loving God believes not only that we ourselves are capable of returning to godliness, but He also empowers us as his emissaries to turn the whole world toward the God of compassionate righteousness and moral justice.

THE ROSH HASHANA PRAYERS: THE JEWISH MESSAGE TO THE WORLD

Hence, we recall on Rosh HaShana the goals of Judaism, and thus our mission. The structure and content of the Musaf service sets forth our most fundamental Jewish beliefs and aspirations. The *Malkhuyot* (Sovereignties) section of Musaf speaks of God's kingship, of an entire world under God. What this means, in effect, is that the only laws that can be promulgated for all of humanity are those which are in consonance with God's laws, the laws of the Ten Commandments, the Noahide ethical laws which are the biblical universal laws of morality, which the Bible calls compassionate righteousness and moral justice. There may be lesser rulers, whether they are called kings, emperors, prime ministers, or presidents, but they must likewise be subject to the moral laws which God has taught. God, after all, is the King of kings, the one Master God over the entire world. This also means that there is no room whatsoever in the world for a totalitarian or despotic leader who rules by force or terror and literally enslaves at least some significant number of the populace under his control. The absolute prohibition of slavery – that no human being is permitted to subjugate another – was taught by the Bible to the world when God Himself took the Hebrews out of slavery in Egypt, and that prohibition clearly wells up from the words of the Bible informing us that God created every human being in His image.[7]

On Rosh HaShana, *Malkhuyot* is introduced by the *Aleinu* prayer. (*Aleinu* is so important that it also forms the conclusion of every statutory prayer service during the year.) The *Aleinu* concludes with the verse from Zechariah 14:9, "On that day [of the acceptance of God by the entire world] the God of Love will truly be One and His name One." The God of Love will rule the world, against all totalitarianism and despotism. In the meantime, says the *Aleinu* prayer, we Jews came into the world accepting this concept of a universal God demanding compassionate righteousness and moral justice. Therefore, our role is to teach this idea to the world because we are mandated by God to be a "kingdom of teachers and a holy nation" (Ex. 19:6).

We must teach, first and foremost, God's love, that God loves everyone and so we must love everyone. That understanding will bring peace on earth – a world of wholeness, a world of love. This is the romance between God, the Jews, and the world. God, in His love, appointed us to deliver His message to the world: the loving parenthood of God must lead to the loving siblinghood of human beings. From this perspective one begins to understand that democracy is built into the

7. See our discussion in chapter 13.

very fabric of the Torah. A government imposed autocratically by means of power and submission is antithetical to the kingship of God that we declare in *Malkhuyot.*

The story is told of a hasidic rabbi who passed away, and left two sons. In the hasidic tradition, the elder son took on the role of being the new *rebbe,* the new leader of his group of Hasidim. Two weeks after the father's passing, the younger son said to his brother, "Father came to me last night in a dream, and told me that I should be the new *rebbe,* not you." The wise elder brother immediately replied, "I understand, but what you've said is not sufficient. It is only when all of the Hasidim will appear to you in a dream and tell you that they accept you as *rebbe,* will you then become the *rebbe*!" The meaning of the parable is clear: No one can foist rule on anyone else; because only God is sovereign; a flesh-and-blood leader must be chosen by at least a majority of those whom s/he wishes to lead. The goal of the Jewish people will only be reached when the world – not just our nation – comes to recognize the sovereignty of the God of Creation and Love in a world filled with compassionate righteousness and moral justice.

While *Malkhuyot* speaks of God and humanity, the next section of Musaf, *Zikhronot* (Remembrances), places before us God's special covenantal relationship with Israel, the mutual faithfulness and commitment which eternally unites us. The Jewish people promise that we will always keep the commandments,[8] and God promises that we will always live as a nation and a separate peoplehood, return to Israel, and ultimately redeem the world (see Genesis 15; Isaiah 2).

God's specific love for the Jewish people is part of *Zikhronot*'s theme, quoting several verses that describe the great passion with which God initially embraced the Jewish people when He took them out of Egypt, and the ardor with which the Jewish people gave God their love. However, *Zikhronot* goes much further, describing God's loving relationship with all of creation and emphasizing the notion that not only Israel is called upon to come close to God, but so are the nations of the world called upon to cast their lot with the one God. *Zikhronot* proclaims that

8. This refers to the "covenant at Sinai," when the Israelites proclaimed, "All that God has spoken we will do and we will understand" (Ex. 24:7).

God is mindful of *all* individuals and nations, each of whom will have a unique mission to fulfill on the road to redemption. *Zikhronot* proclaims that all individuals and nations are remembered by God on this day, and judged according to their actions.

The third and final segment of the Musaf service is *Shofarot* (Sounds of the Ram's Horn). This portion makes the connection between the two moments in history when the sound of the heavenly shofar was and will be heard: one event at Sinai when God revealed to us His Torah, which we accepted for all generations freely and joyously, and the second sound of the shofar which will yet be heard and accepted, not only by Israel, but by the entire world, that will announce the ingathering of the exiles to the Land of Israel, and the final Redemption.

The God of *Malkhuyot* (Sovereignties) is first and foremost the God of creation of all of humanity and the world. The God of *Zikhronot* (Remembrances) is first and foremost the God of revelation and especially in His unique love relationship with Israel, expressed in a Torah which was originally meant for the entire world. The God of *Shofarot* is the God of redemption, when everyone will be joined in a loving relationship with our universal God of Love in a perfected world of redemption.

ROSH HASHANA AND THE SHOFAR DRAW US CLOSER TO REDEMPTION

Lest any of our readers be skeptical about such a claim, I would suggest that in our very times, two thousand years after the destruction of the Second Temple and our exile throughout the world, and some seventy-five years after the Holocaust, we are the fortunate generation that is privileged to see the beginning of the redemption of Israel in a Jewish state, and even the movement of much of humanity toward our God of Love.

Against all the laws of history, which decree total assimilation and the end of peoplehood for those who have been exiled from their homeland even for two *hundred* years – witness the disappearance of the Girgushites and the Canaanites – we have returned to our national state after two *thousand* years of exile. Similarly, after two thousand years of persecution by the majority of the Christians against the Jews, an amazing rapprochement is taking place before our very eyes, whereby the mother religion Israel is being embraced by and is embracing hundreds of thousands and even millions of Christians with mutual respect and a united march toward redemption. Large organizations such as Christians United for Israel (CUFI), Christian Friends of Israel (CFI), and Bridges for Peace work tirelessly in support of the Jewish state and the Jewish people. Within Africa there are many thousands claiming ancestry from the Lost Tribes, similarly desirous of returning to Israel and to Jewish peoplehood.

I believe that much of this is happening in our generation because of the power of *teshuva*, because we have taken, as the Bible prophesied, the first steps in our return to Israel and return to God. Over the last few generations great numbers of Jews have returned spiritually to their tradition. We may certainly declare that Israel has remained faithful to its covenant with God despite persecution and even holocaust, and God has remained faithful to His covenant in providing for the eternity of the Jewish people.

An old woman once found herself all alone in a strange synagogue for Rosh HaShana, having traveled to her non-observant daughter for the holiday. Everyone was wishing everyone else a good year – except for her. She looked upward to God: "You are my only and truest friend, my Father in heaven. But what can I wish for You? Long life? – You are the author of life. Good health? – You live forever. I know what I can wish You, the greatest wish of all: May You, my beloved Parent-in-Heaven, have *naḥas* (true Jewish joy) from your children!"

It is this relationship – God as a parent, we as His children, all of us as siblings – which we crave and for which we strive, throughout the Rosh HaShana-Yom Kippur period. We must do our part, and God then promises that He will do His. And it is this relationship that we keep in the forefront of our mind, as we move to Yom Kippur, the Day of pure and unconditional forgiveness and love.

Chapter 6

Yom Kippur: A Fast Day Festival?

YOM KIPPUR: UNIQUE JOY BECAUSE OF PHYSICAL DEPRIVATION?

Yom Kippur is my favorite festival of the year.

This may sound strange, especially since the gentile world – and also a good part of the non-observant Jewish world – see Yom Kippur as a very bleak and sad day, the very antithesis of a festival. That is no surprise, since this "Jewish festival" is a twenty-five-hour complete fast – no eating or drinking – on which we also are commanded to refrain from wearing leather shoes, using fragrant creams or oils, or engaging in sexual relations. It is almost as if those observing Yom Kippur are somehow in mourning; in fact, many of the prohibitions of the day are the same prohibitions that Jewish law prescribes for those mourning a close relative: not wearing shoes, so that one can actually feel the stones and sharp pebbles beneath his feet, refraining from the pleasures of sexual relations, and from the use of creams and oils used for pampering the physical body. Indeed, it is true that on Yom Kippur we are enjoined from performing acts of physical creativity – use of electricity, cooking, and so forth – exactly as on the Sabbath, but without the Sabbath's concomitant pleasures – sumptuous meals, singing around the table, relaxing and communicating with spouse and children. So, where is the festivity of this festival?

In order to begin to answer this question, let us look at what the Bible has to say about Yom Kippur. In Leviticus (23:32), the Bible describes the character of Yom Kippur: "It shall be a Sabbath of Sabbaths to you." The Bible is calling Yom Kippur not only Shabbat, but *Shabbat Shabbaton,* a double expression of Shabbat – a kind of "Shabbat on steroids." From our previous extensive discussion about Shabbat we know that Shabbat is a day of great festivity and joy, and so it would seem that the Bible, with its double expression of the Shabbat character of Yom Kippur, is declaring Yom Kippur to be an especially festive day.

I believe that the key to understanding Yom Kippur is to be found in an earlier biblical verse: "For on that day [Yom Kippur] He will forgive you, to purify you; from all of your sins before God shall you be purified" (Lev. 16:30). And so it is that, while Rosh HaShana is the first of the Ten Days of Repentance, Yom Kippur is the last and the zenith of those ten days, in which we are promised forgiveness as a result of our repentance, and even, according to one view in the Talmud, being granted automatic forgiveness on that day – even if we have not repented![1]

And so, how could I not be ecstatic about this festival? Our God of Love promises that, on this day, we receive the greatest gift of all – forgiveness – and, once forgiven, I feel myself in the presence of a God of overwhelming love. Indeed, on Yom Kippur, God even invites us into His home for a twenty-five-hour period, during the waking hours of which we are expected to be in the synagogue.[2] As the psalmist says (27:4): "One thing do I desire of the Lord, that which I truly seek: that I may dwell in the house of the Lord all the days of my life, to behold the sweetness of God, and to be a welcome visitor in His abode."

1. See Shevuot 13a. Note, however, that this refers only for forgiveness for transgressions against God. Transgressions against other people can only be forgiven by the wronged people themselves.
2. In many Eastern European communities of the previous generation, the Jewish householder would remain in the synagogue even during the night of Yom Kippur and study together with the rabbi the details of the Holy Temple service.

Note that being in God's presence is to be in the midst of a spiritual and supernal sweetness, flowing not from physical blandishments, but rather from the more profound delight in the spiritual. Remember that one can become "overstuffed" with food, drink, and other physical pleasures, but never from elation emanating from the spiritual. It is only in matters of the spirit that more is always better. A very important aspect of this spiritual joy and sense of well-being is that we ourselves see not only that we are capable of rising above physical temptations and seductions, but also to what extent we can truly delight in the sacred and the spiritual. This is the experience of Yom Kippur!

Our souls sing on Yom Kippur.[3] We are together with a compassionate, loving God who forgives us. And so, I cannot imagine a day more enjoyable than Yom Kippur – a true gift from God. The prayers during the full day that we remain in the synagogue, while steeped in the solemnity of a day full of import, have a festive quality to them, often expressed in their tunefulness. The very confessional section of the prayers, the *Vidui,* in which we mention a catalogue of sins, is sung in a major key! Yes, we are confessing our sins; but we also know that God has promised divine forgiveness, and we rejoice with the confidence of that promise. A recurring line in the *Vidui* states: "And for all of them, O God of forgiveness, forgive us, pardon us, purify us." Although this can sometimes sound like a request, it is meant here to be interpreted as a categorical statement: You forgive us for "all of them." Yom Kippur brings complete forgiveness.

---

3. The source for the deprivations we observe on Yom Kippur is the continuation of the same verse we quoted regarding Yom Kippur as a "Sabbath of Sabbaths" (Lev. 23:32). The Hebrew reads ועניתם את נפשתיכם, usually translated as "And you shall afflict your souls." However, the root of the Hebrew word for "affliction" is ע-נ-ה, a root that can also mean "to sing" or "to respond by singing," as "And Miriam sang (ותען, from the same root) to them: Sing to God..." (Ex. 15:21). The Mishna in Sukka 38a uses the same root to express the singing of Hallel prayer, the Psalms of Praise. Regarding Passover, the Talmud understands the additional meaning of *leḥem oni* (from the same root), the "bread of affliction," to also mean "the bread over which we sing" (the psalms of praise) at the Passover Seder. And so, this phrase, ostensibly about Yom Kippur deprivations, could actually be understood to read, "And you shall enable your soul to sing."

On Yom Kippur there is no food or drink; we rather imbibe the spiritual. Even our intimacy on that day is reserved for God. The mourner removes his shoes because, in his grief, he feels uprooted from the material world; on Yom Kippur, we remove our leather shoes in God's house because we have no need to be rooted in the material world.[4] On Yom Kippur we are much more connected to heaven than to earth.

In God's presence, I am in the presence of eternal love, and nothing can give greater joy. For the individual who treasures the opportunity of spending a full day with God's love and in God's realm, no period in time could be more filled with elation. Hence, one may refer to Yom Kippur as a consummate God-fest by means of a love-fast.

THE FIRST YOM KIPPUR IN HISTORY

The very first Yom Kippur in history eventuated from the egregious "sin of the desert" – the building and worshipping of the Golden Calf by the Israelites, replete with sexual orgies and bestial conduct toward animals and humans, just weeks after receiving the Torah from God. In a sense, so many of our own wrongdoings emerge from a source all too similar to the great "sin of the desert." The idol that the Israelites constructed was that of an animal, alluding to the bestial desires within themselves. And the substance used to construct the calf – gold – alludes clearly to how, often, in pursuit of riches, we commit serious moral infractions.

As the Bible recounts, after the intercession of Moses, God agreed to forgive the nascent Jewish people for this treachery of licentiousness – an affront to the God who had shown them so much love and had revealed Himself to them with His gift of the Torah. This forgiveness came on the tenth day of the month of Tishrei – our Day of

4. When Moses stood in God's presence at the burning bush, God instructed him, "Remove the shoes from your feet, for the place upon which you stand is holy ground" (Ex. 3:5). Shoes, representing material rootedness, had no place as Moses stood in the realm of the purely spiritual. In our early-morning blessings, we recite the blessing thanking God for "providing for all my needs." This blessing (now usually recited in the synagogue) was originally recited just before the individual put on his shoes in the morning. Once again, shoes are the symbol of physical rootedness.

Forgiveness, Yom Kippur – forever ensconcing that day as one full of love and the promise of forgiveness.[5]

On that same primordial Yom Kippur, God revealed Himself once again, in the same place as the initial revelation – Mount Sinai – a revelation of equal importance to the revelation of all of the laws of the Torah. This "second revelation" was not a revelation of laws, like the first, but rather it was a revelation of love, of the names – and, therefore, the characteristics – of God, each of which is an expression of His love: "The God of Love, the God of Love,[6] a God who is compassionate and gracious, slow to anger, abundant in loving-kindness and truth, showing loving-kindness to thousands, bearing iniquity, transgression, and sin, and purifying…" (Ex. 34:6–7). Through this revelation, God defines Himself, first and foremost, as a loving forgiving God, with His very first name repeated twice to signal that he loves us both before we sin, and even after we sin.[7]

TO WALK IN GOD'S WAYS MEANS THAT WE TOO MUST FORGIVE

As we have just explained, the essence of Yom Kippur joy is that Yom Kippur is the day on which God forgives all of us. But do not think for a moment that Yom Kippur is a purely passive festival from our perspective, that it is only a day on which we receive and rejoice at God's forgiveness of us. One of the major commandments in the Torah (Deut. 28:9) is "And you shall walk in His ways." Just as God forgives us, so ought we forgive others who have transgressed against us. And so, a major commandment of Yom Kippur is for us to have forgiven those who have sinned against us before we even enter into the Yom Kippur fast.

One of the most difficult things to do is to forgive others, because the feeling of having been wronged is a very strong one. However, it

5. See Rashi on Taanit 30b, where he examines the chronology of the events of the year following the Exodus and concludes that the second set of tablets – representing atonement for the sin of the Golden Calf – were given on the Tenth of Tishrei.
6. YHVH in Hebrew, which, as we explained in chapter 1, really means "love."
7. See Rashi ad loc., based on Rosh HaShana 17b.

becomes somewhat easier to forgive if, regarding the incident in question, one recognizes that s/he shares at least some measure of guilt for what has occurred.

I am reminded of an incident that came to my attention many years ago in New York regarding a married couple with four children who frequently hosted a young yeshiva student as a regular guest in the house on Shabbat and festivals. The husband changed jobs and began to travel a great deal on business, and his wife continued to host the student. After a time, it became clear that the wife and the student had come close to consummating an affair. The wife confessed this to her husband, and the husband, furious, declared that he could never forgive her, and that he wanted a divorce. As I spoke to him, it became clear to me that despite his great anger and disappointment, he still had feelings for his wife, and especially for the family they had created together. I gently expressed to him that perhaps a contributing factor to that near-tragedy was that he had been a frequent "absentee husband." When I questioned him, it emerged that during his trips his telephone conversations with his wife were *pro forma* at best, and he did not make up for his absenteeism with special attention to his wife when he was at home. This seemed to hit home with the husband, and once he was able to assume at least part of the responsibility for what nearly happened – his guilt, of course, was not as great as his wife's – he was able to find the strength to ask his wife for forgiveness for his part in the calamity, and then to forgive her as well.

To a great extent, that is how the Rabbis of the Talmud portray the basis of God's willingness to forgive us on Yom Kippur. So it is that one of God's attributes, which we cited before, is that He is *noseh avon*: He "*bears* iniquity, transgressions, and sins." He bears our sins, almost takes them upon Himself, as it were, because, as our creator, he has formed within us our weak and even evil instincts. He takes the responsibility.

There is an amazing passage in *Avot DeRabbi Natan*, a midrashic source, chapter 16:

> R. Shimon bar Yoḥai said, "From where do we know that a Jew will never see the face of hell? There is a parable: It is similar to a king of flesh and blood who had a field of the very worst quality. Some people came along and leased the land, for which they would give

> the king ten *kur* of wheat at the end of the year. They fertilized it, tilled it, watered it, and harvested it, but were only able to reap one *kur* of produce for that year. The king said to them, 'What is this?' They said to him, 'Our lord the king, you knew about the poor quality of the field that you gave us, and we produced as much as we could.' So are the Jewish people destined to say before God, '[You must forgive us because] You knew and even implanted within us the *yetzer hara* (the evil inclination), and how it incites us.'"

So may every sinner say to God: "This is how You made me. You cannot hold me culpable as long as I have tried to do my best."

An individual came to the great Baal Shem Tov, the founder of Hasidism, just before Yom Kippur and said, "Please tell me how to forgive before I enter Yom Kippur." The great rabbi answered, "Go to Berel the baker just before Yom Kippur, and watch him. Then you will know how to forgive." The person went to watch Berel the baker in his home just before Yom Kippur. Berel had two lists: one of all of the incidents throughout the past year in which people had wronged him; the second list was a list of favors he had done for people throughout the year. The guest watched raptly as Berel read through both lists and then threw them into the roaring fire. Forgiveness means to completely put out of your mind any wrong that another has done to you and attempt to also put out of your mind the special favors you did for others, for which you may feel that they owe you extra favors. Berel understood that perhaps he may have done something to trigger the negative acts that had been done to him. Moreover, he felt that is was wrong to do good to someone because you expect the other to return your favor. We must do good because it is the right thing to do good, and, under any conditions, if we are praying to God to forgive us unconditionally on Yom Kippur, we must be ready to forgive everyone else unconditionally on Yom Kippur.

APPROACHING YOM KIPPUR IN THE FACE OF HUMAN TRAGEDY

One of the central prayers of Yom Kippur is *UNetaneh Tokef.* The prayer is haunting, even frightening. "On the day of Rosh HaShana it is written, and on the fast day of Yom Kippur it is sealed: How many shall pass away, and how many shall be born, who shall live, and who shall die ... who by water and who by fire ... who by earthquake and who by plague ..." This prayer seems to be emphasizing the extent to which so many aspects of our lives, such as the length of time we live, the quality of our health, and even our financial status, seem to be part of blind fate, or haphazard luck, but certainly out of our hands. At the same time, comes the conclusion of *UNetaneh Tokef*, with the congregation declaring, "But repentance, prayer, and compassionate righteousness remove the evil decree."

Is that really true? Human experience teaches us that righteous action, heartfelt prayer, and sincere repentance will not necessarily cure the patient in the hospital bed.

We have already explained in our chapter on prayer that God does not necessarily control everything that happens in this world, but rather He gives us freedom of choice to act as we wish, even if our acts are against His will, even if they are evil and destructive. We have learned that God created an imperfect world, with natural disasters, wars, and genetic diseases. As we have also said, God made us humans His partners in perfecting that imperfect world, and certainly contemporary medicine, technological advances, and attention to diet and exercise have helped cure many diseases and lengthened life expectancy in advanced countries.

Moreover, the talmudic Sages themselves have asked about tragic occurrences that often befall righteous people and the beneficial events which are frequently enjoyed by the wicked. The conclusion of the Sages (Kiddushin 39b) is that there is no reward for the observance of commandments in this world and that to a great extent (Avoda Zara 54b) "the world goes on in its natural course," largely irrespective of the degree of righteousness of the individual who may be suffering.[8]

8. It must be noted that there are two opposing views within Jewish tradition regarding the directness of God's control of the world: the one we have presented above (which seems to be the more widely accepted one) and the one expressed in Ḥullin 7b by the statement, "No person bruises his finger here on earth unless it was so decreed against him from on high." Also, when we discuss above the principle that "there is no reward for the observance of commandments in this world," it should be noted that the reference is to an *extrinsic* reward. There is, however, the notion of a reward inherent in the commandments themselves: the significance of the Sabbath,

From this perspective, we must re-translate the words at the crescendo of *UNetaneh Tokef* in a more literal way than we did previously: "But repentance, prayer, and compassionate righteousness will *remove the bitter sting* of the decree." (The Hebrew is not *gezera raa,* the evil decree, but rather *ro'a hagezera,* the bitterness of the decree.) For example, we may not be in control of the length of our lives, but we are in control of the breadth and depth of the years that we are given, of the meaningfulness or lack thereof of the time which is within our control.

From an honest religious perspective, this principle of not receiving a reward for commandment observance in this world makes good sense. The God who is lovingly compassionate and righteous would want us to be lovingly compassionate and righteous, not because it will mean that we will not become sick or drown in a tsunami, but rather because that is the right and correct way to live.

The late Yonatan Moshitz, a member of my community in Efrat, was a shining example of this approach to life. Yonatan was afflicted for years with ALS disease, eventually being able to communicate only with his eyebrows. Not only did he not complain through all of this, but he was grateful that he was still alive, conscious, and of sound mind. Despite his physical impairments, he continued to relate to his family members, especially his children, guiding them as they faced crucial life decisions. In the face of his adversity, Yonatan refused to become depressed, and made it known that if one was determined enough, one could rise from a state of depression and despair, and continue to be a loving and beloved parent, son, and friend. No one could express it as eloquently as Yonatan did, in a video he left before his death:

> Depression is a state of mind that is dependent only upon us. Every day, three times a day, we say: "God is good to everyone, and His compassion is upon all of His creatures" (Ps. 145:9). It's just that we're like flies on a giant mural, not able to see the full

for example, with its wonderful familial and communal togetherness. ("The reward for the commandments are the commandments themselves" – *Pirkei Avot* 4:2.) Finally, although there may be no extrinsic reward in *this* world, we do believe in the idea of a spiritual reward after death – in the World to Come.

> picture. What is *mesirut nefesh* (giving up one's physical life for a higher ideal and value)? It's not lying down on the railroad tracks and saying *Shema Yisrael,* but rather it is accepting everything (that comes your way) with love, even though it's difficult to understand the reason for our suffering.

For Yonatan, the question to be asked was not, "Why is this happening to me?" but rather, "What can I find within my present condition to help me understand a higher purpose for this great challenge?" (In Hebrew, not *lama* [why?], but *bishvil ma* [for what purpose?].) And so, Yonatan continued learning and teaching Torah and being especially close to his loving family, continuing to convey to all who came in contact with him the most important and difficult message of all: to try to do one's best even within the most difficult situations, to continue to live a worthwhile life of love and support. This is certainly part of the message of Yom Kippur: even when divested of almost all of one's physical needs, one can still love and be loved. More than any of my teachers, Yonatan taught me the truest lesson of life.

AFTERWORD

Yom Kippur is called in the hasidic tradition the "Day of Holiness." As we have seen, it is a day absent of physical blandishments, but full of love of God and humanity. The truest joy is within God's abode. In a traditional yeshiva, at the conclusion of Yom Kippur, when one would expect the students to quickly adjourn to the dining room for the breakfast meal, one sees something else – extremely joyous singing and dancing for an extended period of time. This is the celebration of the joy of the life of the spirit.

Yonatan Moshitz was not only against depression – he was never depressed. Although he was left only with the joy of the spirit, he felt that joy profoundly, and even more importantly, he communicated that joy loudly and clearly.

And that is how we conclude this day of sanctity – with *Shema Yisrael*: "Hear O Israel, the Lord of Love and the God of Power, are One."

It is the Lord of Love who comes first. In an imperfect world, power may be necessary, but the goal must always remain love and peace.

We then proclaim the verse *Barukh Shem*: "Blessed be the Name of the Glory (*kevod*) of His Majesty for ever and ever." Glory – *kavod* – refers specifically to God's majesty in *this* world, God's immanent presence in *this* world, God's ruling Torah in *this* world. We are stating, loudly and clearly, that more blessed is the glory of the God of Love in this world than is the presence of God in the supernal world of the ethereal heavens.[9] Indeed, what we are saying at the conclusion of Yom Kippur is that we must bring God's laws of love and spirit within our physical world of everyday life and experience.

The very concluding words of Yom Kippur are shouted fervently seven times, as a prayer and as a statement: "*Hashem Hu HaElokim* – the God of Love, He is the power of the world." Love is the great power that is able to transform an imperfect world of earthquakes into a perfect world of snowflakes. It is ultimately the message of Yom Kippur that love can transform our lives and redeem the world. We must take the love of Yom Kippur, which has lifted us into God's supernal world and higher abode for twenty-five hours, and with the power of that love bring it into our physical world, not only in order to transform our world, but also in order to redeem it.

---

9. This idea, that God's presence in this world – brought about by our actions – is even more significant that His presence in His supernal abode, can be interpreted from the seminal verse in the vision of the prophet Ezekiel (3:12): "Then a spirit lifted me up, and I heard behind me the voice of a great rushing: 'Blessed be the glory of the Lord from His place.'" In the Hebrew, the final word of the verse, *mimkomo,* is usually translated as "from His place." However, when the Hebrew letter *mem* is used as a prefix – as it is here – it can mean "from," but it can also mean "greater than." So the verse may well be stating what we have stated above: that the glory of God (His presence in our physical world) is *greater than* (much more significant than) His presence in His ethereal and heavenly world of the spirit.

Chapter 7

Sukkot: God's Homes on Earth

HOSTING THE DIVINE: HOW ISRAEL SURVIVED DESERT/EXILE

Five days after Yom Kippur, we celebrate the festival of Sukkot. The Bible tells us that beginning on the fifteenth of the month of Tishrei, "in modest protective tents (sukkot) shall you dwell for seven days; every citizen of Israel (the Jewish people) shall dwell in sukkot" (Lev. 23:42). The Sages of the Talmud describe the architectural requirements for these sukkot: simple structures standing under the sky, with basic walls and a roof made of vegetation, tent-like in function and appearance, to provide protection in difficult climatic situations.[1] Ideally, every Jew builds a sukka in which he carries on his life for the seven-day duration

1. According to Avraham Even-Shoshan, *HaMilon HeḤadash*, 917–18, the derivation of the word "*sukka*" is from the Hebrew root *samekh-kaf-kaf*, which means "to cover" or "to hide" (in the sense of protecting), and, by extension, "to cover the sukka with *sekhakh*," the noun commonly used for the vegetation with which we create the roof of the sukka.

of the holiday, taking all of his meals in the sukka and, climate permitting, sleeping in the sukka.

What exactly is the symbolism of the sukka, this modest, protective dwelling that stands at the center of this joyous festival?

Historically and biblically speaking, the sukka represents the simple living structures in which the Israelites resided after their exodus from Egypt and through their forty-year-long desert sojourn. From this perspective, the sukka reminds us that God, because of His great love for us, protected us from harm under the difficult desert climatic conditions, with intense heat during the day, piercing cold at night, roaming wild animals, with little water to be found. At the same time, God saw in our readiness to follow Him even under such conditions an important expression of our great love for the Divine: "I remember you for the affection of your youth, the love at our engagement; how you followed after Me in the wilderness, into an uncultivated land" (Jer. 2:2). In effect, we have here an expression of the love-covenant-commitment between God and Israel.

But it is even more than that. One of the great biblical commentators, the Ramban, often explains that "the experiences of our forefathers are a prescription for what will befall the Jewish people in their future." Hence, our desert wandering is a foreshadowing of our two-thousand-year-long exile experience, with unending expulsions and pogroms. Throughout all of this, and despite the fragile nature of our Sukkot existence, we held firmly to our faith that just as we had emerged triumphant from our Egyptian servitude, so would we be brought home to Israel after our many exiles.

It might seem counterintuitive that this festival of reexperiencing – in the humble surroundings of the sukka – life under desert and exile conditions is uniquely called *Zeman Simḥateinu,* the "Festival of our Joy." However, it is important to remember that our sukka/home was meant not only to protect us physically, but also to provide us with the spiritual strength to weather the difficult conditions during our long exile. Therefore, on each night of the holiday, we invite a special guest to the sukka, great biblical leaders who themselves overcame many difficult obstacles. The traditional list of these *Ushpizin* (Hebrew/Aramaic for "guests") includes Abraham, Isaac, Jacob, Moses, Aaron, Joseph, and

David. It has become customary recently to also invite seven *Ushpizot* (the feminine form for "guests"): Sarah, Rebecca, Rachel, Leah, Miriam, Deborah, and Ruth. Our celebrated guests in the sukka are not show business celebrities or corporate executives, but rather individuals celebrated for their wisdom, their holiness, their leadership of the Jewish people as a unique nation, individuals who provided us with the spiritual strength to weather every storm and emerge triumphant. As we sit joyfully in our sukka/home, we realize that, in truth, we really have no need for lavish accoutrements to make our home joyful; it is the spiritual content of our dwellings and the familial love that the sukka engenders that inject the elements of joy and celebration. As the Talmud (Sanhedrin 7a) states, "When love was strong, we could have made our bed on a sword blade; now that our love has grown weak, a bed of sixty [cubits] is not large enough for us."

We also make an effort to invite "living" guests into our sukka, an extended family. We take note that in the Torah the commandment to be joyful on the festivals is always followed by the commandment to feed the hungry and tend to the needy.[2] We are mindful of Maimonides's admonition: "He who eats and drinks [on the festival] only with his wife and family, without giving anything to eat and drink to the poor and the bitter in soul – his meal is not a rejoicing in a divine commandment, but a rejoicing in his own stomach" (*Mishneh Torah, Hilkhot Shevitat Yom Tov* 6:18).

There is a story told about the great hasidic master, Rav Levi Yitzhak of Berdichev (1740–1809). Every year, on the first night of Sukkot, the rabbi, as was the custom in most Jewish communities, would invite the influential members of the community – the wealthy philanthropists, the Torah scholars – to celebrate the holiday with him in his sukka. One year, however, as the festival approached, none of these people had yet received their usual invitation to Rabbi Levi Yitzhak's sukka. When the festival arrived, it turned out that the rabbi had invited as his guests the town's shoemaker, the butcher, a tailor, and many of

2. "You shall rejoice on your festival: you, your son and your daughter, your male servant and your female servant, the Levite and the stranger and the orphan and the widow who are in your gates" (Deut. 16:14).

the usual itinerant beggars. When the incensed "important" community leaders asked for an explanation from the rabbi as to why he changed the usual tradition, he replied,

> You know, there is also a tradition that, in the heavenly abode, God Himself sits in His sukka, made of the skin of the Leviathan, whose meat will be served by God to the righteous in the next world. I have always dreamed of being invited to this great and holy feast, but, alas, who am I? I am an imperfect person, a rabbi in Berdichev – how will I possibly merit to sit in God's presence at the Leviathan feast? Then I thought further. Perhaps if I, here on earth, invite people into *my* sukka who are not usually seen as deserving – the unschooled, the poor – perhaps then I – the undeserving rabbi of Berdichev – might have the chance of being invited by the Holy One to His sukka on High.

There is a touching song in Yiddish, *A Sukkaleh,* which emotionally embodies this aspect of the sukka's meaning. Here is the song, freely rendered into a rhyming English:

> A *sukkaleh,* quite small, wooden planks for each wall;
> Lovingly I stood them upright.
> I laid thatch as a ceiling,
> And now, filled with deep feeling,
> I sit in my *sukkaleh* at night.
> A chill wind attacks,
> Blowing through the cracks;
> The candles, they flicker and yearn.
> It's so strange a thing,
> That as the Kiddush I sing,
> The flames, calmed, now quietly burn.
> In comes my daughter,
> Bearing hot food and water;
> Worry on her face like a pall.
> She just stands there shaking,
> And her voice nearly breaking,

Says "*Tattenyu,* the sukka's going to fall!"
Dear daughter, don't fret;
It hasn't fallen yet.
The sukka's fine; banish your fright.
There have been many such fears,
For nigh two thousand years;
Yet the *sukkaleh*'s still standing upright.

THE FOUR SPECIES: OUR LONGING FOR THE LAND OF ISRAEL

The festival of Sukkot falls calendrically during the month of Tishrei (which is also the month of Rosh HaShana and Yom Kippur). This is the season of the ingathering of crops at the beginning of the rainy season in the Land of Israel. The Bible even instructs us, "And you shall take for yourselves on the first day [of the festival] the beautiful fruit of the *hadar* tree [the etrog or citron], branches of date-palm trees [the lulav], boughs of thick-leaved trees [the *hadas* or myrtle], and willows of the brook [the *arava*]" (Lev. 23:40). This specific vegetation is indigenous to the Land of Israel, and so this emphasizes our faith that we will soon return to Israel and live in Israel and rejoice in its bountiful produce.

THE SUKKA: GOD'S HOME ON EARTH, THE SANCTUARY

There is a fundamental question that we must ask at this point in our study. The Torah commands us to celebrate the three pilgrimage festivals (times when Jews made the pilgrimage to the Temple in Jerusalem) of Passover, Shavuot, and Sukkot. Each of these festivals allows us to re-experience seminal moments in our history: Passover, the Exodus; Shavuot, the Giving of the Torah at Mount Sinai; Sukkot, our desert sojourn.

Yet, there seem to be two problems with the season in which Sukkot falls. We have stated that the sukka represents the tents in which the Jews lived during their desert sojourn, which began with the exodus from Egypt that we commemorate with the festival of Passover, falling in the month of Nisan, in the springtime. On the basis of this history, logic would dictate that the festival of Sukkot – commemorating as it does our desert wanderings – be celebrated soon after Passover and Shavuot, in the springtime or early summer, which would position it as the culmination of the national pilgrimage festivals: Passover, Shavuot, Sukkot. And yet, the Torah mandates that Sukkot be celebrated in the autumn, immediately following the festivals of Rosh HaShana and Yom Kippur. Moreover, the Bible seems to even emphasize that Sukkot falls immediately after Rosh HaShana and Yom Kippur[3] as the culmination of the trilogy of the universal festivals on which we emphasize world redemption. It would seem from this chronology that Sukkot is not only to be considered one of the national pilgrimage festivals, but it is, indeed, the culmination of the trilogy of our universal redemption festivals (Rosh HaShana, Yom Kippur, Sukkot), and is especially connected with Yom Kippur.

Interestingly enough, when the Talmud (Sukka 11b) gives us the explanation for the symbolism of the sukka, it does not immediately provide the symbolism that we have just explained, i.e., the tent-like structures that the Israelites constructed in the desert. That, in fact, is only the second talmudic opinion; the first opinion (R. Eliezer) asserts that the sukka is rather to be seen as the Clouds of Glory (*ananei kavod*) which rested upon the portable Sanctuary commanded by God to be constructed by the Israelites in the desert. ("And they shall make for Me a Sanctuary, and I shall dwell in their midst" – Ex. 25:8.) It is important to note that this symbolism of the Clouds of Glory is the one accepted by the majority of the biblical commentators (Saadia Gaon, Rashi, Ramban, Ḥizkuni, among others). This portable Sanctuary housed the Tablets of Revelation upon which were written the Ten Commandments of God. This Sanctuary was the first stage of what was to eventually become the Holy Temple (*Beit HaMikdash*) in Jerusalem.

3. In Leviticus 23:34, immediately following the commandment of Yom Kippur, the Bible states, "On the fifteenth day of *this* seventh month is the festival of Sukkot for seven days." The Torah's use of the word "this" seems to emphasize the connection between the aforementioned Yom Kippur, which falls on the tenth of the month of Tishrei, and Sukkot, which falls on the fifteenth of *this same month*. The Bible seems to be stating that Sukkot must also be seen as the climax of the Rosh HaShana-Yom Kippur-Sukkot trilogy of festivals.

Of what significance were these heaven-sent Clouds of Glory encompassing the sukka/Sanctuary, that they are eternally memorialized by our sukkot?

You will remember from our Yom Kippur discussion that *kavod* – glory – refers to God's presence on earth. And so, the Bible informs us regarding the Sanctuary, "The cloud covered the Tent of Meeting (*ohel moed,* the Sanctuary) and the Glory of God (*kevod Hashem*) filled the Sanctuary" (Ex. 40:34). And the Bible has explained earlier that it was precisely at the time that these Clouds of Glory filled the Sanctuary that God communicated with Moses and the children of Israel in the midst of His glorious and sacred presence in this sukka on earth – which was, in effect, a "*Tent* of Meeting" between God and Israel. "And I will rendezvous (meet) there with the children of Israel and I will be sanctified by the [clouds] of My glory" (Ex. 29:43). Clearly, the Sanctuary, with its Clouds of Glory and Tablets of Revelation, was the first model of God's home on earth, as the Jews began their history as a free nation with their desert journey.

This Sanctuary in the desert was a temporary structure because it had to be moved from place to place, as the Jews traveled through the desert and established many different encampments. This sukka/Sanctuary would eventually develop into a stationary Holy Temple when the Jews would enter their Promised Land. This is the symbolism of the sukka, a kind of pre-construction of the Holy Temple-in-miniature for the people in the desert. Please bear in mind that the Holy Temple is called in Hebrew a *Beit Mikdash,* a Sacred Home. With the Sanctuary, we are actually creating a home for God, as the Bible instructed: "And they shall make for Me a Sanctuary, and I shall dwell in their midst" (Ex. 25:8).

Fascinatingly enough, this Sanctuary in the desert began to be erected – at least according to the great halakhic sage the Vilna Gaon – only five days after Yom Kippur, and is therefore clearly connected to the opinion of the talmudic Sage who defines our sukka as Clouds of Glory. This is how the Vilna Gaon presents the chronology in his commentary to the Song of Songs:

As we have explained, the Clouds of Glory appeared and began to protect the Israelites in the month of Nisan, when they were taken out of Egypt at the beginning of their desert journey. However, when they sinned with the Golden Calf (just weeks into their trek), the clouds were removed. Those clouds did not return until the beginning of the creation of the Sanctuary/sukka, says the Vilna Gaon. Moses came down [from Mount Sinai] on Yom Kippur, and, on the day after Yom Kippur, assembled the people, and commanded them regarding the construction of the Sanctuary/sukka. This was the eleventh of Tishrei. The people brought their donations for the Sanctuary/sukka for two days, which brings us to the thirteenth of Tishrei. On the fourteenth of Tishrei the artisans received the gold from Moses in order to fashion and assemble the various parts of the Sanctuary/sukka. And on the fifteenth, they actually began to assemble and complete the Sanctuary, at which time the Clouds of Glory returned, as an added confirmation that the Israelites had indeed been forgiven for the sin of the Golden Calf, and the sukka/ Sanctuary would once again become a Tent of Meeting between God and Moses. Therefore, the fifteenth of Tishrei begins our celebration of the festival of Sukkot.

And so, the sukka clearly represents the Sanctuary, the physical structure which "housed" God's presence on earth.

As we explained, at the very conclusion of our Yom Kippur prayers, we pray and state with crystal clarity that our God of Love will become God over the entire world.[4] This is the very essence and the deepest meaning of Yom Kippur. And so, it follows naturally that the true significance of the desert Sanctuary (and ultimately the Temple) is that the Temple is to be a place of rendezvous and dialogue initially between God and Israel, but eventually between God and the world.

Indeed, it is from the Holy Temple that the Jewish people will eventually communicate to all the families of the earth the closing message of Yom Kippur. As the prophet Isaiah explains in chapter 2, verses 2–4:

4. To recall, we close Yom Kippur by declaring the *Shema*, stating that eventually the entire world will accept the One God, followed by "Blessed be the name of the glory of His majesty for ever and ever," "glory" meaning God's presence in our world. Finally, we declare "*Hashem Hu HaElokim*," that God's love takes precedence over His power and judgment, and that the God of Love will ultimately rule the world.

> 2. And it shall come to pass in the end of days, that the mountain of the Lord's house [the Holy Temple] shall be established as the top of the mountains, and shall be exalted above the hills; and all nations shall flow unto it.
>
> 3. And many peoples shall go and say: "Come, and let us go up to the mountain of the Lord, to the house of the God of Jacob; and He will teach us of His ways, and we will walk in His paths." For out of Zion shall go forth the law, and the word of the Lord from Jerusalem.
>
> 4. And He shall judge between the nations, and shall decide for many peoples; and they shall beat their swords into plowshares, and their spears into pruninghooks; nation shall not lift up sword against nation, neither shall they learn war anymore.

This is very similar to the message of the *Aleinu* prayer that we discussed in our chapter on Rosh HaShana: "And everyone will accept the responsibility of Your sovereignty and You shall rule over them soon and forever.... On that day will the Lord of Love be one and His name one." And this is the message of the Sanctuary, by which we bring the lessons of Rosh HaShana and Yom Kippur into God's house on earth: the sukka/Sanctuary. And therefore, we pray for our ultimate sukka/Sanctuary every day of the Sukkot festival, "May the Compassionate One raise up for us the fallen sukka of (King) David."

Similarly, the development of the Sanctuary/sukka into the Holy Temple is strengthened by the total of seventy bullocks that were sacrificed in the Temple throughout the festival of Sukkot, which our Rabbis explain represent our offerings on behalf the seventy nations of the world.[5] This is in sync with the vision of the prophets that eventually all the nations of the world will flock to the Holy Temple in order to

5. Sukka 55b. You will remember that God promised Abraham that he would be the "father of a multitude of nations" (Gen. 17:4) and "In you (Abraham), shall be blessed all the families of the earth" (Gen. 12:3).

learn compassionate righteousness, moral justice, and peace on earth from the Jewish nation, as we have explained.[6]

As the prophet Zechariah (14:16) prophesies, "And it shall come to pass, that every one that is left of all the gentile nations that made war against Jerusalem shall go up from year to year to worship the King, the Lord of Hosts, and to keep the feast of Sukkot." Clearly, the sukka/Sanctuary was meant to include all of humanity.

The Torah further commands: "Every citizen of the Jewish people shall dwell in sukkot" (Lev. 23:42). This commandment teaches that each of our own familial sukkot must function as a mini-Sanctuary! Each of us builds his or her own sukka – a kind of mini-Holy Temple – for the festival, because each of us must internalize our individual responsibility for *tikkun olam*, for bringing the world to the God of Love. In this way, we demonstrate that, indeed, we *can* fulfill the challenge of Yom Kippur; we *can* bring God down to earth, as it were, and create for Him a central home as well as individual homes throughout the world, wherever Jews happen to be. This is the climax of the Tishrei trilogy which expresses our mission to bring blessings to all the families of the earth.

As the Talmud teaches (Pesaḥim 87b), "R. Elazer says, 'The only purpose for God having brought the Jews into exile was in order for converts to join together with them.'"

6. There seems to be a striking difference of opinion between the two great prophets Isaiah and Micah. The four verses previously quoted from Isaiah are repeated word for word by the prophet Micah (4:1–3), to which Micah himself adds (in verses 4 and 5): "But they shall sit every person under his vine and under his fig tree; and none shall make them afraid; for the mouth of the Lord of Hosts has spoken. For let all the peoples walk each one in the name of its god, but we will walk in the name of the Lord our God for ever and ever." Clearly it would seem that Micah may well have understood Isaiah to mean that all the nations will convert to Judaism, whereas Micah himself believed that they will accept the ethics of Judaism, but not necessarily the rituals of Judaism – that there will be ethical absolutism and ritual pluralism. Similarly, there are two different opinions in the Talmud: in Berakhot 57b R. Shimon b. Elazar states that all the gentiles will convert to Judaism. The Rabbis opine that in Israel they will all convert, but not necessarily in the rest of the world. The Rambam (*Mishneh Torah, Hilkhot Melakhim* 12:1) agrees with R. Shimon b. Elazar, and states that the nations of the world "will all return to the true religion."

The idea of every family building and living in a mini-sukka-Sanctuary dedicated to God has encouraged many magnificent mystical prayers and songs, emphasizing the ideal of each individual developing such a mini-sukka-Sanctuary within his/her own soul, in effect a mini-Sanctuary for the God within each of us. Here is one example, the song *BiLevavi:*[7]

Within my heart shall I build a Sanctuary
To honor the glory of our loving God.
I shall place within the Sanctuary an altar
To accept the rays of His glorious splendor.
And for the eternal flame,
I shall take for myself
Some of the fire which fueled the altar of Isaac.
And for my sacrifice,
I shall offer Him my soul,
My unique and only soul.

WILL THE TRUE SYMBOLISM OF THE SUKKA PLEASE RISE

So, which is it? Is the primary symbolism of the sukka the protection of the desert dwelling of the Israelites throughout their exile experience, or does it primarily represent the sukka/Sanctuary, filled with its Clouds of Glory, modeling God's presence within every Jewish home and every Jewish individual throughout the world? Perhaps the answer depends upon where one resides: in the Diaspora, or in the State of Israel. In the Diaspora, the sukka is the flimsy tent of exile, albeit protected by the Divine; nevertheless wind-tossed and tempest-driven, but at the same time filled with the joy of spirituality. If, however, one is privileged to live in the State of Israel, our sukka/Sanctuary represents our Temple-Sanctuary, from which God's loving Torah will spread throughout the world.

7. The words are based on a liturgical poem written by Rabbi Elazar Azkari (1533–1600) and included in *Sefer Ḥaredim,* published during his lifetime.

THE FOUR SPECIES AND WORLD REDEMPTION

The view of Sukkot in its universalistic sense, steeped in the theme of world redemption, also gives us some additional insights into the commandment of the Four Species. As we wave these plants, we emphasize that not only do we pray for the well-being of all the nations of world on Sukkot, but we also pray for the earth's bounty and natural resources which provide sustenance for all humanity. This idea of gratitude for the earth's vegetation expresses Jewish sensitivity to the complexity of our ecosystems, and our responsibility to preserve our environment in the best possible way. This has always been Judaism's "Green Revolution," our commitment to the conservation and crop diversity that will provide food security, safe water, and healthy air for the world's population (e.g., *bal tashḥit,* not to waste or vandalize) – all arising from our God-commanded responsibility to conserve the blessings of the environment with which God has graciously provided us. As the Bible says, "And God took the human being and placed him in the Garden of Eden [our primordial natural environment] to develop it and to take responsibility for it" (Gen. 2:15).

There are two acts that we perform with the Four Species. In the first, we merely take them up together and recite the blessing, thanking God for the beauty and nutritive value of our vegetation. But then, during the Hallel (the joyous Psalms of Praise) section of the prayer service, we profoundly thank God for the physical world, for nature round about, as we wave the Four Species in six directions – the four points of the compass, upward, and downward. On one level, this act demonstrates our belief in the ubiquitous nature of God: that "the earth is filled with His glory" (Is. 6:3) – a message similar to the closing words of the Yom Kippur service.

But there is another aspect to our waving of the Four Species, an action that expresses complete redemption, a period when the earth will provide sufficient sustenance for all of humanity, a world of plenty which will truly be worthy of hosting the Divine in its midst. As the psalmist declares, "Let the heavens be glad, and let the earth rejoice; let the sea and its fullness shout exultantly. Then [at the time of the redemption] shall all the trees of the forest sing for joy" (Ps. 96:11–12). In a redeemed world, *everything* – animate and inanimate – will sing praises to God and revel in the joy of His perfected world.[8]

THE MIDRASH EXPANDS AND FANCIFIES THE FOUR SPECIES

Hence, it becomes clear that uniting the entire world under God is the primary goal of this Rosh HaShana-Yom Kippur-Sukkot period of the year.

The Sages of the Midrash (Leviticus Rabba 30:14) explain that the Four Species symbolize the most important aspects of the human being: The etrog (citron) represents the heart, signifying love, which must be the guiding force of uniting humanity. The lulav (date palm) symbolizes the spine, the physical aspect of the human being, which must work with all its strength toward bringing people together. The *hadas* (myrtle) is symbolic of the eyes: how one internalizes what one sees, how one must look for the unity within everything and everyone. Finally, the *arava* (willow) represents the lips: how one speaks – hopefully with words of love. This obvious message of the Four Species is for all of humanity to utilize its most important human endowments for the sake of world unity.

Our Sages also explain the Four Species in a way that relates only to the Jewish people, so that we may prepare ourselves for our mission to unite humanity. In this allegory (Leviticus Rabba 30:12), the Sages tell us that the Four Species represent four types of Jews: The etrog, which has both taste and fragrance, is the Jew who has a knowledge of the Torah and who performs good deeds. The lulav, which has taste but no fragrance, is the Jew with Torah but without good deeds. (That seems self-contradictory, but unfortunately there are many who enjoy

8. This idea is reminiscent of our discussion in our chapter on Shabbat of the Havdala blessing that concludes the Sabbath. We stated there that, at the time of redemption, darkness will be emblazoned with light, the profane will be elevated into the sacred, and the nations of the world will be as one with Israel. Both our statements, here and there, explain that in the redemption time, the entire world will joyously express the love of the Divine.

the Torah as intellectually challenging, but unrelated to their actions and lifestyle.) The *hadas* has fragrance but no taste, and so it symbolizes the Jew with good deeds, but no Torah. Finally, the *arava*, with neither taste nor fragrance, is the Jew with neither Torah nor good deeds. Clearly, the message is that all Jews must stand together and embrace each other, since the commandment is to take *all four species together*. If one is missing, the mitzva is not fulfilled. One must love everyone unconditionally, even those who are not yet ready for redemption. Even the willow, with no Torah and no good deeds, must not be isolated, but rather be brought close. If s/he understands that s/he is also loved, slowly but surely s/he may change her/his ways. Love breeds love, and if we love the other, it will bring them to love us, and perhaps even to love the way of life and the prescription for life that has taught us to love unconditionally. As the Mishna in *Pirkei Avot* (1:12) states: "Be among the disciples of Aaron: Love peace, pursue peace, love humanity, and bring them close to Torah."[9]

HOSHANA RABBA AND THE MESSAGE OF THE ARAVA

The joy of Sukkot reaches its pinnacle on the seventh and final day of the festival. This day even has a special name: Hoshana Rabba, the Day

9. But we must not love others *in order* that they come to love us and our lifestyle. As long as the other is a moral human being, we must love him unconditionally. Note that the Mishna does not say "*in order to* bring them to Torah." The Mishna merely says that very often it will happen that way. There is a well-known story in the Talmud (Berakhot 10a):

> There were once some criminals in the neighborhood of R. Meir who caused him a great deal of trouble. R. Meir accordingly prayed that they should die. His wife Berurya said to him: "How do you assume [that such a prayer should be permitted]? Is it because it is written (Ps. 104:35) 'Let *ḥatta'im* (sins) cease'? Is it written *ḥotim* (sinners)? It is written *ḥatta'im*! (sins). Further, look at the end of the verse: 'And let the wicked people be no more.' Since the sins will cease, there will be no more wicked people! Rather pray for them that they should repent, and they will no longer be wicked." He did pray for them, and they repented.

Berurya's great message of "hate the sin, not the sinner" is very pertinent here.

of Great Salvation. During the first six days of the holiday of Sukkot, the custom is for all the worshippers to encircle a Torah scroll (held at the *bima,* the desk from which the Torah is read in the synagogue) with everyone holding all Four Species for one circuit around the *bima.* On Hoshana Rabba, all the Torah scrolls are removed from the ark and held at the *bima,* with each worshipper joining the procession, taking all Four Species and encircling the *bima* seven times. Each circuit is in the name of one of the seven "guests," the *Ushpizin,* whom we have already met in the sukka, and in commemoration of the custom during the Temple period of encircling its altar seven times on Hoshana Rabba. During these processions, each worshipper joins in the procession to the accompaniment of special prayers and songs to God with the refrain of "*Hosha na*" – "Please save us now." (The Hebrew word *na* can be translated both as "please" and as "now."[10])

You will remember that specifically this festival of Sukkot is called *Zeman Simḥateinu,* the "Time of our Rejoicing." It is difficult to describe in words the beauty and grandeur that pervades the synagogue on that day: all of the Torah scrolls, replete with their colorful festival mantles, held at the *bima* and the majestic processions with the Four Species and their magnificent colors of yellow and green.

The consummate joy of this festival is also expressed by the Mishna in Tractate Sukka (5:1–4), as it magnificently describes the Temple celebration every evening of Sukkot: exuberant celebrations in Jerusalem, replete with candles, torches, songs, and dances. Rabbis juggled, the Levites played instrumental music, and everyone joined in the festivities.

This heightened joy and gratitude is certainly connected to the fact that Sukkot is the season of the ingathering of the crops and the plentiful vegetation. This, too, adds to our happiness because we have greatly benefited from the rains which blessed the earth and its produce

10. For example, in Genesis 18:21 the verse begins with God saying: ארדה נא ואראה, "I will go down *na* and I will see..." *Na* here must be translated as "now," because "please" would make no sense; God does not have to ask anyone's permission. There are many other biblical examples like this.

for this festival of ingathering. The Mishna also speaks of a daily ceremony during Sukkot called *Simḥat Beit HaSho'eva*, the "Joy of the Water Drawing." In this ritual, water was drawn from the Shiloah pools outside of Jerusalem, exultantly carried to Jerusalem to be presented to God as the libation, the liquid part of the sacrifice, on the altar of the Temple. During the rest of the year, this libation offering consisted of wine. During this Sukkot festival of the ingathering, the libation was water – God's gift of the blessed rains.

From this description, one might have thought that the seventh day should have been the climax of the festivities. Is it not strange that the ritual chants of Hoshana Rabba are characterized by the sudden intrusion of heartfelt and plaintive petition, "Please save us now" (*Hosha na*) which seems to create a certain dissonance, to say the very least.

With the understanding that this ritual was created in an agricultural society for which the single most important element, critical to economic survival, is rain from the heavens, it is easy to imagine that in the midst of their rejoicing for this year's bountiful crop, the Israelites would be very much concerned with the coming season's rain and the coming season's produce.

And so, the Mishna in Tractate Rosh HaShana (1:2) declares that "on Sukkot, we are judged regarding water [rain for the coming year]." And so, in the midst of this joyous day, we plaintively and repeatedly call out to God, "*Hosha na*" – "Please save us now"; and we name the very day Hoshana Rabba, the "Day of the Great Salvation." We are hopeful that God will provide us with plentiful rain and produce for the coming year.

At this point in the Hoshana Rabba ritual, as we have concluded our seven circuits around the Torah desk, we lay aside the etrog, the *hadas*, and the lulav, and take up only the *arava*, the willow. The logic of this is that the willow is most identified with water, because it generally grows close to water. The Torah (Lev. 23:40) refers to the *arava* as "willows of the brook." Some even have the custom of, at this point, waving the *arava* in all directions, and up and down, just as we waved the Four Species together. We are now, in effect, asking for rain for the coming season.

THE STRANGE RITUAL OF STRIKING THE ARAVA UPON THE EARTH

At the conclusion of these prayers, the halakhic custom is to take the willow and strike it against the earth two or three times, in effect expressing our wish that the earth will continue to bring forth produce during the coming year, which we pray will be one of plentiful vegetation. By this act we are stating that we will make all of our efforts to till, plant, and harvest, but we ask God to help us with plentiful rain to make the harvest a bountiful one. We strike the symbol of water upon the ground, in effect asking God to water the dry earth.

Especially in light of Judaism being practiced today in a more industrial, rather than in an agricultural society, there is yet another level of meaning to what many may consider a strange ceremony, the striking of the willow on the ground. The symbolism of water for the Jewish mystics was not so much rainwater for vegetation as it was for the life-giving waters which began the entire process of the world's creation, which, as we have seen, was an expression of God's love and giving-ness, especially when He created the first human being: "And the spirit of God hovered over the face of the waters.[11] And God said, 'Let there be light, and there was light'" (Gen. 1:2–3). Life-giving water, free-flowing water, thus became the symbol of God's loving-kindness. Moreover, the earth – which holds the water back from inundating, by actually placing a stop order on the waters – symbolizes within kabbalistic thought God's *gevura,* His law and power of limitation. Hence, when the *arava,* symbolizing water and love, strikes the earth, symbolizing limitation and law, we are, in effect, praying to God that His love (the *arava*) overcome even the laws of nature and provide Israel with generous bounty for the coming year.[12]

---

11. Rashi comments on this verse, "The Throne of Glory stands suspended in the air and hovers over the face of the waters by means of God's breath and His speech like a dove hovers over her nest (of chicks)." The image is one of loving by means of protectiveness, without pressing down too hard.
12. According to the Zohar, the most difficult story in the Torah is *Akedat Yitzḥak,* the near-sacrifice of Isaac. The Zohar explains that, when God commanded Abraham, the embodiment of loving-kindness (*ḥesed*) to take Isaac, the embodiment of *gevura,* strict law and power, and to bind him on the altar, God was saying to Abraham,

And if, indeed, the *arava*, according to the Midrash, represents the Jew with neither Torah nor good deeds, we can see how emblematic is the choice of the *arava* for our rain-*ḥesed* prayer. God's loving-kindness extends even to those Jews who seem to be without merit altogether, just as Yom Kippur is a day of forgiveness even for Jews who do not meaningfully repent. We symbolically conclude Hoshana Rabba with the willow alone, representing God's unconditional love for His people and His world.

SHEMINI ATZERET: THE POWER OF RAIN

Immediately following Sukkot, we celebrate the one-day (two days outside of Israel) festival of Shemini Atzeret, the "Eighth Day of Assembly," which is tied to Sukkot (the "Eighth Day"), but is also seen as a festival unto itself in that we no longer live in the sukka, nor do we take the Four Species. The novel idea of this festival is that this is the first time during the fall season that we are praying for rain in each of our *Amida* prayers.[13] We praise God as "He who causes the winds to blow and the rain to fall," which we introduce with beautiful cantorial poetry, tuneful verses describing the power of rain to give life and sustenance to everyone. Our prayer for rain carries with it a similar message to our sacrificing the seventy bullocks in the Temple on behalf of all the nations of the world: rain is a universal need; we are praying for everyone.

Rain and water have an additional symbolism within the prophetic books of the Bible. In chapter 36 of Ezekiel (vv. 24–28), the prophet images water as the catalyst for cleansing the exiled Jewish people, and bringing them back to their land:

---

symbolically and mystically, that your love, Abraham, must "bind" (subdue) Isaac's law, that your compassion will triumph over Isaac's power of strict justice. And so we take the *arava*, the symbol of God's loving-kindness and beat it on the earth, a symbol of God's law and power, our "action prayer" for Hoshana Rabba, as we stand assured that God's love will overtake the laws of nature, which may well have been "slated" for a year of drought.

13. We did not pray for rain on the Sukkot festival itself, although it would have been logical to do so from a seasonal point of view, because rain would prevent us from living in the sukka, the central commandment of that festival.

> For I will take you from among the nations and gather you from all the countries, and I will bring you to your land. And I will sprinkle pure water upon you, and you will be pure; from all your impurities and from all your abominations will I cleanse you…that you will walk in My statutes and you will keep My ordinances and do them. Then will you dwell in the land that I gave your fathers, and you will be a people to Me, and I will be to you as a God.

Rain, as we have just explained, is a universal symbol of God's loving-kindness for all of humanity. From this perspective, the prayer for rain of Shemini Atzeret becomes not only a prayer for Israel, but for all humanity.

SIMḤAT TORAH: THE REJOICING OF OUR TORAH, A TORAH FOR THE WORLD

Shemini Atzeret is also celebrated with an additional theme, the "Festival of the Rejoicing of the Torah," Simḥat Torah. (In the Diaspora, Simḥat Torah is celebrated on the second day of Shemini Atzeret; in Israel, where only a single day of Shemini Atzeret is celebrated, Simḥat Torah is observed on Shemini Atzeret itself.)

Simḥat Torah is a day of dancing and singing in the synagogue with the Torah scrolls, a day given over to the celebration of Torah, the climax of the autumn festivals, the climax of the Jewish year. We imitate with the Torah scrolls the same seven circuits in the synagogue that we did with the Four Species on Sukkot; Torah is our ultimate nutritional source, the nutrition of the soul, and the very purpose of our nation.

But how did Shemini Atzeret become Simḥat Torah?

Originally, there were two customs regarding the weekly Torah reading: In the Land of Israel, the full Pentateuch was completed over a period of three years (some groups had the custom of three and a half years) – the triennial cycle. In Babylonia, the whole Torah was read over the period of one year – the annual cycle – at the conclusion of which they would celebrate the culmination of the Torah readings. This meant that throughout the countries of exile, those Jews who came from Babylonia would have one Torah-reading cycle, and those Jews who came from Israel would have another – a rather confusing situation which did not allow for a universal celebration at the conclusion of the Torah-reading cycle. After the end of the geonic period (c. 1038 CE), it was decided that Jews everywhere follow the annual cycle – completing the Torah in one year and concluding it on Shemini Atzeret, the beginning of the new year. Many scholars believe that the wide observance of Simḥat Torah on Shemini Atzeret began then.[14] And so, from a calendrical perspective, Shemini Atzeret became Simḥat Torah, as well as a rare expression of a universally accepted decision on behalf of Jewish unity.

But there is even a much deeper thematic connection between Shemini Atzeret and Simḥat Torah. The Talmud in Bava Kama 82a compares the Torah to water, explaining that, just as one cannot live for three days without water, so one cannot live for three days without Torah, quoting the verse from Exodus 15:22, "And they went three days in the wilderness, and found no water." Therefore, we read the Torah in the synagogue on Shabbat, Monday, and Thursday, so that there is never a three-day interval without Torah. And so, our prayer for water – for rain – on Shemini Atzeret/Simḥat Torah bears an additional nuance: just as physical life cannot go on without water, so spiritual life cannot go on without Torah. As we say in the blessing before *Shema* in our daily evening prayers: "For it [Torah] is our life and the length of our days." Throughout our four-thousand-year history, there is no question that the Jewish people could not have lived as a separate and unique nation had it not been for the Torah, which kept them alive as a unique people. Whenever we rejected Torah observance, we assimilated into the nations round about, such as the once-proud Jewish community of Alexandria, Egypt, which, after the death of the great Alexandrine Jewish philosopher Philo (c. 50 CE), declined rapidly through assimilation. The assimilation rates in the United States today are frighteningly high, especially in those sectors of the Jewish population that are unaffiliated and, sadly, untouched by Torah.

But we believe that Torah is life giving and life sustaining not only for the Jewish nation. As we have seen within the liturgy of Rosh

14. Avraham Yaari, *The History of the Festival of Simḥat Torah* (Jerusalem: Mosad Harav Kook, 1964), 15–16.

HaShana and Yom Kippur, as well as in the rituals of Sukkot, we believe that Torah is necessary for the world. Without the Abrahamic message of compassionate righteousness and moral justice, without Isaiah's vision of a world without weapons of war, there will be no world, especially in our era of nuclear capabilities.

Fascinatingly enough, there was a custom on Simḥat Torah during the sixteenth and seventeenth centuries in both European and Oriental Jewish communities to take the Torah scrolls outside of the synagogue and dance with them on the streets, bringing the Torah out into the world. And even more to the point, these congregations would invite members of the gentile community to join our celebrations in honor of the Torah,[15] a Torah not just for the Jews, but a Torah for the world.

In reference to our statement about the nuclear age in which we live, one might well say that the most important message of Torah, the deepest message of the words of the prophet Isaiah, proudly adorning Dag Hammarskjold Plaza at the United Nations, can, perhaps, be summarized in a simplistic manner as "Make love, not war." In the words of Rabbi Akiva: "'You shall love your friend like you love yourself' (Lev. 19:18), this is the great principle of Torah" (*Midrash Torat Kohanim* 12). And so, the rabbis have instituted as the climax of the three universal festivals of Tishrei – Rosh HaShana, Yom Kippur, and Sukkot – the festival of Simḥat Torah, a festival, as we have now seen, dedicated to the all-embracing concept of Torah for the world.

15. Ibid., 255–56.

Chapter 8

Hanukka: The Victory of Light

THE FIRST HUMAN CELEBRATES A PRIMORDIAL WINTER SOLSTICE FESTIVAL

The Talmud tells a fascinating story that may very well bear on the initial origins of Hanukka, the "Festival of Lights," as it is called by the Books of the Maccabees as well as by the famous Jewish/Roman historian Josephus Flavius (37–100 CE). We celebrate Hanukka on the twenty-fifth day of the Hebrew month of Kislev, and December 22 begins the period when daylight is becoming longer (December 22 is the shortest daylight day and so known as the winter solstice[1]), after which the

1. The winter solstice is the timeframe of many festivals. It is worth noting that the point that Hanukka begins is on 25 Kislev and the date of Christmas is December 25. Many historians make connections between some of the customs of Christmas – such as gift giving, lighting candles, and feasting – and those of the Roman Saturnalia. See Bruce David Forbes, *Christmas: A Candid History* (Berkeley, California: University of California Press), 9–10. It is also noteworthy that the African American festival of Kwanzaa begins on December 26 and lasts until January 1. Kwanzaa also contains the theme of lights, with a special seven-branch candelabrum being kindled each night of the festival.

sunlight each day in the Northern Hemisphere begins slowly to begin its growth, spreading light and warmth. This fascinating "coincidence" harks back to Adam, the very first human being, as the Talmud (Avoda Zara 8a) recounts the tale:

> When Adam the first human being saw that the amount of light each day was slowly but progressively diminishing after June 21 – the longest day of the year with the greatest amount of sunlight and so known as the summer solstice – he (Adam) said, "Woe is me! Perhaps because I sinned [by eating the forbidden fruit in the Garden of Eden], the world is becoming dark around me, and will return [to the primordial state of] chaos and disorder. This must be the death that was decreed upon me from Heaven!" He arose and spent eight days in fasting and prayer. Once he saw that the season of Tevet [the winter solstice] was approaching, and saw that the day was beginning to lengthen again, he said, "This is the regular order of the world." He went and observed a festival for eight days. Upon the next year (Hebrew: לשנה האחרת) he observed both periods as days of festivities. Adam established these festivals for the sake of Heaven, but they [the nations of the world] established them for the sake of idol worship.

The holiday of Hanukka is not openly mentioned in this fascinating story, but it is not hard to see Hanukka between the lines of the talmudic description of an eight-day festival of light celebrated after the time of the winter solstice, when periods of sunlight in the days begin to lengthen.[2] And it is most logical to identify a calendrical connection between Hanukka (which begins on the twenty-fifth of the Hebrew month of Kislev) and Christmas on the twenty-fifth of December, Hanukka in praise of God having created the world with periods of light always

2. There is even a striking linguistic point. This story contains the expression "upon the next year" (Hebrew: *leshana haaḥeret)* referring to when Adam began to observe his new festival. Exactly the same phraseology, an unusual Hebrew phrase, is used in the Talmud's story (Shabbat 21a) of the Hanukka war (discussed at length in this chapter) and the establishment of the festival of Hanukka.

following periods of darkness and Christmas celebrating the birth of "God's only begotten son" (which, to the Jewish mind, sounds like idolatry), but with both festivals celebrating light after the passing of the winter solstice. In any case, there seems to have been a powerful desire, at this very dark time of the year, to find ways of celebrating light, which they did just as the daylight was beginning to increase. Indeed, it was the historian Josephus Flavius who first called Hanukka the "Festival of Lights." As he wrote: "And from that time [of the Hanukka story] to this [his time of writing] we celebrate this festival and call it φώτα, 'Lights.'"[3]

GREEK CULTURE AND THE JEWS OF JUDEA

In order for us to understand the festival of Hanukka as we celebrate it today, we must review the forces and events in Jewish history that led to its creation. In the year 586 BCE, the First Temple in Jerusalem was destroyed by the warlord Babylonians in their conquest of Judea (the Land of Israel), in the wake of which most of the Jews of Judea were deported to Babylon. They developed a thriving Jewish community in exile; in 539 BCE, Cyrus, king of Persia, who in turn had conquered the Babylonian Empire, gave permission for the Jews of Babylonia to return to the Land of Israel and rebuild their temple. A sizable number of Jews returned, and, in the days of the prophets Haggai and Zechariah, rebuilt the Holy Temple, which was consecrated in 516 BCE.

The next several hundred or so years constituted a productive and calm period for the Jews of Judea as well as for the Jews in Babylon. The Persians treated them well, allowing them to practice their religion and conduct the rites of the Temple in full,[4] with the priestly class (the *kohanim*) in control of Jewish independent Judea.[5] The Jewish population grew during this period, from a total of 70,000 in all of Judea when the Jews first returned, to a population in Jerusalem alone of 200,000 by

3. Josephus Flavius, *The Antiquities of the Jews,* translated by William Whiston (London: George Routledge and Sons, Limited, 1900), XII:325.
4. Paul Johnson, *A History of the Jews* (New York: HarperCollins, 1987), 87.
5. Victor Tcherikover, *Hellenistic Civilization and the Jews* (New York: Atheneum, 1970), 39.

the third century BCE.[6] They had apparently learned the lesson clearly enunciated in the Bible: If Israel forsakes God's Torah, God will forsake Israel and send them back into exile. When they return to God, Torah, and Israel, they will prosper, especially in Israel.

Beginning in 334 BCE, Alexander the Great, king of the ancient Greek Kingdom of Macedon (and later king of Greece), began a series of military campaigns toward his goal of conquering the ancient world, in which he was eminently successful. In addition to power, Alexander the Great had a very strong cultural agenda for his conquered lands; his goal was to Hellenize, to spread and inculcate Greek culture to all of the peoples under his influence.

It is important to understand the massive power and influence of Greek culture in Alexander's time and beyond it. The Ancient Greeks were the cultural leaders of the ancient world. The beauty of their art and the startling realism of their sculpture (e.g., the work of Praxiteles), the depth of the philosophical works of Socrates, Plato, Aristotle, their literary masterpieces and plays including the Homeric epics, the tragedies of Aeschylus, Sophocles, and Euripides, the dazzling sweep of their historians, Herodotus and Thucydides, the excitement of their athletic games which highlighted their impressive physical prowess – all of these captivated and profoundly engaged huge sectors of the ancient world, and form much of the basis of Western culture to this day. Alexander was determined – apparently with the best of intentions – to bring the entire world under the pervasive influence of Greek culture. He was a successful conqueror with an unmistakable cultural mission.

Interestingly enough, although Alexander conquered and subjugated virtually all of the lands of the Middle East, he – amazingly – did not extend his political and cultural control to Judea. There is a rather fascinating and charming story that attempts to explain this anomaly in the Talmud (Yoma 69a):

> When Alexander the Great set out to destroy the Temple in Jerusalem, and thereby remove Jewish independence from Judea, the high priest Simon the Just donned his priestly garments and

6. Johnson, *History of the Jews*, 97.

> walked all night to greet Alexander. At the sight of the venerable Simon, Alexander, totally out of character, fell prostrate at the high priest's feet. When Alexander was asked why a great king like himself should bow down before this Jew, he answered that he now is seeing in the flesh a great sage and prophet who visited him in his dream before every battle, blessing him with success!

Although this story is a bit fanciful, it does explain the historical fact that the Jews of Judea were granted independence, enabling them to carry on their religious and communal lives, much as they had done under the Persians.[7] The high priest continued to rule as before and Mosaic law remained in force among the Jews as it had been previously after their return from exile.

THE CULTURAL CLASH LEADS TO A JEWISH CIVIL WAR

But military and political stability were not features of the ancient world. After the death of Alexander the Great in 323 BCE, the control of Judea passed through a succession of kings called the Ptolemies, against whom the Seleucids, or Greek-Syrians, made war. Ultimately, the Seleucids prevailed, leaving Judea technically under Seleucid control, but as a suzerainty in which the Jews of Judea remained essentially independent and were allowed to be ruled by the high priest of the Temple as before. In 175 BCE, Antiochus IV Epiphanes (a Seleucid) assumed power, initially preserving the good relationship with the Jewish community, and maintaining the laissez-faire relationship toward the Jewish political control over Judea that had generally existed from the time of the Ancient Persians to the time of Alexander the Great.

However, by this time, the masses of Jews of Judea, and even of Jerusalem, were not at all as faithful to Torah teachings as they had been previously. They could not help but be affected by the intellectual and financial allure of the Hellenism that was overtaking the literate world at that time. And so the Jews were essentially divided into two groups, or parties: There were certainly the traditionalists, who remained staunch

7. Tcherikover, *Hellenistic Civilization*, 49.

defenders of the Torah and its commandments, and the rituals of the Temple. But the universal allure of Hellenistic culture gave rise to a pro-Seleucid party, often referred to as the "reformers" or "Hellenizers," composed of the more aristocratic upper stratum of the priestly class, eventually including even the high priest himself (first Jason and then Menelaus).[8] This elite minority were challenged and entranced by the logic of Greek philosophy, which dealt with the weighty intellectual issues of the day and emphasized theoretical meditation over the practical morality of Jewish ethics, systematic logic over helping those in need.[9]

Moreover, the Greek system of thought did not see an invisible God at the center of all existence who bequeathed to Israel a Torah with an entire halakhic system of conduct from cradle to grave, replete with rites of passage, festivals, and rules for interpersonal relationships based on "You shall love your neighbor as you love yourself, I am the Loving Lord."[10] For the Greek Hellenists, not God but rather the human being was perceived as being the center of all ideals and philosophic meditation. As the Greek philosopher Protagoras said, "The human being is the measure of all things."

I am reminded of the famous "Riddle of the Sphinx" from the great Ancient Greek play *Oedipus Rex* by Sophocles: "What goes on four in the morning, on two in the afternoon, and on three in the evening?" The answer, of course, is "the human being" – as an infant he crawls on four, as an adult he walks on two, and as an elderly person he walks on three, supported by a cane. The great classicist C. M. Bowra stated that for the Greeks, the answer "human being" was not only the solution to

8. Tcherikover, *Hellenistic Civilization*, 81.
9. Philosopher William Barrett (1913–1992) notes this dichotomy as the essential difference between what he calls "Hebraism" and Hellenism: "The distinction … arises from the difference between doing and knowing. The Hebrew is concerned with practice, the Greek with knowledge. Right conduct is the ultimate concern of the Hebrew, right thinking that of the Greek" (*Irrational Man: A Study in Existential Philosophy* [New York: Anchor Books, 1958], 62).
10. The psalmist declared, "I place the Loving Lord before me always" (Ps. 16:8). The Torah states clearly, "You have been taught to know that the Loving God is God, there is none beside Him" (Deut. 4:35).

the Riddle of the Sphinx, but the answer to *any* important question; the human being is the measure of all things.

How alluring it must have been to see celebrated the beauty of the human figure – with the consequent emphasis on developing that body through athletics, sports, games, and competitions, with the gymnasium as the primary social center. It is not difficult to imagine the "embarrassment" of the "primitive" Jews, mocked above all by the Hellenists because of their insistence upon circumcising their eight-day-old sons, which Greek culture decried as a desecration of the body's perfection.

Indeed, for the Greeks, beauty was truth. How magnetic it was to hear that physical appearance was all-important, and it must have been "refreshing" to many of these Jews to sense the emphasis within Hellenistic culture on physical and sexual pleasure – the enjoyment of the "here and now." It is also important to remember that Greek culture was the world's culture – the signature legacy of Alexander the Great. Everyone wants to be "up with the times," to be modern and enlightened. In Judea at that time it meant to immerse oneself in the arts, sports, and philosophy of Hellenistic civilization, an ethos well known to the more worldly aristocratic and politically involved priestly class of the Jewish elite as a result of their travels abroad and meetings with foreign leaders.

Conversely, the traditionalists still believed in the truth of the Torah and the Jewish traditions. For them, as we have seen, it was not the human being, but rather the Divine Being, who was the measure of all things and the ultimate decisor for all actions. Hence, Jewish tradition dictates that circumcision for males is a most important ritual which even brings the would-be convert into the Jewish tradition, precisely because it expresses a willingness to shed blood in one's very organ of propagation to ensure the continuity of one's faith from generation to generation. Only those who are willing to give up their lives and even the lives of their children – most paradoxically and counterintuitively – for the continuity of a faith dedicated to marital and familial faithfulness and to the sanctity of the physical, over and above the perfection of the physical, will guarantee a world of peace and redemption which is the goal of Judaism. It is not beauty which is truth, but it is the Loving Lord your God (and His commandments) which are truth and therefore are truly beautiful. "The Lord God is truth" (Jer. 10:10).[11]

The traditionalists had a burning love and a fervor for Jewish law and Jewish custom, for the invisible God who created the world and taught the lifestyle that included our Holy Temple rituals and strict rules of ethics and morality, which would eventually redeem humanity in a world dedicated to peace, justice, and compassion rather than physical prowess and perfection, to the development of heart and soul more than mind and body. Most importantly, they believed that they were responsible to pass down their higher values and divinely mandated lifestyle to the next generation. For them, extreme Hellenism posed a lethal threat to Judaism and its Torah. A civil war between Jew and Jew, traditionalist versus Hellenist, was now developing in Judea.

ANTIOCHUS JOINS THE WAR ON THE HELLENISTS' SIDE

It must be understood that the Jewish reformers, with their strong adherence to Hellenism and their unconcealed contempt for Jewish tradition, held the real power in Judea at this time. Even the high priesthood became progressively Hellenized, which can even be seen in the names of the high priests, which, over time, moved from Simon the Just, to Onias (a Hebrew name, *Ḥonyo,* meaning "God has compassion"), to Yehoshua ("God is our salvation"), whose name changed midway in his tenure as high priest from Yehoshua to Jason.[12] The last in this order of high priests was Menelaus (a fully Greek name), who ruled the high

11. Indeed, the Greek notion that the human being is the measure of all things is the central tenet of atheism, which sees the human being as having dethroned God. The author and philosopher Ayn Rand (1905–1982) was a primary proponent of atheism. In her novels, her brilliantly drawn characters proclaim the human being as the center of everything. In *The Fountainhead,* Wynand wants something sacred. He asks architect Howard Roark if he's ever built a temple. He wants a temple built to Dominique Wynand – and he hires Roark to build it. Roark accepts the commission to build a temple to the heroic human spirit, with muscular form as the central object of worship in this temple, the ultimate in modern idolatry. The sacred truth of love and commitment is beyond physical depiction!
12. Josephus, *Antiquities of the Jews,* V:1.

priesthood by terroristic means,[13] and who even brought Hellenism into the very Temple precincts. The Hellenizers, as a result of their response to the allure of Greek culture, converted Jerusalem into a πώς (*polis* – a town), introduced Greek customs into Jewish life, built a gymnasium (in the area of the Temple), and began to bring the Greek gods to Judea.[14] (You will remember that the Greek gods were created in the image of humans; the Jewish view is, of course, that humans are created in the image of God.)

By this time, there was a true civil war raging in Jerusalem between the Hellenizers and the traditionalists.[15] At this point, the Hellenizers invited Antiochus, the Greek-Syrian monarch, to abandon his laissez-faire approach to the Jews in the interest of quelling the raging civil war by vanquishing the religionists. Antiochus then began to issue his draconian edicts against major areas of Jewish observance: the Sabbath, circumcision, study of the Torah. He even went so far as to erect an idol of Zeus in the Temple. Violation of Antiochus's decrees brought torture and slaughter to the perpetrator. But it must be remembered that it was not the monarch of Greek Syria who had initially pushed the reformers into Hellenism. Much the opposite: the Jewish reforming Hellenists encouraged the king to support their Hellenistic cause and thereby bring peace to Judea as a true satellite of Hellenistic Syria. It goes without saying that as soon as Antiochus became an active supporter of Hellenism in Judea, Judea lost its initial internal independence harking back to Alexander the Great. Now an anti-religionist Antiochus was in full control. It seemed almost certain that the Hellenists allied with Antiochus would crush the cause of the traditionalists and that Hellenistic culture would prevail in Judea even in the *sanctum sanctorum*, the Holy Temple in Jerusalem.

Clearly, this was the beginning of a civil war – a cultural/religious war – within Judea. The first "act of war" on the part of the traditionalists

13. Tcherikover, *Hellenistic Civilization*, 172.

14. Ibid., 117.

15. Modern scholars support the idea that the "Hanukka Revolt" began as a Jewish civil war. See Tcherikover, *Hellenistic Civilization*, 206. See also Joseph P. Schultz, *Judaism and the Gentile Faiths: Comparative Studies in Religion* (Fairleigh Dickinson University Press), 155.

took place in the town (now a modern Israeli city) of Modi'in, near Jerusalem. A company of Syrian troops came to the village to compel the Jewish inhabitants to bow down to pagan gods. Old Mattathias, of the priestly class but a traditionalist, refused to obey the order; he then saw a Hellenizing Jew bowing down to the idol. He rose up and slew not only the king's commissioner, whose task it was to enforce idolatry, but he also slew the Hellenizing Jew, and then fled with his sons to the hills.[16] Thus truly begun the "Hanukka War," an uprising of Mattathias the Hasmonean and his guerilla army against the Hellenists and their allies, the Greek-Syrian king's forces.

THE TRADITIONALISTS' VICTORY OVER HELLENISM AND THE ESTABLISHMENT OF THE HANUKKA FESTIVAL

With the more aristocratic and wealthier Hellenistic Jews having joined in the battle with the powerful army of Greek Syria and King Antiochus, it would certainly seem improbable to have foreseen a victory for the traditionalists. Yet, the dedication and zeal of the Maccabees, fighting for the sake of the Lord of Israel and His Torah on behalf of the Jewish political and religious internal independence of Judea, ultimately drove all of the Hellenizers and Greek-Syrians out of the area around Jerusalem and reclaimed the Temple on the twenty-fifth day of the winter month of Kislev, 164 BCE. This battle was a most glorious victory of the "few against the many, the wicked into the hands of the righteous" (from the *Al HaNissim* prayer). In less than three years, this untrained but fiercely dedicated and brave group, led by Mattathias's son "Judah the Maccabee," supported by the religious Jews who had remained committed to Jewish tradition, were able to declare unconditional victory!

Upon reentering the Temple, the victors purged it of its desecration by the opposing forces. As a sign of their victory, they rekindled the Menora, the giant candelabrum in the Temple, symbolizing the fact that it was the light of God's Torah of morality and truth that vanquished the darkness of pagan Hellenism, with its emphasis on physicality. "For the candle is the commandment and the Torah is light" (Prov. 6:23).

16. This story is told with great drama in First Book of Maccabees, chapter 2.

The Rabbis of the Talmud (Shabbat 21a) recorded that the victors found only enough pure oil to burn for one day – but to keep the Menora eternally alight, they needed seven more days in order to secure more oil. Miraculously, that initial cruse of oil lasted for eight days, which inspired the eight-day celebration of Hanukka – our Festival of Lights.

As a result of the victory, the Hasmoneans would be installed as the governing group in Judea, once more ensconcing Jewish law and tradition as the prevailing mandate and message in the Holy Land. Independent Jewish rule would last for about two hundred years, until the destruction of the Second Temple by Roman invaders.

WHY TWO MIRACLES? THE MILITARY VICTORY AND THE MIRACLE OF THE LIGHTS

There are two essential rabbinic sources regarding the Hanukka story.[17] One is the special Hanukka prayer called *Al HaNissim* (literally, "For the Miracles"), traditionally attributed to Johanan the high priest (also called John Hyrcanus) (164–104 BCE), who was the nephew of Judah the Maccabee and the third Hasmonean ruler of Judea following the Hanukka victory. This prayer is recited in the *Amida* devotion in each of the prayer services of all eight days of Hanukka, and in the Grace After Meals. This prayer recounts what seems to be a review of the Hanukka war: "In the days of Mattathias the son of Johanan, high priest, a Hasmonean, and his sons, when the evil Greek kingdom rose up against Your nation Israel, to make them forget the Torah and to transgress Your laws." It thanks God for "standing by them in the times of their troubles, pleading their cause … and avenging their wrong, delivering the strong into the hands of the weak, the many into the hands of the few, the impure into the hands of the pure, the wicked into the hands of the righteous." It sees the miracle of Hanukka exclusively as a military victory. While there is a mention of the lighting of candles – "Afterward they (the

17. There is actually a third late mishnaic source, *Megillat Taanit* (probably composed between 41 and 70 CE), from which the talmudic text is derived, but, for our purposes, the portions in that text about the military victory, the polluting of the oil, and the establishment of the festival are almost identical to the text of Shabbat 21a.

Hasmoneans)...purified your Sanctuary and kindled the candles in the courtyard of our sacred precinct" – there is no mention of what we would call the great miracle of the day, the one small cruse of pure oil with the seal of the high priest sufficient only for one day which miraculously lasted for eight days, enough time for them to secure sufficient oil to keep the Menora alight for as long as necessary – the great miracle of the lights! And neither is there mention of the earlier civil war between the Hebrew Hellenists and the Hebrew traditionalists. I would maintain that this *Al HaNissim* source is dealing with the Hanukka victory that we have celebrated throughout the generations, the final epic war of the Greek-Syrian monarch and his army (perhaps joined by a small number of Hellenistic-reformist Jews) against the masses of traditionalist Jews, who desired both religious as well as political independence for Judea; these were the forerunners of the Religious Zionists today, who were fighting for both religious and political independence. It is certainly obvious that the Greek Empire had a larger and more powerful army than did the Hasmoneans, and so the military miracle certainly is deserving of major mention!

The other source is the Talmud (Shabbat 21a). This source reads:

> What is Hanukka? Our Rabbis taught: On the twenty-fifth of Kislev commence the days of Hanukka, which are eight, on which a lamentation for the dead and fasting are forbidden. For when the Greeks entered the Temple, they defiled all the oils therein, and when the Hasmonean dynasty prevailed against them and defeated them, they made search and found only one cruse of oil which lay with the seal of the high priest, but which only contained sufficient oil for one day's lighting. However, a miracle was wrought there, and that oil burned for [the necessary] eight days to produce enough oil for the Menora to be rekindled in perpetuity. The following year these days were appointed a festival with the recitation of Hallel [Psalms of Praise] and thanksgiving.

Here, in contrast to the *Al HaNissim* prayer, the military victory is not at all emphasized; it is only touched upon with two words (one in Hebrew – *u'natzaḥum*), "defeated them," without any detailed discussion of the disparity of forces between the Greeks and the Jews and the miniscule likelihood of a Jewish victory, as is found in the *Al HaNissim* prayer. The emphasis here, rather, seems to be upon the eight-day oil miracle.

By way of further comparison, in *Al HaNissim*, the enemy is the "evil Greek kingdom" against God's nation of Israel, whereas in the talmudic source, it was merely a case of "Greeks" (not the "evil monarchy of Greece") who entered the Temple precincts and defiled the oil. There is no mention of a civil war between two national armies, Hebrew traditionalists against Hebrew Hellenists, although there is mention of a victory of "the Hasmonean dynasty," the Hebrew traditionalists!

It is here important and relevant to understand that, technically, a gentile (Greek-Syrian) is not empowered to defile a pure substance to be used for ritual purposes. Since the sanctity of the oil for the Menora only applies to Jews, only Jews can defile those oils.[18] Hence, in the talmudic source, the "Greeks" who entered the Temple and defiled the oil could not have been the Greek-Syrians; it could only have been the Hellenizing Jews who entered and polluted the oil's sanctity. You will also remember that the initial war was a civil war within Judea – Jewish traditionalists versus Jewish Hellenists. Hence in this record of the Hanukka story and miracle, it was not the "evil Greek kingdom" that rose up against "Your nation Israel" (as in the *Al HaNissim* prayer) but rather the Jewish Hellenists!

This leads to the following important conclusion: The story told by the talmudic source in Tractate Shabbat is telling of one element of the battle, which was the religious struggle between Jew and Jew, a story that is separate from the story told by *Al HaNissim* of the great military victory against the Greek-Syrian empire, against Antiochus and his forces who joined the Hellenistic Jewish group to help fight the Jewish traditionalists.

In the civil war between Jew and Jew, the enemy was my Jewish Hellenist brother, who, taken in by the allure of Hellenism, was hellbent

18. The *Baal HaMaor* (Rabbi Zerachiah HaLevi of Girona, 1125–1186) in his commentary on Avoda Zara 24a (according to the pagination of the *Rif*) makes a similar point regarding the inability of a non-Jew to spiritually pollute a substance of purity and, therefore, we must be speaking of Jews who did this act.

to recreate God in the image of man. This was a religious war between two groups of Jews, the radical "reformers" and the traditional religionists – two Jewish political parties, if you will. Since this was a war of Jew against Jew, the military victory is not the one which our Sages would wish to emphasize. To the contrary, I would argue that the message of the book of Genesis – and especially the last portion of the first book of the Bible, which presents the lives of our patriarchs and matriarchs – is how important it is that the children of Jacob-Israel come together and coalesce into twelve tribes of unity. Judah was able to effectuate that unity, and only when true unity of the family of Israel is realized will we be able to reach out and unify the world (Gen. 49:10). I believe it is for this reason that our Hanukka celebration each year coincides with the biblical readings of the fraternal strife within Jacob-Israel's family. "The actions of the fathers is a signpost for future generations," and it is only after the descendants of Jacob-Israel will unify, as they did under Judah at Jacob-Israel's deathbed, that the Messiah will begin to show his presence. And we dare not sit back and wait for the Messiah to come; we must now stand together as a nation dedicated to compassionate peace, justice, and loving-kindness, among all the children of Jacob/Israel – especially now that we have returned to our Jewish State of Israel.

At the end of the day, therefore, it is the religious miracle that appears in Tractate Shabbat that we are celebrating. That one small cruse of oil, sufficient to light the Menora for one day when eight days were necessary to make more sacred oil, the *religious* miracle, the miracle of the lights, that is what we are celebrating, rather than the miracle of the military victory. It would seem that our Sages did not want to glorify the civil war between Jew and Jew! To the contrary, when Jews disagree with other Jews about the rituals in the Temple and the religious values and ritual activities of the Jewish lifestyle, the Jewish Hellenists ought to be vanquished by intellectual and religious dialogue, with words and ideas, not with swords and stones. We must inspire our errant brothers with love and inspiration, not with swords and physical destruction. We must enlighten those who would oppose tradition with the sacred beauty, the life-enhancing morality, and the universal love and peace which emanate from Torah. "For the candle is the commandment, and the Torah is light" (Prov. 6:23). We dare not wage war unto death against our brothers, no matter how misguided they may be. It is always our responsibility to return them to their consciences with love and with Torah.

The major enemy was, of course, the Greek-Syrian autocrat Antiochus, who wanted to cancel Jewish independence in the Land of Israel, to take control over Judea and the Judeans politically and religiously, and to prevent us from observing our ancestral laws. This was a war of Religious Zionism which had to be fought, even unto the death, for the right to live independently and freely Torah-true lives in our own Jewish homeland. As the Hasmoneans declared by their active war against Antiochus in the land of Judea – much before Patrick Henry – "Give us internal political and religious freedom or give us death!"

And so, the miracle of the small cruse of oil has become ensconced as the central miracle of Hanukka, and the religious focus of its observance. While we are grateful for the military victory over those who would destroy us, the major enemy at the time of Hanukka was Hellenism. It was an attractive ideological and cultural enemy that was ready to take away our independence in Judea as well as our spiritual anchor in a loving God and His ethically imbued Torah. Hence, the Sages decreed that our eternal commemoration of Hanukka is not with a military symbol, certainly not with a civil war against our own brothers and sisters, but rather with the message of the Menora, a mandate for bringing more light and love into the world through the Torah. And we dare not allow any other nation to destroy our Torah light; much the opposite – God explained to Abraham at the very dawn of Jewish civilization that by means of our spreading the light of Torah, throughout the world "all the families of the earth will be blessed" (Gen. 12:3).

As we behold the beautiful Hanukka candles burning each night of the festival, we think back to that primordial festival of the first human being, realizing that our task, as was Adam's, is to fill the world with light and love.

The ultimate victory of Hanukka was a religious one, declaring clearly that the light of Torah will vanquish all darkness and that even when the darkness is at full strength, the light will always appear! Even the military victory, important as it was, must take second place to the victory of Torah. After all, our tradition declares, "The paths of Torah are sweet and pleasant paths, and all the roads of Torah must ultimately lead to peace."[19] Hence, we do not place spears in our windows on Hanukka; we place lights. Yes, we thank God for the military victory, but we celebrate the ability it gave us to live as an independent nation under the Menora light of Torah, love, and peace.

GREEK CULTURE AND THE JEWISH STUDIES CURRICULUM

Must Greek culture – philosophy, aesthetics, gymnastics, and theater – be excluded from the Jewish curriculum of study?

The Talmud (Bava Kama 82b) makes a startling statement: "Cursed be the person who raises pigs, and cursed be the person who teaches his son *ḥokhmat Yevanit*," usually translated as "Greek wisdom," i.e., Greek philosophy. One may have thought that herein lies the answer to our opening question: Judaism forbids Greek culture! Indeed, the very talmudic passage cited above goes on to tell of an incident which seems to support a blanket prohibition of Greek culture. The Talmud suggests that the reason for the curse was an incident between two warring brothers who were in charge of the daily sacrifices in the Temple. As part of the story, an "old man" who, the text says, was familiar with *ḥokhmat Yevanit,* whispers something to one of the brothers, which caused him to supply a pig for the Temple sacrifice. This only adds fuel to the fire of forbidding Greek wisdom for all Jews for all time.

However, the Rambam, the major talmudic commentator and legal decisor in Jewish history, very counterintuitively interprets the term *ḥokhmat Yevanit* in this passage as a special "code language," with no relationship to Greek thought or philosophy,[20] and it was this code language that was forbidden forever after. Apparently, the great philosopher and legalist, the Rambam, was not in favor of banning

19. See Proverbs 3:17.
20. See Rambam, Commentary on the Mishna, Tractate Sota, chapter 9, mishna 14. The Rambam there concludes this comment by saying that this "code language" of the Ancient Greeks, to which he refers as "hints and riddles," no longer exists, strongly indicating that there is no longer any prohibition at all in connection with this "code language," and certainly not with Greek wisdom.

Greek philosophy and culture, and, indeed, often quotes Aristotle,[21] sometimes to agree with him and sometimes to disagree, but always with great respect. This was historically the way that mainstream Judaism looked at science and Western philosophy, and this includes the greatest of our talmudic scholars throughout the ages.[22] In truth, for the early Greeks and Hebrews, Hellenism encompassed philosophy, science, the arts, theater, and gymnastics, and within the context of our discussion concerning "Greek wisdom," the Talmud (Shabbat 75a) declares: "R. Yehoshua b. Levi in the name of Bar Kappara: Whoever knows how to delve into the science of astronomy and philosophy but does not do so, about him does Scripture state: 'The works of the Loving Lord they do not look upon and the products of His hands they do not see!' (Is. 5:12)."[23]

Indeed, the question of whether it is advisable or not to study Greek philosophy and culture is actually a difference of opinion between two ways of interpreting a fascinating verse. After the flood, Noah offers a rather ambiguous blessing to his sons Japheth (Hebrew: *Yafet*, which means "beauty," among whose descendants in the Bible are identified with the Ancient Greeks[24]) and Shem, the progenitor of Abraham, and, therefore, the Jewish people.[25] Japheth traditionally represents Greek culture, beauty, and philosophy and Shem represents the pure values of Torah and belief in God. Noah says, in Genesis 9:27, "May God extend

---

21. There are many instances of this in the Rambam's *Guide for the Perplexed*. Examples: On the theory of time (part I: chapter 73); on the nature of the motion of matter (part II: Introduction: proposition 25); on the eternality of the universe (part II: chapter 13). There are many others.
22. The brief exception to this was the ban by the Rashba (Rabbi Shlomo ben Aderet from Provence, 1235–1310) in 1305 against the study of philosophy and science. However, the ban was only applicable to students under the age of twenty-five, because the concern was that these secular studies were being given primacy over the study of the Torah. See Asher Benzion Buchman, "Abraham and Sarah in Provence," *Hakira: The Flatbush Journal of Jewish Law and Thought*, vol. 6 (2008), 223.
23. A fuller treatment to this fascinating issue may be found in my study "Science and Philosophy in the Beit Midrash," in my book *The Living Tree* (Maggid Books, 2014), 3–7.
24. Gen. 10:2.
25. Gen. 11:10–27.

beauty to Japheth, and let Him dwell in the tents of Shem." This verse has been explained in many ways, but essentially there are two world views contained in two different interpretations of this verse.

The first way of reading the verse is, "May God extend beauty to Japheth, and may He (God) dwell in the tents of Shem." According to this reading, indeed there may be much beauty within Japheth (Greek culture), but God Himself and the unique truth within His Torah is only to be found within the tents of Shem (Jewish tradition), to the exclusion of Japheth. The Talmud in Tractate Megilla 9b, however, gives another interpretation: "'May God extend beauty to Japheth, and may Japheth dwell in the tents of Shem' – the beauty of Japheth within the tents of Shem." According to this interpretation, there are many wonderful and edifying ideas to be learned from Greek philosophy, as long as the Greek ideas are compatible with, and ultimately defined by, the eternal values of the Torah.[26]

AFTERWORD

It was the eighth night of Hanukka in Kiel, Germany, a large port city on the Baltic Sea with 250,000 German citizens and a Jewish population of 522 people. On that year, 1932, the last night of Hanukka fell on Friday evening, and Rabbi Akiva Boruch Posner, spiritual leader of the Kiel's Jewish community, kindled all of the eight flames.

Rabbi Posner's wife, Rachel, looked out of their window, to the building across the street, the Nazi headquarters in Kiel, displaying the dreaded Nazi Party flag, emblazoned with its huge swastika, draped over the building. Perceiving from what she saw as the huge and stark contrast between two world views, she felt compelled to immortalize the moment. With the eight lights of the menora glowing brightly in her window, Rabbi Posner's wife, Rachel, snapped a photo of the menora

26. This talmudic passage invokes our verse as granting permissibility to write a Torah scroll in Greek, stating that "the beauty of Japheth (the Greek language) will be in the tents of Shem (the Torah scroll)." But many have extended the meaning of this teaching beyond the technical point of writing the scroll in Greek because of the beauty of the Greek letters and language to bringing other aspects of Greek culture under the aegis of Torah.

which included the Nazi building and flag in the background. After the film was developed, she wrote a few lines in German on the back of the photo. "*Hanukka, 5693 [1932]. 'Judah dies,' thus says the Nazi banner. 'Judah will live forever,' thus say the lights.*"

Just a few days later Germany had parliamentary elections, and on January 30, 1933, Adolph Hitler was appointed chancellor of Germany.

Eighty years later, for a commemoration of Kristallnacht, the "Night of Broken Glass," November 9, 1938, which denoted the onset of the Holocaust, the president of Germany, Frank Walter Steinmeier, asked Rabbi Yehudah Teichtel, formerly the chief rabbi of Germany, "What would be the most meaningful way for Germany to commemorate the eightieth anniversary of Kristallnacht?" Rabbi Teichtel answered, "I was sent to Berlin by my late mentor and teacher, the great Lubavitcher Rebbe. He always taught, 'At the place of the greatest darkness, there you must bring the greatest light.' Let us erect a giant menora at the Brandenburg Gate, the site of many of Hitler's virulent, hate-filled, anti-Semitic speeches, inciting a nation to genocide and hate." And so, in that very place, the government of Germany erected a menora, representing the freedom of the human spirit, the power of light over darkness, the triumph of love over hate. On December 3, 2018, eighty years after Kristallnacht, on the first night of Hanukka, Rabbi Teichtel, assisted by the president of Germany, Frank Walter Steinmeier, kindled the first Hanukka candle which shed its light over the Brandenburg Gate.

"Judah will die." Thus says the flag. "Judah will live forever." Thus say the lights.

POSTSCRIPT
THE MIRACLE OF MILITARY VICTORY OR THE MIRACLE OF LIGHTS?

Question: Why wasn't that great military victory sufficient? Why did God have to create yet another miracle – which effectively teaches the same lesson about the small amount that stretches and expands to become a much more significant amount – of the small cruse of pure oil sufficient for one day, which managed to bring light to the Menora for eight days? Furthermore, they did find enough oil for one day; hence, if the miracle was only for the requisite seven additional days, why do we celebrate the festival for eight (and not merely seven) days?

The sainted Rabbi Elijah of Vilna (of the eighteenth century), known as the Vilna Gaon, notes that if one counts from the very first word of the Bible, *Bereshit* ("In the beginning"), the twenty-fifth word is "*or*," "light," as in the verse "And the Almighty declared 'Let there be light' (Gen. 1:3)." When we remember that the military victory – and onset of the festival of Hanukka – takes place on the twenty-fifth of the Hebrew month of Kislev, and that Hanukka is known by the Book of the Maccabees and by the Second Commonwealth historian Josephus as the "Festival of Lights" (*Ḥag HaUrim*) after the miracle cruse of oil, the "coincidence" noted by the Vilna Goan is nothing less than startling. And in order to understand in depth the message of this "coincidence," we must bring to mind a most profound insight of my teacher and mentor, Rabbi Joseph B. Soloveitchik.

"Why does our Bible open with the story of the creation of the cosmos and not with the first of the commandments?" queries our classical commentator Rashi. Rabbi Soloveitchik answers that the story of the creation of the world includes the very first commandment as well. After all, the central injunction of our Bible is the command that we "walk in (God's) ways," act in accordance with the basic "traits" attributed to the Divine: "Just as He is compassionate, so must we be compassionate; just as He is filled with loving-kindness, so must we be filled with loving-kindness" (Sota 14a).

Similarly, if God created the world, we too must emulate that creativity; we too must become creators. And if the Almighty stood at the abyss of the darkness of the deep and created light – and indeed, this was His first act of creation – so must we enter places of darkness and bring light. This is precisely the meaning of "perfecting the world," *tikkun olam*, the God-given task to Israel to be "a light unto the nations." (See the *Aleinu* prayer, prescribed to be recited at the end of every statutory prayer.) All it takes is a little bit of light to push aside a great deal of darkness.

Rabbi Prager, sainted editor of the Beit Yaakov magazine and acclaimed witness of the Holocaust, writes of a young boy in Auschwitz whose bar mitzva was on the first day of Hanukka. He painstakingly collected strips of fat to craft a makeshift "candle," and invited a small group to celebrate with him after midnight in his "bunk." And so, in the blackness of the night, in the hellhole of Auschwitz, a small band of wasted, frightened Jews huddled together to watch the bar mitzva boy light the "candle" and intone the blessings and join with him in the traditional Hanukka songs. Just as they were beginning to feel themselves transported to an almost forgotten time of love and light, a Nazi guard entered, shot into the air, and barked at the youth at the center of the nocturnal activity to put out the candle. The bar mitzva boy looked unwaveringly into the eyes of the Nazi.

"We Jews do not extinguish light," he said. "We make light – that is our task in the world!"

Inexplicably, the Nazi guard turned and strode out without a word.

The Jewish mission in the world is to add to God's light and push away the world's darkness, which, unfortunately, remained from the beginning and threatens to overwhelm creation. This is what it means for us to function as God's partners. And that is the higher meaning of the miracle of the Menora light. We must add our "human" light and our act of "enlightenment" to God's initial light, which is always present. And that is likewise the miracle of the first day: our realization that we must add our own light to the already existent divine light in order to perfect an imperfect, incomplete, world, waiting for us to partner with God in creating light! And as we enlighten, pushing back the chaos and the darkness, humanity will be redeemed and the light of the moon will equal the light of the sun.

Chapter 9

Purim: A Jewish Victory in the Diaspora?

THE JEWS OF ANCIENT PERSIA: FROM QUIET ASSIMILATION TO THREAT OF GENOCIDE

The drama that unfolds in the Scroll of Esther (the "Megilla") takes place in the fifth century BCE, during the period in which the overwhelming majority of Jews were living in exile in Persia, after the destruction of the Temple of King Solomon in 586 BCE and the concomitant loss of Jewish independence with the fall of Jerusalem. Just fifty years later, in 536 BCE, Cyrus, king of Persia, gave permission for the Jews living in exile in Persia to return to Judea (Israel) and to rebuild the Temple! Although the Jews gratefully set about rebuilding the Temple, contributing generously to the effort, only a small portion of the Jews comfortably ensconced in Persia relocated "home" to Judea; in large measure it was only the poor who actually returned to Jerusalem, with the overwhelming majority of Jews remaining in the Persian Empire. Those are the Jews whom we meet in the biblical Scroll of Esther.

It is also interesting to note a striking similarity between the situation of our return – or lack thereof – to the Jewish state in 1948 from comfortable Diaspora communities like America and Canada despite the possibility of a return to Zion following our victorious War of Independence. Indeed, there are many parallels and dangers that Jews in the American diaspora can avoid by studying the story of Purim and the Jews in the Persian diaspora so many centuries ago.

The Megilla opens in the palace of Persian King Ahasuerus, a powerful monarch, running his country as an oligarchy with a small group of advisers who were the "power behind the throne." The action begins with a detailed description of a six-month-long drinking feast given by King Ahasuerus for the nobles and officials of Persia and Media of the 127 provinces of his kingdom, taking place in his lavish palace, described in detail by the text, using – surely with intended irony – many of the same descriptive terms used by the Torah in describing our sacred Sanctuary.[1] This half-year-long revelry concluded with a seven-day drinking feast for the inhabitants of the capital city of Shushan, rich and poor, including its Jewish community.

A separate drinking feast for the women was organized by Queen Vashti in the pavilion of the royal courtyard. At this feast, Ahasuerus gets thoroughly drunk and at the prompting of his courtiers, orders his wife Vashti to display her "beauty" before the nobles and populace, wearing her royal crown (and, perhaps, *only* her royal crown). Her refusal leads Ahasuerus to have her removed from her post. Ahasuerus then orders all young women to be presented to him, in a "nocturnal beauty contest" (or a sexual "audition"), so he can choose a new queen to replace Vashti. One of these is Esther, who was orphaned at a young age and was being fostered by her uncle Mordecai.[2] She finds favor in the king's eyes, and is made his new wife – the queen. According to

1. The Talmud (Megilla 12a) compares the lavish description in the Book of Esther (1:4) of Ahasuerus's grandiose palace with the same Hebrew words used in the Torah for the priestly garments worn in the Holy Temple (Ex. 28:2). For example, the royal color *argaman,* a shade of purple, appears repeatedly in the book of Exodus in the description of the Sanctuary, and is used in Esther 1:6 to describe the king's palace.
2. Although the Megilla text 2:7 seems to identify Mordecai as either Esther's uncle or cousin, the talmudic Sages (Megilla 13a) say that Mordecai took Esther as a wife, interpreting this from the word *bat* (daughter) in the same verse. *Bat* is similar to *bayit,* "house" or "home," a word that in talmudic parlance is frequently used to refer to the wife.

Mordecai's instructions, Esther does not reveal her origins and her Jewish identity.[3] Apparently, Mordecai is anxious to have Esther chosen queen; he is clearly jockeying for power in the highest echelons of the Persian kingdom! Undoubtedly the picture of the Jewish community, including Esther and Mordecai, is of a culture quickly assimilating into Persian drink-fests and sexual orgies – including intermarriage with Persian aristocracy!

Shortly afterward, Mordecai, who seems to have been in some respect an adviser to the king,[4] discovers a plot by two palace guards, Bigthan and Teresh, to kill Ahasuerus. Based on his testimony they are apprehended and hanged, and Mordecai's service and loyalty to the king is duly noted in the daily record of the court.

Ahasuerus then promotes one of his advisers, Haman, to the position of his grand vizier. By granting Haman a great deal of power, Ahasuerus in effect transformed his oligarchical form of government – with a small group advising the king – into a dictatorship, with Haman at the helm, second only to the king. Haman has virtually become the potentate; in effect, due to the apparent weakness of Ahasuerus, he has become the *de facto* ruler of the kingdom. Hence, Haman now enjoys all of the deference due to the absolute ruler, including all of the fealty and the formal obeisance customarily accorded a sovereign.

Mordecai, sitting at the palace gates that once denoted his influence as adviser to royalty, now must show deference to Haman. But he does not; he refuses to bow and prostrate himself as Haman passes by, as do all others. And so, Mordecai falls into Haman's disfavor. Having found out that Mordecai is Jewish, Haman plans to kill not just Mordecai but,

3. This may indicate that although the Persians had never persecuted the Jews, there may well have been some strong anti-Jewish currents in Persian society – enough to cause Mordecai to adjure Esther not to reveal her background. The presence of latent anti-Semitism in Persia is made clear toward the end of the Megilla (9:1) where, in the same verse, reference is made twice to "the enemies of the Jews," and "their (the Jews') haters."
4. This opinion is based upon the verse (2:21), "…and Mordecai sat at the king's gate…" "The obvious inference is that Mordecai was by this time a known figure, deeply involved in the intrigues of the court" (Yoram Hazony, *The Dawn: Political Teachings of the Book of Esther*" [Jerusalem: Shalem Press, 2000], 29.)

perhaps drawing upon strains of anti-Semitism heretofore dormant in Persian society, to commit genocide against the entire Jewish minority in the empire. Obtaining Ahasuerus's permission and funds to execute this plan, he casts lots (*purim*) to choose the date on which to do this – the thirteenth of the month of Adar.

MORDECAI AND ESTHER RESPOND TO THE PERSIAN PLAN OF GENOCIDE

When Mordecai finds out about the plans, he understands that the assimilation of the Jewish community has gone much too far; he embarks upon a major public demonstration of repentance! He dons sackcloth and ashes, a sign of mourning, publicly weeping and lamenting, together with many other Jews in Shushan and other parts of Ahasuerus's empire doing likewise, as an expression of widespread penitence and fasting.

Esther discovers what has transpired. There follows an exchange of messages between her and Mordecai, with Hathach, one of the palace servants, as an intermediary. Mordecai, aware that mass murder is imminent, requests that Esther immediately intercede with the king on behalf of the embattled Jews; she replies that nobody is allowed to approach the king without being summoned, under penalty of death. Mordecai, in a moment of great drama and pathos, warns her that she dare not hide behind anonymity, that even her status as queen of Persia will not save her; she dare not think that she will be safer in the palace than any other Jew, for rabid anti-Semitism does not make exceptions! Indeed, warns Mordecai, "if you remain silent at this time, then salvation and deliverance will come to the Jews from elsewhere, but you and your father's house will perish, and who knows if, just for [the situation at] this moment, you attained royalty?" (4:14).

Esther, deeply moved by Mordecai's challenge, asks him to declare a fast for all the Jews; she, too, will fast and pray for three days, after which she will approach the king to seek his help, despite the Persian law against her doing so. She concludes by saying, "If I perish, I perish" (4:16).

On the third day, she seeks an audience with Ahasuerus, to which he acquiesces. Esther then invites Ahasuerus to a feast with her in the company of Haman. During the feast, she again invites the "ménage à trois" to attend a further feast the next evening. Clearly Esther is planting jealousy against Haman in the heart of Ahasuerus. Why else would Esther spoil a private tête-à-tête between Esther and Ahasuerus with the presence of Haman?! Nevertheless, Haman returns home overjoyed at his having been invited to yet another banquet with the king and queen. Unfortunately, Haman's good cheer is spoiled by Mordecai's refusal to bow down to him; egged on by his wife Zeresh and his friends, he builds a gallows for Mordecai, with the intention to hang him there the very next day.

As we have suggested, it is quite obvious that Esther's strategy of these two invitations was to raise feelings of jealousy in the heart of the Persian emperor. He expected a tête-à-tête with Esther; now these feasts would be a ménage à trois – Esther, Ahasuerus, and Haman. Esther's strategy may well have been effective, because that night Ahasuerus suffers from insomnia, perhaps brought on by his concerns about a clandestine relationship between Esther and Haman. When the court's daily records are read to him to help him fall asleep, he learns of his life having been saved by Mordecai who had discovered a plot against him. Ahasuerus asks whether anything was done to reward Mordecai and is told that nothing was done.

Just then, Haman appears, prepared to ask the king to hang Mordecai the next day. King Ahasuerus never gives Haman the opportunity to make that request, but rather asks Haman what he thinks should be done for the man whom the king wishes to honor. Certain that the king is referring to Haman himself, Haman says that the honoree should be dressed in the king's royal robes and led around on the king's royal horse, while wearing the king's royal crown. To Haman's shock and horror, the king instructs Haman to render such honors to Mordecai. This is the beginning of Mordecai's rise and Haman's fall. Haman returns home depressed and angry, only to hear his wife Zeresh "rub it in" by saying, "If Mordecai, before whom you have begun to fall, is of Jewish seed, then you will not prevail against him; but you shall surely fall before him" (6:13).

Later that evening, Ahasuerus and Haman attend Esther's second banquet and, responding to the king's offer of granting whatever she may wish, she dramatically reveals her Jewish identity with the words "Let my soul be given to me at my request, and my people at my entreaty" (7:3). She discloses that Haman is planning to exterminate her people, which means that she, too, would be murdered. Ahasuerus becomes enraged and orders that Haman be hanged on the very gallows that he had prepared for Mordecai. Furthermore, Mordecai is installed as primary adviser to the king, in place of Haman. The Jews are then given permission by the king to defend themselves in battle against the king's forces coming to enforce Haman's decree (which, the Megilla says, could not be rescinded); the Jews are victorious. Great rejoicing takes place, and the festival of Purim is established.

QUESTIONS ON THE STORY

There are a number of glaring questions on this story and the manner in which it is written.

Question 1: Throughout the entire Five Books of Moses, and virtually throughout all of the other books of the Bible, God's name appears with great frequency, almost in every verse. After all, in a very real sense, He is the main character of the Bible! Amazingly, in the Scroll of Esther, God's name does not appear even once. As if this was not astonishing enough in itself, this book gives rise to an important festival of the Jewish people – the festival of Purim – on which we are presumably thankful to God for saving the Jewish community of Persia from annihilation! So why is God absent in the very textual source for our Purim celebration? This question begs for an answer.

Question 2: The morality of the Bible clearly outlaws acts of adultery. In early biblical times, such transgressions were – at least officially – punishable by death. So how could Esther have possibly agreed to that "nocturnal beauty contest," and how could Mordecai have agreed to let Esther place herself in that situation?[5]

5. The Talmud (Sanhedrin 74b) discusses the requirement to forfeit one's life rather than commit any of three major sins, one of which is that of publicly violating a sexual prohibition of the Torah. The Talmud wonders why Esther was not required to give up her life rather than have relations with Ahasuerus, because this was an act that, while not committed publicly, was known by all. The Talmud answers that Esther was sexually passive in the relationship, and so she did not willfully commit

Question 3: We must ask why Mordecai refuses to bow down to Haman. There is full halakhic agreement that one is permitted to bow to a ruling official as a show of respect. Why did Mordecai risk his own life and, as it turned out, the lives of all of the Jews, by refusing to perform an act that was permissible by Jewish law?[6]

Question 4: How do we celebrate Purim? Most of the celebration of the festival seems very logical. We read the Scroll of Esther (the "Megilla") publicly twice: once on the night of Purim and again during the day. We give food gifts to each other (called *mishloaḥ manot*) and we give gifts to the poor (called *matanot la'evyonim*). Finally, there is the Purim meal (called *Seudat Purim*), a very festive meal, usually held on the afternoon of the holiday, with much singing and joy. All of this happiness arises from the knowledge that, although anti-Semitism persists, the Jewish people are strong, and will always "win in the end," exactly as Haman's wife Zeresh told him in the Scroll of Esther. These "communal commandments" of giving gifts serve to strengthen the Jewish community, to gladden everyone's heart, and to be sure that no one is left out of the festivities.

However, in connection with this meal, the Talmud[7] has a rather shocking directive, and the *Shulḥan Arukh*, the Code of Jewish Law,[8] brings it as an integral part of the Purim observance: "A person must become inebriated on Purim until he does not know the difference between 'Cursed be Haman' and 'Blessed be Mordecai.'" What could this be? A commandment to get drunk? This would seem to go against everything that Judaism preaches! We are always expected to act with holiness and to remain aware of what we are required to do and what

---

the act. This answer is somewhat difficult to understand, because it seems that Esther's winning the nocturnal beauty contest would be unlikely if she were sexually passive. Our answer in section 6 of this chapter suggests a different approach.

6. The Midrash in Esther Rabba 7:8 tries to answer our question by saying that although it would have been permissible for Mordecai to bow down to Haman, Haman was wearing the figure of an idol around his neck, and so it would have appeared that Mordecai was bowing to the idol – which is prohibited. Clearly, the Midrash is searching for a reason, since there is no hint from the text that Haman was wearing the figure of an idol.
7. Megilla 7b.
8. *Shulḥan Arukh, Oraḥ Ḥayim* 695:2.

we must not do. One cannot maintain that state of awareness in a state of inebriation.[9]

Question 5: Finally, there is a strong custom of masquerading on Purim – wearing masks, wearing costumes. The great halakhic decisor Rabbi Moshe Isserles (1530–1572) even permits men and women to dress as the opposite gender,[10] something generally prohibited the rest of the year. What is the purpose of all this, and what relationship does it have to the meaning of the Purim festival?

THE VERY FIRST JEWISH DIASPORA: WHAT CAN WE LEARN FROM IT?

Purim is a Diaspora festival. It takes place in the Diaspora, and there is no mention at all of the Land of Israel in the Scroll of Esther. Therefore, in order to deeply understand the holiday – and to answer the questions we have posed – we must go back to the very first Jewish diaspora, the diaspora of Egypt, recounted in the biblical book of Exodus.

The book of Exodus begins with a very brief review of the arrival of the seventy members of the house of Jacob-Israel into the Egyptian exile, a narrative that was recounted in detail in the book of Genesis. The opening verses of Exodus recall that Joseph, the favorite son of Jacob, became second-in-command to Pharaoh in Egypt. The development of the Hebrews in the Egyptian exile is carefully described in verse 7 of the opening chapter: "And the children of Israel were *fruitful,* and were *swarming* all about and they grew to be *many,* and they were *very, very*

9. Some of the commentaries try to find ways to perform this commandment by other than actually drinking a great deal of an alcoholic beverage. For example, the Rambam (*Hilkhot Megilla* 2:15) suggests that one should drink a little more than his or her usual measure, until one dozes off. Rabbi Moshe Isserles, the Ashkenazi voice in the Code of Jewish Law (*Hilkhot Megilla, Oraḥ Ḥayim* 695:2), echoes this and points out that while sleeping, of course, one cannot make a differentiation between cursing Haman and blessing Mordecai. Others suggest that one should only drink if he knows that what will come out of his mouth in an inebriated state are words of holiness. The general custom that has developed is of drinking on Purim, but not to inebriation. (It goes without saying that in any case of danger to health, or with minors, no drinking should take place on Purim.)
10. Commentary on *Shulḥan Arukh, Oraḥ Ḥayim* 696:8.

powerful, and the land was *filled* with them." This description by means of seven verbs, adjectives, and adverbs can be superficially seen as painting a very positive picture of the Israelites succeeding, multiplying, and even growing powerful within the Egyptian diaspora.

To a great extent, this "successful integration" seems to have also characterized the nature of the Jewish community in Persia, many millennia later. The Jews are living in Shushan the capital city, Mordecai is described as "sitting at the gate of the king," reserved for advisers and important citizens, and the entire Jewish community is invited to the party of Ahasuerus. The Jews in Persia, to all intents and purposes, are a respected and developing minority.

However, we must go back and look more deeply into the prototypical Egyptian diaspora. In the aforementioned verse in Exodus 1:7, as we have said, there are seven expressions[11] (in Hebrew) that describe the development of the Jewish people in Egypt. Most of those terms express praise of the increase in number and power of the Jews. However, within this verse there are *double entendres*. The word *vayishretzu*, which can also be translated as "they spread out," which would imply benign growth, literally means "they swarmed," which is an expression usually related to a detestable, creeping reptile. There is a strong hint here – from the Divine Narrator – that all is not so well in what seemed like a successfully growing Egyptian diaspora community. The Jews of Egypt are not preserving their distinctiveness; the "swarming" expression indicates that they are partaking of the Egyptian diet, not only the foods and drinks that are traditionally permitted to them. And the coda of the verse, "and the land was filled with them," also hints that there are disturbing currents within the Egyptian Jewish diaspora. The Midrash[12] on this verse explains the land being "filled with them" as meaning that the Jews of Egypt – before the enslavement, of course – were found in places where they should not have been – the "hang-out places" of Egypt, their equivalent of less-than-respectable places of recreation and

11. The seven expressions (seven denoting completeness) are "fruitful," "swarmed," "many," "powerful," "very much" (Hebrew, *bimeod meod* – counting as two expressions), "and the land was filled with them."
12. *Midrash Tanḥuma* (Buber) 6.

self-indulgence. In short, this pregnant verse telegraphs to us the sweeping assimilation of the Jews into the wider community and the loss of their distinctive values, the paradigm of disaster for their community and for all future Jewish diaspora communities.

The verses we have quoted are followed by verses which seem, at first blush, to be *non sequiturs*. "And there arose a new king in Egypt who did not know (or 'revere the memory of') Joseph. And he said to his people, 'Behold the people of Israel are greater and stronger than we are. Let us outsmart them, lest they increase, and, if there is a war, that they join our enemies and make war against us, and leave the land'" (Ex. 1:9–10). It may be that the biblical text is showing a cause-and-effect relationship. The self-insertion of the Jews into Egyptian society and the absorption of Egyptian – but not Jewish – customs and lifestyle brings on the (probably irrational) fear by Pharaoh and his people of being "taken over" by the Jews – a familiar feature of the history of anti-Semitism.

It is also possible, on a more theological level, to view this juxtaposition of verses as sin and punishment. The Jews were losing their value system to a less moral Egyptian one; they were assimilating and so their enslavement was a sign of divine displeasure with their extreme acculturation. [13]

It is almost as if God is saying to the Jewish people,

> It is true that I have a covenant with you and that you will always remain an eternal people even after you leave your national homeland and birthplace and go into a diaspora situation. What will enable you to do that successfully is by remaining true to the laws and customs of the Torah; thus you will remain a separate people in your diaspora. Of course you are expected to be good and productive citizens wherever you live,[14] but you must also remain a people set apart by virtue of your commitment to higher

13. The *Zohar Ḥadash, Yitro* 31a, says that, of the mystical fifty gates of impurity, the Jews in Egypt had reached the forty-ninth.
14. The prophet Jeremiah, in his letter to the Jewish exiles in Babylonia, emphasized this idea: "Thus said the Lord of Hosts, the God of Israel, unto all the exiles whom I have exiled from Jerusalem unto Babylon: Build houses and dwell in them; and

> standards of morality and ethical conduct as well as a unique ritual tradition that will enable you to maintain your separateness. If, however, you fall into the trap of assimilation, and you forget your traditional commitments, there will arise a ruler in that diaspora who will persecute you and will not allow you to assimilate.

The Torah is merely warning us that when we become more gentile than the gentiles, it will not make us more acceptable to our non-Jewish neighbors. Actually, the opposite is often true: as absurd as it seems, they will see us as trying to take over their country and the native culture will attempt to destroy the Jewish interlopers!

ANSWERS TO THE QUESTIONS

Why Is God's Name Absent?

So, why does God's name not appear in the Scroll of Esther? Perhaps it was because God did not belong there, because the picture of the Jews in Persia is a picture of a Jewish community in the midst of assimilation. God was simply not a factor for the Jews of Persia. For these Jews, as we have mentioned, the king's palace was a kind of substitute for the Sanctuary. The Jews attended Ahasuerus's party, apparently with no thought about the non-kosher status of its food and drink. The Megilla even goes so far as to say that although the Hebrews were not forced to drink the non-kosher wine,[15] they nevertheless drank to inebriation! God's laws were not pertinent for them, and so God's name does not appear.

Indeed, the Persian exile produced a much more assimilated "Jewish" community then did the Egyptian exile! The Midrash (Leviticus Rabba 32:5) says that in the Egyptian exile, the Jews remained distinctive in that they did not change their names or their Hebrew language. Yet here, in the Persian diaspora, the very names of the heroes and heroines of the Megilla testify to their profound assimilation! Not only do they

---

plant gardens and eat their fruit... and seek the peace of the city in which I caused you to be exiled, and pray unto God for it; for in its peace you shall have peace" (Jer. 29:4–7).

15. Est. 1:8.

adopt Persian names, but they take on the names of Persian idolatrous deities! Esther may be the Hebraification of the goddess of fertility and sexuality, Ishtar or Astarte, and Mordecai of Marduk, the god of war. How can God be present, if the Persian gods are present?

How Could Esther, with Mordecai's Approval, Enter the "Nocturnal Beauty Contest"?

Regarding our essential question about both Esther and – especially – Mordecai seeming to have no problem with Esther's entering the "queen contest," and, after winning, going to live with a pagan king, the famous traditional commentator Avraham ibn Ezra quotes an opinion (which he goes on to reject) that Mordecai was afraid that if Esther had revealed her origins, she would not be taken as queen.[16] In other words, Mordecai, also influenced by the weight of Persian culture, really did want Esther to be queen, despite the halakhic problems. Assuredly Mordecai's desire for Esther to be accepted as queen of Persia was for the good of the Jewish community; if a problem of anti-Semitism arose, she could help fix it from a position of power. And it was also likely that Mordecai was not displeased with his having a close relative as queen of Persia; he could then play the "court Jew," with a great deal of influence in the corridors of power. The picture, however, is very clear; Esther and Mordecai are certainly mostly concerned about the viability of the Jewish community in Persia, but they have also assimilated into the immoral and hedonistic lifestyle of Persian nobility!

Why Did Mordecai Refuse to Bow to Haman?

What about Mordecai's refusal to bow down to Haman? As we explained, with Haman's rise to near-absolute power, a sea change had occurred in

16. See Ibn Ezra on Esther 2:10. Ibn Ezra rejects this opinion, as well as another that he quotes, which says that Mordecai prophetically knew that Esther would be the instrument of salvation for the Jews, and so he must send her to the contest. He gives a third opinion, which he accepts, that Esther was taken by force to the contest (apparently against Mordecai's will), and was able to keep Jewish tradition secretly (he gives the examples of Sabbath observance and refraining from non-kosher food) within the palace. We have chosen to accept his first opinion, which we see as closest to the simple meaning of the text.

the governance of the Persian Empire. No longer was Persia being run by an oligarchy – a small group of advisers to the king as is stated early in the Scroll of Esther; now, Persia had a true totalitarian rulership, with Haman's power unrivaled.[17] Therefore, Mordecai simply could not give Haman the honor of obeisance, because he knew that in a totalitarian state the Jews would then have no chance of long-term survival. Totalitarianism could not coexist even with an assimilating form of Judaism. In addition, in the ancient world, a totalitarian ruler was similar to a god; people actually prayed to such a potentate. And so, Mordecai's public and visible obeisance to Haman would be akin to idol worship – a "red line" for the Jews. As we say in the daily *Aleinu* prayer, "The Lord is God in the heavens above and upon the earth below; there is none other." Even the assimilating Jews in Persia were still faithful to the one God of Israel and the world, even while they compromised on Jewish morality and sanctity.

Why Do We Masquerade on Purim?

And why a masquerade celebration on Purim? Throughout most of the Megilla, Mordecai and Esther were masquerading as Persians. With their fully Persian names and their aristocratic positions in the Persian aristocracy, they were seen as an integral part of Persian culture. They may have kept Jewish tradition privately – although to what extent we cannot be sure – but publicly, they were most probably "more Persian than the Persians."

However, it is fascinating that, at the moment of truth, Mordecai and Esther return to their real selves, and take off their masks. When Mordecai realizes that Haman has become godlike in power and that the Jewish community is about to be destroyed, he "goes public," and makes a demonstration on behalf of the Jews.

17. The level of Haman's power was so great that, when it came to the issuing of his decree of genocide against the Jews, he did not see fit to discuss it with the king's "cabinet." Even when he came to the king for "permission" to exterminate the Jews, he did not feel the need to fully explain his reasons to the king. Just the offer of money into the king's treasury (3:9) was sufficient for the king to sign off on the decree. Haman was truly in full power.

At first Esther does not quite understand – or does not wish to understand – the gravity of the situation, until Mordecai, as we have said, inspires her with his words: "Do not think to yourself that you will escape Jewish destruction because you are living in the palace of the emperor. If you remain silent at this time, then salvation and deliverance will come to the Jews from elsewhere, but you and your father's house will perish! And who knows if, just for [the sake of the situation at] this moment, you attained royalty?" (4:13–14). In effect, Mordecai is now saying: "Esther, this is your moment of truth! We must be who we really are, no matter what the consequences." Esther now understands Mordecai's message to her: that she – even as the queen – will not be saved if the Jews are destroyed. Ultimately she is a Jew, not a Persian! Esther rises to the occasion; she takes off her mask, and she places her life on the line, comes forward as a proud Jewess to attempt to save her people in her moment of truth.

Drinking on Purim Revisited?

When the Talmud says that there is an obligation to drink on Purim until one can no longer distinguish between cursing Haman and blessing Mordecai, is the Talmud then saying that drinking on Purim to inebriation is a beneficial and divinely commanded act? Moreover, Mordecai is the hero and Haman is the villain! So is it not salutary to distinguish between them?

In order to understand the need to drink on Purim until we can no longer distinguish between blessing Mordecai and cursing Haman, we must first turn to our first question: Who is the true hero of the Megilla? Undoubtedly at this point, it was Mordecai and Esther, who have emerged as true Jews, and placed their lives on the line for their Jewishness. But who was it who initially reminded the Jews that they were Jews? In strange sort of a way, it was actually Haman who reminded the Jews of who they were, with his virulent anti-Semitism, with the very decree that forced them to admit their true identity. Had it not been for Haman and his desire to commit genocide against the Jews, Persian Jewry was well on the way to assimilating into oblivion. Therefore, Haman can well be considered one of the "heroes" of the Scroll. Just as in the first exile in Egypt it was Pharaoh who enslaved the Hebrews just as they were assimilating throughout

Egypt, and thereby prevented their total assimilation, so here in Persia, it was Haman who ironically reminded the Jews of their Judaism. However, if we have to wait for Haman's evil decree to remind us of our Jewishness by almost destroying us, it is well-nigh impossible to rejoice over such a victory. Hence, we require the power of liquor to enable us to rejoice at a victory which comes at such a heavy price. Had it not been for Haman, the Jews in Persia would have completely assimilated! Strangely and most ironically, Haman's evil decree against Judaism saved the Jews from totally identifying as Persians!

PURIM'S LESSON: DIASPORA AS ONLY TEMPORARY RELIEF

With this vulnerability and this uncertainty, can Jewish life flourish in the Diaspora? Jewish history teaches that if at all, it will only give us respite for a limited period. Indeed, perhaps the two most successful Diaspora communities were in Babylon, which flourished for over a thousand years and which produced the remarkable literature called the Babylonian Talmud, and in the United States of America, wherein Jews have been living in freedom and success since colonial times. But we learn from our history – and certainly from the Scroll of Esther – that once we leave our historic homeland, it becomes difficult for a people transplanted into a foreign culture to truly retain their original Jewish identity. They may begin by only masquerading as gentiles, but, generally speaking, the Jewish identity will soon be completely forgotten and the masquerade will become the reality. That is what happened to the once-proud Jewish community of Alexandria, Egypt, which, even during the life and certainly after the death of the great Alexandrine Jewish philosopher Philo (c. 50 CE), declined rapidly through assimilation. Even the Bible that they read was the Septuagint, the Greek translation of the Bible. American Jewry today is intermarrying at an alarming pace, and Jewish affiliation is at an all-time low.[18]

18. For example, according to the well-accepted Pew Report of 2013, among Jews who have gotten married since 2000, about six in ten have a non-Jewish spouse. Moreover, only fifteen percent of the respondents said that being Jewish is mainly a matter

And the only reason that the Babylonian Jewish community lasted for more than a thousand years is that the ruling governments allowed us to have a state within a state: with a Jewish exilarch, with a Jewish judicial system, with a Jewish educational system for the Jewish population of Babylon. Without such a Jewish state within a state, the prospect of retaining a Jewish culture within a foreign environment is very close to zero. Even regarding Babylon, if you were to visit Babylon (present-day Iraq) today, you would see no vestige whatsoever of the once-proud Jewish community which flourished there!

In addition to the "enemy" of assimilation, we know from the history of the Jewish Diaspora that anti-Semitic Hamans will always arise, often at the most unexpected moments. Witness Hitler and Nazi Germany, whose massive and organized killing destroyed six million Jews, sixty-three percent of Europe's Jews, many of whom were devout in their observance. Even in post-Holocaust Europe and America today, anti-Semitism and assimilation are combining to make the Jewish communities negligible in every community outside of Israel – where the Jewish population is literally exploding!

DID MORDECAI MAKE A MISTAKE?

We must remember that our Torah morality, ethics, and rituals are not easy to maintain, especially not in a Diaspora situation, where the entire culture militates against Judaism. We have a covenant with God, who has promised us that ultimately we will return to our homeland, as

---

of religion. Also, twenty-two percent describe themselves as having "no religion"; that figure is thirty-two percent for millennials. Fully two-thirds of the Jews who say they have "no religion" say that they are not raising their children Jewish or partially Jewish! Finally, sixty-one percent of respondents said that no one in their household is a member of a synagogue or temple. A whopping seventy-one percent said that no one in their household is a member of any Jewish organization other than a synagogue or temple. ("A Portrait of Jewish Americans" [Pew Research Center, October 1, 2013], 7–9, 181. https://www.pewresearch.org/religion/2013/10/01/jewish-american-beliefs-attitudes-culture-survey/). According to research carried out by the Rabbinical Center of Europe in 2014, intermarriage rates (without meaningful conversion) among European Jews are even higher, reaching an average of eighty-five percent!

many of us have done, sometimes under difficult conditions. Judaism will triumph at the end – but only when we are redeemed within our ancestral homeland! The Pentateuch concludes with the Hebrews meriting the blessings only after the tribes are returned to their homeland after a difficult diaspora!

Hence, as we are told in the very final verse of the Megilla, Mordecai is only accepted as a true leader by the *majority* of his brethren.[19] Why? It is instructive to note that Haman's edict of destruction was issued on the thirteenth day of the month of Nisan. However, the edict stated that the actual mass murder would take place eleven months later, on the thirteenth of the month of Adar.[20] Mordecai used this time in order to arrange for a demonstration on behalf of the Jews, warn Esther that she must make herself known to Ahasuerus as a Jewess, and arrange a meeting between them that would end with the monarch's complete condemnation of Haman.

I would suggest that perhaps Mordecai did not use those eleven months well. Conceivably he should have acted like a true Jewish leader and done everything in his power (à la Ze'ev Jabotinsky[21]) to galvanize a mass effort of the Persian Jews to move to the Land of Israel, a move which, as we have mentioned, had already been permitted years before by Cyrus. But even though it was obvious from Haman's edict – on which the king had happily signed off – that the Jews were not welcome in Persia, Mordecai apparently felt that mass transfer to Israel was not the right approach. Mordecai should have understood that given the enmity of the Persians toward the Jews, the exile in Persia would never have a happy ending.[22]

19. See Megilla 16b, "'By the majority of his brethren,' but not by all his brethren. This teaches that some members of the Sanhedrin parted from him."

20. Est. 3:12–13.

21. Ze'ev Jabotinsky (1880–1940) was a founder of the Revisionist Zionist Movement in Europe. Deeply concerned with the threats to Eastern European Jewish communities, he prepared an "evacuation plan" that called for the evacuation of the entire Jewish population of Poland, Hungary, and Romania to Palestine. In 1938, he said, "Catastrophe is coming...the volcano that will soon spew out its flames of extermination." His plan met with disapproval in several quarters and was never implemented.

22. It is difficult not to see a parallel in our own day that in spite of the rise of anti-Semitism to alarming levels in many countries, there is extreme hesitation on the

Mordecai's approach worked on an interim basis, but even after the Purim salvation, the Jews were just as vulnerable as they had been before. According to that final verse of the Scroll of Esther, the majority of Mordecai's brethren agreed with his decision, but there may well have been a significant minority who felt that the correct solution would have been to abandon the vulnerable Diaspora existence and relocate to the Land of Israel.

Indeed, the Talmud[23] states clearly that every festival in the Hebrew calendar (including the rabbinic holiday of Hanukka) calls for the recitation of Hallel (Ps. 113–118), but that no Hallel is to be recited on Purim. The Talmud explains this ruling by saying that "we are still servants of Ahasuerus" – that the victory of Purim is a very transient one. The Talmud goes on to note that the very first verse of Hallel (Ps. 113:1) states, "Halleluyah! Praise, you servants of the Lord, praise the name of the Lord." The Talmud reasons that we cannot recite that verse – and, therefore, the entire Hallel – because it is impossible to serve God to the fullest extent as long as the Jewish community is subject to the wishes and whims of a foreign ruler – the very definition of the Diaspora situation. Even though it seemed as if Mordecai and Esther succeeded through their approach, they really did not – at least not in the larger sense. We cannot properly praise God with Hallel on Purim – the very picture of Jewish vulnerability in the Diaspora – because we are still "servants of Ahasuerus." Those Persian Jews who remained "servants of Ahasuerus" were still slaves to a foreign culture and foreign values and therefore could not sing the praises of Hallel and engage in a full, loving relationship with God. Perhaps this is why we are obliged to get drunk on Purim.

I understand that for many readers our interpretation of the Megilla is different from the one usually given: that the victory is complete, that Mordecai and Esther were truly extremely righteous individuals, and that God's presence, albeit mostly hidden, will guarantee ultimate Jewish success, even in the Diaspora. Having said that, the glory of our

part of Jewish leaders to suggest a mass exodus of their Jewish populations to the State of Israel.

23. Megilla 14a.

Jewish texts lies in the many possible – and different – ways of understanding them. Jewish tradition teaches that there is not only one true interpretation, but that there are many possible interpretations which may all be true at the same time.[24] In addition, I honestly believe that our interpretation is closest to the literal meaning of the text, and when the Rabbis decreed that there is to be no Hallel on Purim because "we are still servants to Ahasuerus," this was a clear position statement by our Sages that Purim is not a complete festival, and that the victory of Esther and Mordecai was, at best, only temporary.[25]

And so, in a certain way, Purim may be seen as an "anti-holiday," the only holiday which requires "artificial alcoholic stimulation" to feel joy – because the joy in the Diaspora is, at best, only temporary. That is why we drink until we can no longer distinguish between "cursing Haman and blessing Mordecai." Both of their "solutions" – Haman's edict of destruction and Mordecai's planned defenses – would, nevertheless, end in the loss a Jewish future into the Messianic Age. Exile from our homeland Israel will always destroy us, either physically or spiritually.

In the final analysis, the ultimate place in which Jewish communities will truly find "light and gladness and joy and honor" (Est. 8:16) – ultimate victory – is in Israel. And we still await the true universal redemption, when all the nations of the world will accept the majesty of the Loving Lord: "From Zion will come forth Torah and the word of the Loving Lord from Jerusalem, when nation will no longer lift up sword against nation and humanity will no longer engage in war" (Is. 2:2–4).

---

24. There are many sources that express this idea. The Talmud in Eruvin 13b, discussing the differing opinions of Hillel and Shammai, states that "these and these are the words of the living God." Avraham ibn Ezra, in a poem that concludes his commentary on the Torah, says, "There are seventy [often denoting a very large number] faces [or facets] to the Torah."
25. Rabbi Yoel Bin-Nun, a deep thinker and creative expositor of the Bible, suggests that when the Talmud teaches that the Jews of Persia were still "servants of Ahasuerus," it means that they continued to need special permission from the king to defend themselves, as is evident from the Megilla. Today, with the establishment of the State of Israel, Jews can defend themselves without asking for permission from others. Effectively, the Hallel that we do not recite on Purim is the one that we recite on Israel Independence Day.

Chapter 10

Raḥamim BaDin: Kill or Convert Amalek?

A LIFE-CHANGING STORY

The year was 1952. I was twelve years old, living with my family in Brooklyn. On *Shabbat Parashat Ki Tavo,* I made the two-mile walk to the Klausenberger Beit Midrash in Bedford-Stuyvesant, Brooklyn (formerly the Beth Moses Hospital, where I was born). I had heard about the Klausenburger Rebbe – Rabbi Yekusiel Yehudah Halberstam – survivor of Auschwitz and charismatic leader of his Hasidim. I had learned about many of the sacrifices the Rebbe had made to help his people during the Holocaust; although he was offered an escape visa to America, he refused to accept it – since it would have required him to leave his Hasidim behind. He had, indeed, suffered horribly in Auschwitz but remained an inspiration for all who came into contact with him. When the Jews were liberated he was too ill with typhus to be moved. Now that he was well enough to have been brought to America, and to be the leader of a congregation close to where I was living, I very much desired to pray with him.

Parashat Ki Tavo contains the *Tokheḥa,* the lengthy, horrific description of curses that would befall the Jewish people if they, as a group, did not keep the laws of the Torah. The age-old custom in all the congregations where I have been is that the Torah reader chants these verses very quietly and very quickly, so as not to dwell upon punishment and destruction. On that Shabbat, when the reader reached the *Tokheḥa* section, that is exactly how he began to read – quietly and quickly.

Suddenly, the Rebbe, who was standing in front of the ark ramrod straight, called out, in Yiddish, one word: "*Hekher!*" ("Louder!"). The Torah reader stopped, confused. There was total silence. It couldn't be that the Rebbe would defy Jewish tradition and want the *Tokheḥa* read loudly! Assuming that he had heard incorrectly, the Reader resumed chanting, quietly and quickly. This time the Rebbe's voice was a shout, an angry shout in his voice and look in his eyes, and what he said was unmistakable: "*I said, 'Louder'! Let God hear! We have already had all of the curses; we have nothing to be afraid of! Let God hear the curses, and let Him now bring the blessings which the Torah promises will follow the curses!*"

I was bathed in sweat. Many of the congregants were sobbing quietly.

After the service, the Rebbe turned to the congregation. The anger of moments before was gone, and in his eyes there was only love. He said, "It is time for the blessings. And indeed, they are already coming, but not here in exile; as promised, in our homeland, Israel. And so, we must move to Israel. Let everyone pack up for the last time." And, in fact, in a most brave and tradition-breaking move for Hasidim, the Rebbe and his Hasidim relocated to Kiryat Sanz in Netanya, Israel.

There is a sequel to this story. Many years afterward, I was speaking in a synagogue in Surfside, Florida, called "The Shul," under the rabbinic leadership of Rabbi Sholom Lipskar. It was *Parashat Ki Tavo,* and I told this story. At *Seuda Shelishit,* a gentleman approached me, and told me how moved he was by the story. He said, "I was with the Klausenberger Rebbe in Auschwitz." He recounted to me that, as part of the same work force in the camp, he and the Rebbe often stood together as they did their backbreaking work. On Shabbat, and on Yom Tov, when, of course, they had to work, the Rebbe would mouth the words of all the Shabbat prayers as he did what he was forced to do, and then would move on to whispering all of the *zemirot,* the Shabbat songs that are traditionally sung around the table during the three Shabbat meals.

At *Seuda Shelishit*, the third meal, as the holy Sabbath is waning it is customary to recite Psalm 23, and the Rebbe sang-whispered this as well. When the Rebbe came to the haunting verse "Yea, though I walk through the valley of the shadow of death, I will fear no evil, for You are with me; Your rod and Your staff, they comfort me," he did not pause between the words in the traditional way, but, rather, he punctuated it differently. *Gam ki elekh begei tzalmavet* – "When I walk through the valley of the shadow of death" – *lo ira* – "I will not fear" – and then he paused. "But *ra* – what is bad, what is difficult for me, what gives me great pain – *ki Ata imadi* – is that You, God, are with me here in Auschwitz." "Even God," said the Rebbe, "is also imprisoned, *afilu der Aibishter is farshklaft*, the One on High is also in chains!"

I did not understand what the gentleman was telling me. If God is imprisoned, then how will Israel be redeemed? If God is imprisoned, who will destroy our historic archenemy Amalek who is embodied in all of our enemies; Haman was Amalek, Hitler was Amalek. And what did the Rebbe really mean when he said that God was also in captivity in Auschwitz?

Yes, Hitler, his minions, and his collaborators were the embodiment of Amalek, the archenemy of Israel. I would like to add to my discussion about Purim a suggestion about the eventual destruction of Amalek, about who will destroy Amalek, about how Amalek will eventually be blotted out, about who will free God, about who will free Israel, and about who will ultimately redeem the world from its evil. Only when Amalek is truly destroyed will the world truly be redeemed!

WHO WILL DESTROY AMALEK?

There are two major sources in the Bible about the destruction of Amalek, which are read publicly prior to and on Purim. The first is in Exodus chapter 17:

> And the Lord said unto Moses: "Write this for a memorial in the book, and rehearse it in the ears of Joshua: for I will utterly blot out the remembrance of Amalek from under heaven." And Moses built an altar, and called the name of it *Adonai-nissi*, the Loving

> Lord is my banner. And he said: "The hand (of Amalek is) upon the throne of God: The Loving Lord will wage war with Amalek from generation to generation." (vv. 14–16)

These verses describe an ongoing war between God and Amalek, "from generation to generation." The throne of God and Amalek are engaged in battle. It is clear from this that God will ultimately destroy Amalek: "I (God) will utterly blot out the remembrance of Amalek from under heaven."

However, in Deuteronomy chapter 25, we find a sharp contradiction to the previous verses:

> Remember what Amalek did to you by the way as you came forth out of Egypt; how he accidentally came upon you by the way, and cut off all the weak stragglers in your rear, when you were faint and weary; and he feared not God. Therefore it shall be, when the Loving Lord your God grants you respite from all your enemies round about, in the land which the Loving Lord your God gives you for an inheritance to possess it; you shall blot out the remembrance of Amalek from under heaven; you shall not forget.

Here, we have a dramatic description of the evil nature of Amalek: You must remember that which Amalek did to you when you were leaving Egypt, when they came upon you, when they took as their victims those who were lagging behind, the weaker vessels, the old, the infirm, the disabled, the women, the children; these were the fodder upon which Amalek fed.

In these verses, the struggle is between Israel and Amalek (not between God and Amalek, as it seems from the previous verses). Therefore, when you are freed from difficulty with other nations (this seems to hint at the Messianic Era), it is *you* who must blot out Amalek from under the heavens.

Here, it is clearly a commandment for the *Jewish people* to blot out Amalek: "*You* shall blot out the remembrance of Amalek from under heaven."

So, which is it? Will God blot out Amalek, or must we – the Jewish people – do it?

THE REDEMPTION OF PURIM: HOW IMPORTANT IS IT?

It seems clear that the redemption of the world cannot come until Amalek – the personification of evil – is destroyed. Therefore, in order to arrive at a resolution to our question "Who will destroy Amalek?" we must study the concept of *geula,* redemption.

We have two festivals in the Jewish year that celebrate redemption: Purim and Passover. The story behind each of these redemptions is very different. On Passover, the redemption was dramatic, and God's hand was visible: the Ten Plagues, the Exodus itself, the release from slavery, the Splitting of the Reed Sea. Passover introduced an entirely new reality to the Jewish people; they were free and independent, leaving exile and marching toward their new homeland, the Land of Israel.

On Purim, however, the redemption was very different. True, the Jews of Persia were saved from the genocidal plan of Haman, but, at the end of the story, the Jews were still in exile, in Persia. They did not leave for the Land of Israel. The Talmud (Megilla 14a) suggests that this is the reason that we do not recite Hallel – the Psalms of Praise – on Purim; the story both began and ended in exile. As we have noted, this may also be the reason that God's name is not mentioned at all in the Book of Esther; on Purim, God did not truly redeem Israel; "we were still servants of Ahasuerus," even at the end of the Megilla Scroll.

However, there is a very interesting difference of opinion among the Rabbis in Megilla 6b which sheds light on the issue. The Gemara raises an important question: In a Hebrew leap year, which contains two months of Adar – the month of Purim – in which Adar do we actually celebrate the holiday, the reading of the Book of Esther, and the other commandments of Purim?

According to R. Eliezer b. Yosi, we read the Megilla (and celebrate Purim) in the first month of Adar, invoking the rule of *ein maavirim al hamitzvot* – "We do not put off the performance of a mitzva." We perform commandments at the earliest possible time; thus, we observe Purim in the first month of Adar, rather than wait an entire month to perform the mitzva.

R. Shimon b. Gamliel disagrees. He insists that we are to read the Megilla in the *second* month of Adar, because *mismakh geula ligeula adif* – it is more important to connect redemption to redemption, to place the redemption of Purim adjacent to the redemption of Passover, which falls in the month of Nisan, following the second month of Adar.

It seems that R. Shimon b. Gamliel – and the halakha is decided according to his opinion – understands that the two redemptions, of Purim and of Passover, are somehow connected, and somehow parallel. Certainly, connecting Purim to Passover lends great importance to Purim's redemption, despite its not having effected an essential or fundamental change in the status of the Persian Jews.

The Rambam echoes and emphasizes this view of the importance of the Purim redemption, and therefore, of the Purim holiday itself. In *Hilkhot Megilla* 2:18, he makes a startling statement:

> All of the books of the Prophets, and all of the Writings, will be annulled in the days of the Messiah. The only exception is the Book of Esther, which will still stand like the Five Books of Moses and like the laws of the Oral Torah, which are never annulled. Although the memory of the troubles will be annulled, as it is written (Is. 65:16), "For all of the first troubles have been forgotten, and have been hidden from My eyes," the days of Purim will not be annulled, as it is written (Est. 9:28), "And these days of Purim will not pass from among the Jews, and their memory will not end from among their descendants."

Apparently, according to the Rambam, Purim and its redemption are exceedingly important, even to the extent that its story – the Book of Esther – will outlive most of the books of the Bible, alongside the Five Books of Moses, in the time of the ultimate redemption, the time of the Messiah! This certainly gives a hint of the importance of connecting Purim to Passover on the calendar.

However, Purim still appears to be one of the lesser festivals. After all, as the Talmud (Megilla 14a) expresses it, – we are still servants of Ahasuerus, meaning that since there really was no essential change in the status of the Jews of Persia, we are really celebrating salvation of the Purim Jews from death, but not eternal redemption for Israel in its classical sense. Moreover, logic would dictate that the more involved God is in a particular redemptive act, the greater the redemption. When there is *hester panim*, when God "hides His face," so to speak, as in the Book of Esther, the redemption is of lesser status. So what does the Rambam mean when he speaks of the special redemption of Purim, linking it to Passover and connecting it to the Messianic Age?

THE REDEMPTION OF PESAḤ: PRAYER VERSUS ACTION

The apex of the Passover redemption is generally seen as the Splitting of the Reed Sea. There, after all, is where God seems to change natural law, turning sea to dry land in order to redeem the Jewish people. This is the experience about which the Sages declare that what the simplest uneducated individual saw of God at the Reed Sea, even Ezekiel did not see in his most intimate visions of the Almighty.

Yet, if we look closely at the biblical text, there seems to be a difference of opinion between God and Moses as to how important the role of God is in this acme of redemption.

The Jews are being pursued by the Egyptians, who want to bring them back to Egypt and slavery. The sea is in front of them, the Egyptian army behind them. The Jews panic. And when the Jews panic, they *kvetch*, they complain:

> And they said unto Moses: "Because there were no graves in Egypt, have you taken us away to die in the wilderness? Why have you dealt thus with us, to bring us forth out of Egypt?" (Ex. 14:11)

Moses tries to reassure them, understandably, by invoking the power of the Loving Lord of Salvation:

> And Moses said unto the people: "Fear not, stand still, and see the salvation of the Loving Lord, which He will effectuate for you today; for what you have seen in Egypt today, you will never see again. The Loving God will battle for you; you hold your peace!" (Ex. 14:13-14)

This seems right. It was through God's authority that the Exodus occurred, and Moses tries to reinforce the people's faith in the saving power of God. However, God will have none of it.

> And God said unto Moses: "Why are you crying out in prayer to Me? Speak unto the children of Israel, that they go forward." (v. 15)

God is essentially telling Moses, "By referring the people to Me, you are not exercising proper leadership. Just tell the people to get moving!" Ibn Ezra interprets this to mean that with 600,000 males, indeed they should have fought the Egyptians!

Rashi's comment on these words is even stranger, and seems to go against all of Jewish tradition regarding prayer. Rashi explains that when God says to Moses, "Why are you crying out to me?" we can learn that Moses prayed to God (the Hebrew *tze'aka* means to cry out in prayer). According to Rashi, God is telling Moses, "This is not the time for a lengthy prayer, when the Jewish people are in such trouble." This seems strange! If the time when the Jews are suffering is not the time for a lengthy prayer, then when would be the proper time? When else should they pray?

Rashi's comment on God's insistence that the Jews move forward at the sea, and not indulge in lengthy prayer, teaches us a deep truth. When Jews are in trouble, do not make lengthy prayers; rather, perform lengthy actions, and say shorter prayers.

This is a message of the Passover redemption that we often miss. Of course, God played a leading role in our salvation from Egypt and slavery. However, God Himself taught us that we must "move forward" with our own action in order for the redemption to be realized. First and foremost, divine redemption will take place on the shoulders of Israel.

THE CRUCIAL ROLE OF ISRAEL ON THE PATH TO REDEMPTION

God speaks to the prophet in Isaiah 45:7:

> I form the light, and create darkness; I make peace, and create evil; I am the Lord, that does all these things.

God creates evil? How can that be? God is good! I suggest that while God does not actually *create* evil, He has created the human being who has the potential, and the free choice, to choose to do evil – even unto Auschwitz.

God has created an imperfect, incomplete world, and He has created the human being in His image, as His partner to perfect the world. The clearest statement of this fundamental idea is the statement in Genesis 2:15 that God placed the human being into the Garden of Eden (the primordial world) "to develop it and to take responsibility for it."

A further proof of this freedom of choice is the Ramban's interpretation of the seminal verse (Gen. 1:26) "Let us make the human being in our image, after our likeness." To whom is God speaking? The Ramban says that God is speaking to the animal world that he had created on that primordial sixth day. God was saying to the animals: "Let us make the human being in our image. You and I will be partners in this human being." And then God breathes the soul-breath of life into the human, so that, in addition to his animalistic features, he will also be part God. It will be up to the human being which part he or she chooses to take precedence. Will it be the animalistic side, which speaks of brute strength to dominate those who are weaker, giving in to every appetite, or will it be the godly side, which strives to help and support the weak, and to control the craving for power over all? The choice belongs – fully and completely – to the human being.

This doctrine of free choice, so central to Jewish thought, also applies directly to the notion of redemption. The Jewish people must choose redemption *by their actions* in order to be redeemed!

TEACHING THE WORLD: THE TASK OF THE JEWISH PEOPLE

God makes two promises to us: First, that the Jewish nation will never be destroyed.[1] And second, that ultimately, the Jews will choose

1. This is clear from the verse in Leviticus 26:44, "And yet for all that, when they are in the land of their enemies, I will not reject them, neither will I abhor them, to

God and godliness.[2] Our task is to teach God and godliness to the world.

Just before declaring the Ten Commandments, God charges us with being "a kingdom of priests and a holy nation" (Ex. 19:6). Rabbi Ovadia Sforno understands the phrase "kingdom of priests" as implying that our task is "to teach [the Torah to] the entire human race, that all of them should call upon the name of God."

Judaism is a religion for the world. Sforno's comments echo that idea, which finds its origins in Genesis 12:3, where God promises Abraham:

> And I will bless them that bless you, and those that curse you I will curse; and in you shall all the families of the earth be blessed.

And the Torah is explicit about the "subject matter" which we must teach the world, in Genesis 18:19:

> For I have known (loved) him [Abraham, and by extension, the Jewish people], because he has commanded his children and his household after him, that they take responsibility for the pathway of the Loving Lord, to do acts of compassionate righteousness and moral justice.

TWO IDEOLOGIES REGARDING THE NATURE OF THE HUMAN BEING

Going back to very early history, there were two ideologies about the nature of the human being. The most popular one was that that the

destroy them utterly, thereby breaking My covenant with them, for I am the Lord of Love their God." This divine covenantal promise harks back to Genesis 15, the Covenant Between the Pieces.

2. Deuteronomy 30:2: "You shall return unto Hashem your God and you shall listen to His voice, according to all that I command you today, you and your children, with all of your heart and all of your soul." Some commentators see this as a commandment (the Hebrew is ambiguous), but others see it as a promise or a prediction. The Ramban seems to view it as both.

human being is a complex animal, and, as in the animal world, only the most powerful survive. This was the view in virtually every civilization in the ancient world: the Greeks, Sparta, Rome, Persia, Babylon. In the modern world we have seen this ideology expressed in Nazi Germany, under Soviet rule, and in murderous regimes all the way to ISIS and the jihadists of today. Just as in the animal world, power was the prime arbiter of human existence. In this worldview, war is idealized; the stronger army wins, and "to the victor belong the spoils."

The leaders of each of these groups have chosen the animal within them as the dominant force within their personalities, their strivings, and their goals. Those individuals – and those whom they influence – believe only in the survival of the fittest. They believe that power is the main goal in life. They truly believe that they have the entitlement (by virtue of their power) to control the weakest elements of their societies.

These individuals, and these nations, are represented by Amalek.

The opposing ideology is expressed by the Jewish people alone – that compassionate righteousness and moral justice will ultimately trump power, and that morality and peace will ultimately take over the world. Judaism believes that in order to do "compassionate righteousness" and to teach it, we must choose the godly portion of our makeup, not our animalistic side.

Amalek took the weak as its victims. They took them as their "right." Nietzsche suggests that the reason for anti-Semitism is that Judaism – through its emphasis on compassionate justice – tries to curb the power of the most powerful, and, of course, the powerful violently resent and resist that curbing. This is the reason for world anti-Semitism.[3]

---

3. Nietzche's relationship with anti-Semitism is complex and the subject of much scholarly discussion. But he seems to make clear what we have said above in this quote from his book *Beyond Good and Evil*:

> All that has been done on earth against "the nobles," the "mighty," the "overlords"... is as nothing compared to what the Jews did against them: the Jews, that priestly people who were only able to obtain satisfaction against their enemies and conquerors through a radical revaluation of the latter's values, that is, by an act of the most spiritual revenge.... It was the Jews who... dared to invert the aristocratic value-equation... saying, "The wretched alone are the good ones, the poor, the helpless, the lowly.... You who are powerful and noble are to all eternity the evil ones."

Israel and Amalek represent absolutely polar opposite ideologies. And so, Amalek – in all his forms – has fought against Israel for generations, as the verse above from Exodus proclaims.

"YOU SHALL NOT FORGET": FORGET WHAT?

The verse from Deuteronomy that commands us to blot out the memory of Amalek concludes with the warning, "You shall not forget." But what is it exactly that we are not to forget?

A similar problem arises in the Torah shortly after these verses. In *Parashat Ki Tavo,* we have the section called *vidui maasrot.* The Jew in the Land of Israel during the time of the Temple is commanded, after he has completed the giving of his required tithes, to make a formal statement that he has done so. However, at the beginning of this declaration, he includes a curious pronouncement. Here is the complete verse (Deut. 26:13):

> Then you will say before the Lord your God: "I have put away the hallowed things out of my house, and also have given them unto the Levite, and unto the stranger, to the fatherless, and to the widow, according to all Your commandment which You have commanded me; I have not transgressed any of Your commandments, and I have not forgotten."

What a strange way to end the performance of a commandment! Of course you have not forgotten; you just performed the commandment!

Rashi explains that the individual is stating that he did not forget to recite a blessing over the commandment. But this is difficult, because even if one does not recite a blessing over a commandment, but performs it, his performance is considered to be valid.[4] So what is it that this tithe giver has not forgotten?

4. This point is widely discussed, but we generally rely on the conclusion of the Jerusalem Talmud at the beginning of chapter 2 of Tractate Berakhot – that if one forgets to recite a blessing on a biblical commandment, the performance of the commandment is still valid.

By way of an answer, let us turn to the *Kuzari*, the seminal work of Rabbi Judah HaLevi (1075–1141, Spain). According to the format of the *Kuzari*, the king of the Khazars asks the rabbi/philosopher questions about Judaism. There are only two questions to which the rabbi admits he has no answer. The king asks, "I note that you mention the Land of Israel in your prayers with great love and devotion. And yet, here you are, not living in Israel, but living with us, the Khazars. Why are you inconsistent on this matter?" The rabbi admits to the king that he has no answer to this question. "*Boshtani*, you have shamed me," responded the rabbi, not yet on the road to the Jewish homeland.[5]

The other question to which the rabbi has no answer, concerns the status of the Jewish community as poor and degraded.[6] The king suggests to the rabbi that the Jewish people are perceived as being weak – in exile, without a homeland, subject to the whims and vagaries of their host countries. Perhaps, the king reasoned, Jewish devotion to helping the weak is simply because the Jews are weak themselves and they want everyone to help them. Jewish concern for the poor is simply a self-serving idea for the Jews in exile. But, he continued, if Jews had a land and were strong and powerful, they might well act like all of the

5. *Kuzari*, II:23–24.
6. This is the relevant text of the *Kuzari*, I:113–15:

> The Rabbi: I see thee reproaching us with our degradation and poverty, but the best of other religions boast of both. Do they not glorify him who said: He who smites thee on the right cheek, turn to him the left also; and he who takes away thy coat, let him have thy shirt also. He and his friends and followers, after hundreds of years of contumely, flogging, and slaying, attained their well-known success, and just in these things they glorify. This is also the history of the founder of Islam and his friends, who eventually prevailed, and became powerful. The nations boast of these, but not of these kings whose power and might are great, whose walls are strong, and whose chariots are terrible. Yet our relation to God is a closer one than if we had reached greatness already on earth.
>
> Al Khazari: This might be so, if your humility were voluntary; but it is involuntary, and if you had power you would slay.
>
> The Rabbi: Thou hast touched our weak spot, O King of the Khazars. If the majority of us, as thou sayest, would learn humility toward God and His law from our low station, Providence would not have forced us to bear it for such a long period. Only the smallest portion thinks thus.

other strong and powerful nations, ignoring the weak, and even taking advantage of them.

The rabbi had no answer. He admitted that, because of the status of the Jewish people – in exile, without power – they had never been tested in this matter.

In order to understand why the tithe giver announces that he did not "forget," we must recall the verses about Amalek in Deuteronomy – just a few verses before the strange statement of the tithe giver. The commandment is to blot out the memory of Amalek, but it is preceded by an important clause: "When the Lord your God grants you respite from all your enemies round about… [then] you shall blot out the memory of Amalek; do not forget."

The tithe giver, when he says, "I did not forget," is proving the king of the Khazars wrong. The king had said, "If you would have your own land, if you were not in exile, if you were powerful, then you would become just like Amalek: not only would you not help the 'weaker vessels' – the poor, the stranger, the disadvantaged – you might even take advantage of them, and oppress them, enslave them, and even kill them." But the tithe giver is saying,

> No. I have now returned from exile to my own land. I have power. *But I have not turned into Amalek.* I have blotted out the Amalekism within me. I have power, but I will never use it to oppress the weaker vessels. As you see, I have given all my tithes – to help and give support to these vulnerable members of society. I am a Jew – the opposite of Amalek. Helping the weak, and not taking advantage of them, is the only way the world will be perfected. I have not forgotten.

PURIM: EVERYTHING WORKS OUT – BECAUSE JEWISH ACTION MAKES IT HAPPEN

In the Book of Esther, it looks as if God is acting from behind the scenes – indeed God's name does not appear in the Megilla Scroll even once – and everything seems to work out. Even before the crisis with Haman's decree, the king got angry with Vashti, and Esther was appointed queen, setting the stage for her to intervene. Just that night, before the planned hanging of Mordecai, the king had insomnia and needed to be read the Book of Records. Just when they required a tree to hang Haman on, someone pointed out that a hanging tree had been prepared for Mordecai. And so forth. It all works out.

But, in two cases in the Megilla, it doesn't work out.

Esther needed to go to the king to plead for her nation. When Mordecai tells Esther to go to the king, she could have said, "What an amazing coincidence! The king just summoned me." Given the other "happenstances," that is what we would have expected. But that is not what happened. Esther had not been summoned for thirty days, and she knew that if she initiated the meeting, and the king was not in the mood, he could kill her. She had to put her life on the line. Esther's heroic *action* – not another happenstance, not even God behind the scenes – had to be central in bringing about redemption of Purim.

The second incident in the Megilla which needed human – Jewish – action was the question of the status of Haman's decree after he was unmasked and discredited. Given the "flavor" of the Megilla, we would have thought that Haman is dead, so his decree is annulled. But that is not what happened. Permission is given by the king for the Jews to defend themselves from the Persian anti-Semites. The Purim redemption arrived through action – fighting – not only through God's manipulation of events from behind the curtain.

The message is strong: Redemption – in every form – comes, yes, from God, but only eventually, and only with active participation – often at heroic levels – even to the point of sacrificing Jewish lives! We are God's partners. God is waiting for us. We must act – first. No better example can be found than the initiative taken by Nahshon ben Aminadav plunging into the Reed Sea even before it split.[7] He is remembered eternally for his understanding that redemption demands sacrificial human action.

This will explain a difficult and almost inexplicable verse in Exodus that we quote here again:

7. Numbers Rabba 13; Sota 37a.

> And he said: The hand [of Amalek is] upon (against) the throne [*kiseh*] of God: the Loving Lord will wage war against Amalek from generation to generation.

The verse is difficult, in part because of the unusual form of words common in biblical usage: "throne" (Hebrew: כסא *kiseh)* is missing a letter; God's name is missing two letters (the *vav* and the second *heh*). Rashi on this verse actually says it: God's name and throne are not complete – God's loving-kindness cannot be manifest as long as Amalek is in the world. As the parallel commandment in the book of Deuteronomy (25:19) makes clear, Israel must first begin to destroy Amalek, evil incarnate.

This is exactly what the Klausenberger Rebbe was saying. During the Holocaust Auschwitz took over. Hitler took over. Amalek took over. When Amalek takes over, God also becomes imprisoned. When Amalek takes over, God's being – the Loving Lord – is incomplete. God's goodness is incomplete. The Rebbe was actually saying, "We need people to redeem God. We are human beings created in God's image, God's full – and even senior – partners. Israel must come to the rescue."

That is what the Klausenberger Rebbe meant when he said that God was in chains in Auschwitz – and that we had to take Him out. God is waiting for us to redeem the world, and to redeem God along with the world! We must begin the act of destroying Amalek!

BLOTTING OUT AND REMEMBERING: HOW IS THAT POSSIBLE?

There still remains one question in our analysis of the destruction of Amalek. There is a major problem with the Amalek verses in Deuteronomy. On the one hand, we are commanded to "remember what Amalek did to you." On the other, we are told, "Blot out the memory of Amalek." How is this possible? How can you remember Amalek and blot out the memory of Amalek at the same time? It seems to be an insoluble logical contradiction.

But it is not.

When the Torah commands us to physically destroy the seven nations preventing us from conquering the land, the Torah's language

(Deut. 20:17) is very explicit: *haḥaram taḥarimem,* you shall utterly destroy them. However, regarding Amalek, the Torah does not explicitly tell us to physically destroy them. The word *timḥeh* is used – "blot out (erase)." So, how can we blot out Amalek, yet remember what he did to us?

Perhaps if we investigate the origin of Amalek, we may find the solution.

The Talmud (Sanhedrin 99b) explains by discussing Timna, the mother of Amalek:

> [Timna] sought to convert. She came before Abraham, Isaac, and Jacob, and they did not accept her. She went and became a concubine of Eliphaz, son of Esau, and said, referring to herself: It is preferable that she will be a maidservant for this nation, and she will not be a noblewoman for another nation. Ultimately, Amalek, son of Eliphaz, emerged from her, and that tribe afflicted the Jewish people. What is the reason [that the Jewish people were punished by suffering at the hand of Amalek]? They should not have rejected her when she sought to convert.

From Timna's womb came Amalek, who afflicted Israel, and who represents the archenemy of Israel in every generation, from Pharaoh who enslaved us, to Haman who wanted to kill us, to Hitler who wanted to destroy not only the Jews but Judaism entire.

Timna, a royal princess, wanted to attach herself to the Jewish people – to such an extent that she was willing to give up her royal status in order to do so. After being rejected by Abraham, Isaac, and Jacob, she became a part of the "Abrahamic family" by marrying Eliphaz the son of Esau. Their son was Amalek, who is the eternal enemy of the Jewish people. Fascinatingly, the Talmud sees the birth of Amalek as a punishment for Israel, because the Jewish leadership prevented Timna's conversion.

I want to make a radical, and yet logical, suggestion. There is a way to both blot out Amalek, and yet still remember what he did to us. That is by converting Amalek to Judaism. If Amalek converts, I am not permitted to remind him of what he was – and so he is "blotted out." We are forbidden to remind a convert that he was once of a different faith.[8]

We were punished, the Talmud says, for not accepting Timna for conversion. The *tikkun*, the repair, for that would be for us to convert Amalek, Timna's son! And, it is amazing that the Talmud hints at a precedent for the conversion of Amalek. The Talmud in Tractate Sanhedrin 96b tells us that "the descendants of Haman taught Torah in Bnei Brak." Haman, of course, was a direct descendant of Agag, king of the Amalekite nation. Therefore, these "descendants of Haman" were also descendants of Amalek. If they were "teaching Torah," they no doubt had converted to Judaism.

Even more amazingly, we know that Rabbi Akiva lived in Bnei Brak and served as a rabbi and yeshiva head there.[9] We also have the tradition that Rabbi Akiva was descended from converts.[10] Therefore, could one of these "descendants of Amalek" have been Rabbi Akiva, probably the greatest of Jewish intellectual and spiritual leaders? Perhaps. So it can be said that our tradition proposes that at least one "Amalekite" actually did convert to Judaism.

The Talmud (Berakhot 57b) quotes R. Shimon b. Elazar, who states that ultimately everyone in the world will convert to Judaism, deriving his opinion from the verse in Zephaniah 3:9 – "For then will I turn to the peoples a pure language, that they may all call upon the name of God, to serve Him with one consent."

The Rambam actually codifies this idea as halakha in *Hilkhot Melakhim* 12:1, where he writes that in the Messianic Era the wicked of the nations of the world (presumably this includes Amalek) will join the Jewish people.

---

8. Bava Metzia 59b.
9. Shabbat 32b.
10. The Rambam, discussing the line of transmission of the Oral Tradition, says the following in his introduction to *Mishneh Torah*: "Rabbi Akiva ben Yosef received the tradition from Rabbi Eleazar the Great. Yosef, his father, was a righteous convert." The Rambam is clearly saying that Rabbi Akiva's father was a convert to Judaism according to our mishnaic tradition.

> Israel will dwell securely together with the wicked gentiles…. They will all return to the true religion and no longer steal or destroy. Rather, they will eat permitted food at peace with Israel.

It would seem that, in those days to come, everyone will convert to the "true religion." Everyone will be together. And, presumably, Amalek will be no more – blotted out, not by physical destruction, but by his having converted to Judaism.

It is very possible that killing will not be an option in messianic times. In the achingly beautiful verse of Isaiah 11:9:

> They shall not hurt nor destroy in all My holy mountain; for the earth shall be full of the knowledge of the Lord, as the waters cover the sea.

There will be no physical destruction at all on God's holy mountain. Rav Kook derived from this that in those times, there will be no animal sacrifices in the Third Temple – only meal offerings, because there may be no destruction of animals. He writes in *Olat Re'aya* (vol. 1, p. 292), first quoting the verse from Malachi 3:4: "Then shall the grain offering of Judah and Jerusalem be pleasant to the Lord as in the days of old and as in the ancient years." He continues, giving his explanation to the verse: "In the future, the abundance of knowledge will spread to and penetrate even animals...and the 'sacrifices' which will then be from grain, will be as pleasing to God as in days of old (when there were animal offerings)."

And if animals will not be destroyed in the Messianic Age, certainly human beings will not be destroyed! Amalek will not be killed in war or even by the Sanhedrin as punishment. Amalek will be reborn into Judaism as righteous converts, children of Abraham and Sarah[11] – or, at the very least, children of Noah (see Micah 4:1–5).

Finally, the famous mishna in Avot 1:12:

11. In truth, Amalek is already a descendant of Abraham and Sarah, inasmuch as he is descended from Isaac's son, Esau.

> Hillel says, "Be of the disciples of Aaron, loving peace and pursuing peace, loving *all humanity* and bringing them closer to Torah."

We will remember what Amalek did to us. We will convert Amalek, and Amalek will then be blotted out, his memory erased, because we can never remind a convert of what he was, of how he acted, before his conversion.

And so, Amalek will disappear from the world, not by death or destruction, but by finally becoming part of that goal promised at the dawn of our people by God to Abraham: "In you shall be blessed *all* the families of the earth."[12]

---

12. Some readers may find my reading of the obligation to "blot out" Amalek difficult to accept. I would like to bring support for this idea from Rav Avraham Yitzhak HaKohen Kook, the first Ashkenazi chief rabbi of pre-state Israel who writes: "The attribute of love inherent in the souls of the righteous encompasses every element of creation, sparing nothing – not a single nation, nor a single language. Even Amalek, designated for destruction 'under the heavens,' can, through purification, ascend to its lofty root above the heavens, so that all is part of the highest form of love. However, achieving this transcendence requires great strength and immense purity" (*Middot HaRe'aya, Ahava,* paragraph 6).

    At the same time, I would like to emphasize that until we succeed in achieving this goal, it is incumbent upon the people of Israel to recognize the dangers presented by those people who reject the godly soul-breath breathed into man at the time of Creation, choosing to revel in their animalistic features. Israel must defend herself against her enemies and take up arms to defeat them.

Chapter 11

The Hebrew Lunar Calendar: A Path to Freedom

THE LUNAR CALENDAR: THE FIRST HEBREW REBELLION AGAINST EGYPTIAN SLAVERY

Our sacred Bible commands that we sanctify each month – each new moon – beginning with the first month, Nisan. The biblical command – in accordance with the interpretation of the *Midrash Mekhilta* to Exodus 12:2 – reads as follows:

> The renewal of this month shall be for you the (semi-festival) of the Beginning of the Months (Rosh Ḥodesh), and this (particular month of Nisan) shall be for you the first of the months of the year.

To be sure, the biblical text immediately continues with the first Passover commandment given by God to the Hebrews still in Egypt, "On the tenth day of that month (Nisan) every individual shall take a lamb,… a lamb for each household…to be examined (and held over until) the fourteenth day of that month when they shall slaughter it" (Ex. 12:3–6). But why should the Passover freedom festival be introduced by the seemingly unrelated command of Rosh Ḥodesh, renewing and sanctifying the first month – and every month – of the calendar year? What is the theological connection between the new Hebrew lunar calendar with its emphasis on the moon and the festival of our independent nation of Israel? And why is this command of Rosh Ḥodesh, the renewal of the month, the very first commandment given to Israel, as our tradition maintains?

It would seem to me that there ought to be other more worthy commands to come first, like "You shall love your fellow like yourself" or "Remember the Sabbath day to keep it holy."

And strangest of all, the month of Nisan is not the first month of our calendar year. Open any Hebrew calendar and you will see that it begins with the month of Tishrei, since Rosh HaShana is on the first day of Tishrei, the beginning of every year with the festival of "New Year," the anniversary of the day in which "the world was conceived." Tishrei is, in actuality, the seventh month, counting from Nisan which is the first month of the months. Why two first months, one for the months (Nisan, the month of Jewish liberation, Passover) and one for the years, connected to Rosh HaShana? What is our calendar teaching?

Perhaps we will be able to answer our questions by first examining the literal meaning of the Rosh Ḥodesh verse as it appears in the Bible, which we have not translated literally at the beginning of this chapter, but which we have chosen to translate in accordance with the *Midrash Mekhilta* (ad loc.) for reasons which will soon become clear. The literal reading of this verse is as follows: "This month (of Nisan, the month of the Passover spring festival) shall be for you the beginning of the months; it shall be for you the first of the months of the year." Rashi, the most classically accepted among the early biblical commentators, maintains that the above rendering is most in accord with the literal meaning of the words (the *peshat*). However, he only presents this reading in his commentary after he first cites the reading based on the *Midrash Mekhilta* with which we began this chapter, which I will now set down in greater detail than it appears in my initial rendering:

> Moses was anguished about identifying the birth of the new moon, as to how much light of the moon must be visible in the blackened skies in order to renew and sanctify each of the new months and proclaim the semi-festival of Rosh Ḥodesh (in our context, on the first evening of the month of Nisan). And so, the Creator, the Holy One, Blessed be He, actually showed Moses the appearance of the first slivers of the renewed moon in the heavens, pointing out (as it were): "When you see it looking like this, *renew* the moon and declare the new month. When you see it looking like this, sanctify the moon and declare the new month" (*Midrash Mekhilta*, ad loc.).[1]

But still we must ask once again, what has Rosh Ḥodesh, the renewal and sanctification of each new moon, to do with the rebellion of the Hebrew slaves against their Egyptian masters, which is the *raison d'être* for the festival of Passover and the designation of Nisan as the first month of the months? And why is Israel's obligation to renew and sanctify the advent of each new moon the very first commandment of our Bible? And what is the point of two "first months of the years," Tishrei in the fall at Rosh HaShana time and Nisan in the spring at Passover time?

Let us examine in depth the symbolism of the sun as contrasted with the symbolism of the moon. Then the message of the lunar calendar, as well as the response to our questions, will clarify why this first commandment is the key to our understanding the first theological rebellion against Egyptian idolatry.

---

1. It is interesting to conjecture as to why Rashi places the midrashic explication as his initial interpretation and the *peshat* as a second and alternative interpretation. I believe it is because the *peshat* renders the second half of the verse a repetition of the first: "This month shall be for you the beginning of the months; it shall be for you the first of the months of the year." According to this midrash, however, the first part of the verse comes to teach the commandment of renewing and sanctifying each month, the semi-festival of Rosh Ḥodesh, while the second part of the verse declares the Passover month of Nisan as the first month of the Hebrew calendar year.

THE PESSIMISTIC AND IDOLATROUS MESSAGE OF THE CYCLICAL SOLAR CALENDAR OF EGYPT

It is important to note that the landscape and culture from which the soon-to-be-freed people of Israel emerged was the mighty civilization of Egypt, for whom one of the chief gods of their pantheon was Ra, the sun god. Indeed, one of the most powerful and long-lasting Pharaonic dynasties assumed the hereditary family name Rameses, literally "The son (*meses*, Egyptian for son) of Ra" (which means "evil" in Hebrew and refers to the sun god in Egyptian). And the Egyptian calendar was – and is – based completely upon the sun, around which the Earth circles during its 365-day journey in space, which comprises one solar calendar year. The seasons of spring, summer, autumn, and winter – so vital for farmers and human subsistence on grain, vegetable, and fruit production – are dependent upon the angle of the Earth to the sun during the Earth's yearly movement around the sun.

Of greatest symbolic significance is that the sun remains completely static and fixed in space; the Earth and the moon together both revolve around the sun, while the sun remains stationary and unmoving.[2] And this is precisely what makes the concept of a world "under the sun" problematic for our Hebrew Bible, as we shall see.

Listen to the biblical words of the book of Ecclesiastes (*Kohelet*), attributed to King Solomon, biblically called the wisest of men. Our Sages suggest that the Scroll of Ecclesiastes was penned at the end of his life, with more than a small dose of pessimistic cynicism, and he opens his scroll with a rather pathetic analysis of human life *under the sun*. Remember, too, that since the Earth's movement around the sun determines the passage of a year, the human relationship to the sun reflects the human relationship to time and thereby to one's lifespan or lifetime in general "under the sun," through the eyes of Kohelet. Take note that we measure the quantitative period of the life of an individual in years.

Ecclesiastes 1:1–11:

2. Clearly, our understanding of the solar system today differs from that of the ancient world. Nevertheless, they still perceived the sun as unchanging and the moon as being in constant state of change, waxing and waning over a thirty-day period.

> The words of Kohelet,[3] the son of David, king of Jerusalem: Futility of futilities, everything is futile! What profit does a person have for all the labor which he toils beneath the sun? One generation goes and one generation comes – but the Earth endures forever. And the sun rises and the sun sets – then to its place it rushes, and there it rises again. It goes toward the south and veers toward the north; the wind goes round and round, and on its rounds, the wind returns.[4]
>
> All the rivers flow into the sea, yet the sea is not full; to the place where the rivers flow, there they flow once more.
>
> Whatever has been is what will be, and whatever has been done (before) is what will be done (again).
>
> There is nothing new beneath the sun!
>
> Sometimes there is something of which one says, "Look, this is new!" – (but nay) it has already existed in the ages before us!
>
> There is no recollection (זכרון) of the former ones, and neither too of the latter ones that are yet to be, there will be no recollection by those of a still later time.

And so, the message of a solar calendar: cyclic regularity. An endless circular repetition, lasting 365 days, year after year. The solar calendar emphasizes the centrality of the sun and our existence in the world that is "under the sun" defines time based on it, and frames our lives as an endless cyclical process that seems aimless: an eternal journey

3. In actuality, says Ibn Ezra (ad loc.), it was the words of King Solomon, but called *Kohelet* because of the assemblage of so many streams of wisdom in his words. The Hebrew word for futility is *hevel*, which means breath or exhalation; in cold air one's exhaled breath appears like a small cloud, which quickly evaporates and disappears into nothingness. The true wisdom of Kohelet lies in his final message; after understanding the futility of a life dedicated to wealth, pleasure, fame, or power, he concludes with the ultimate advice for the true seeker, "The sum of the matter, when all has been considered, revere God and keep His commandments for that ought be the whole of human pursuit" (Eccl. 12:13).
4. In actuality, the sun remains static and stationary, it appears to the human spectator to move in an arc-like motion from east to west and back again, cyclically and repetitiously.

to nowhere. Hence the solar calendar – emphasizing the centrality of the sun and a world under the sun – provides for and is the measure of time, and time is the quantitative measure or period of our individual lifespans or lifetimes. Time, therefore, as the dimension within which all humans live, has human existence locked into a cyclical and seemingly purposeless pattern, doomed to meaningless and directionless circular, repetitive movement to nowhere. This is reminiscent of the Greek myth of Sisyphus, in which all of human activity is metaphorically described as gruntingly pushing a boulder to the top of the mountain, watching it fall to the bottom, struggling again to exert the requisite energy to push it up again, only to watch it fall again, and again, and then again, and again – *ad infinitum.*

And similarly Shakespeare's Macbeth sees the human being held captive by an unfeeling, unending iterating and re-iterating time, against which he lashes out accusingly, "Tomorrow and tomorrow and tomorrow creeps in this petty pace… to the last syllable of recorded time…. [Life] is a tale told by an idiot, full of sound and fury, signifying nothing."

Most damaging of all is how Kohelet discounts human activity and creativity: "What profit does a person have for all the labor he toils under the sun?" If time is cyclical, absent of ultimate purpose or destination, if all we may look forward to is another tomorrow not at all qualitatively different from yesterday or even from the day after tomorrow, if humanity is trapped in Sartre's *No Exit*, if human activity remains devoid of effectuating any significant change or meaningful accomplishment, then the sensitive and thinking person will find himself enslaved – even paralyzed – by the eternal repetitious and inexorable time, which only seems to be mocking him. He finds himself encircled by a constant merry-go-round which is not at all so merry, which has taken him from a dark and silent womb – leading him into many experiences, at best unfulfilling and at worst debilitating – and finally bringing him to a dark and silent tomb of emptiness and nothingness, ultimately under the unmoving and unchanging sun, from womb to tomb.[5]

5. The Hebrew term for grave – קבר – is used often by the Talmud as a synonym for womb – רחם – especially in the marital *nidda* laws.

> The Past is *History*, not worthy of remembrance;
> The Future is *Mystery*, without promise or even hope;
> The Present is *Momentary*, a human cloud-breath of vapor (Hebrew: *hevel*) devoid of substance or significance.

THE OPTIMISTIC AND REVOLUTIONARY MESSAGE OF THE MOON

In order to understand our first commandment to renew and sanctify the moon, we must review briefly the situation of the Hebrews at the time of God's command. They had left Canaan in time of famine for Egypt, a large seventy-people-strong family, to become reunited with their leader brother Joseph, the grand vizier of Egypt. The times changed, a new pharaoh emerged, and although the family grew greatly and prospered, they became enslaved by the Egyptians and served their foreign masters for more than two hundred years. Egypt, the "Gift of the Nile," had become a mighty empire, and had made a great divide between the native Egyptians and the foreign refugees, believing that to the more powerful host country belong all aliens as slaves. The Hebrews were treated with especial harshness, and God tells Moses He has seen their suffering and informs them – with five different expressions of redemption – that He will take them out of Egyptian servitude and into freedom in their original homeland Israel, the Promised Land of the covenant (Ex. 6:6–8). The Hebrew slaves will be freed, declared God, and, indeed, God smites Egypt with nine plagues – but Pharaoh still refuses to let them leave. God then warns them of a tenth and final plague, the death of all of the Egyptian first-born sons, including the son of Pharaoh himself; but to no avail! God then informs Moses that Pharaoh nevertheless will still refuse to allow the Hebrews to exit Egypt! (Ex. 11:9).

It is at this most sensitive moment, when logic would dictate that the Hebrews are filled with disappointment and despair – believing that Egypt will never grant them exodus to freedom, that the world of Egyptian mastery and Hebrew slavery will never change under the sun, that Egyptian society would never condemn servitude, that the Egyptians are locked into enslaving the Hebrews and the Hebrews are locked into serving as slaves to the Egyptians – it is at this critical juncture of the narrative that God commands Moses and Aaron to create the first Hebrew calendar. This lunar calendar differs from the solar calendar of the Egyptians, offering a clear signal that the Hebrews will separate from the Egyptians by waging at least a cultural rebellion against Egypt. And the Hebrews were to renew and sanctify the emerging new moon with Nisan as the first of the months of the new lunar calendar. This calendar begins with the month of Passover: "This renewal of the moon (the Hebrew word "*ḤoDeSH*," month, may, with different vocalization, read "*ḤiDuSH*," renewal, change!), shall be for you the beginning of the months (the semi-festival of Rosh Ḥodesh at the start of each month), and this particular month of the year (Nisan, the month of the Passover spring festival, when the flora and fauna of all of nature is being renewed in Israel) shall be for you the first of the months of the year" (Ex. 12:2, in accordance with the midrashic explication of the *Mekhilta*, and see Rashi ad loc.).

We have queried the significance of this particular commandment of the renewal and sanctification of the new moon of Nisan at the moment that Israel heard that despite God's promise of freedom they are doomed to remain slaves to their Egyptian masters. You will remember that "life under the sun," under a sun god and a solar calendar, only reinforced the status quo, the static and stationary master-slave society in Egypt, inexorably militating against freedom, change in status, and revolution "under the sun" as explained by Kohelet. God's response is a new command to be focused on the moon, to take note of the changes of the moon, and to bless the renewal of the moon every month. Indeed, the renewal of the months and the sanctification of the months are a biblical command, based upon the lunar calendar beginning with Nisan.[6]

The moon is very different from, even antithetical to, the sun. The moon is in constant motion, revolving around the planet Earth and completing each revolution every twenty-nine and a quarter days, thereby creating the lunar months. In addition and at the same time, the moon and the Earth together revolve around the sun in an elliptical circuit which takes 365 days, creating the solar year and effectuating the four seasons, dependent upon the relative closeness of the Earth to

6. See Rambam's *Sefer HaMitzvot*, positive commandment 153.

the sun. (Our new Hebrew lunar calendar was astronomically crafted to adjust to the solar calendar in accordance with the seasons, so that Passover is always celebrated at the same time each year as the early ripening barley gifts were brought to the Temple and similarly so that Shavuot always corresponded with the harvest festival of the first fruits and newly ripened wheat.)

With this understanding, we can also explain why there are two "first months" in the Hebrew calendar. The first day of the first month Tishrei of every new year, Rosh HaShana, is the anniversary of the day upon which "the world was conceived," יום הרת עולם, at the start of the solar year for all mankind. But in actuality, Tishrei is the seventh month from Nisan, which is the first month of the lunar months, when the Hebrews were freed from slavery as an independent people. When we think of Rosh HaShana, with everyone praying to be worthy of another year of life, we must remember that our quantitative lifespans – how many years we live – is dependent upon God alone, hidden from every mortal. But how we spend the months of whatever time God places at our disposal, how we live the lives we are given month to month, day to day, minute to minute, that is very much within our power. Hence, whereas the length of our lives depends on God, the months are very much ours to determine – whether we sanctify them or desecrate them is the true test facing every individual. Hence the commandment of this first of the months Nisan – "This month is *for you*" – applies especially to the newly freed Hebrews, who must bring about change within their own characters and personalities, eventually within all humanity, in accordance with God's will, and specifically under the changing moon rather than under the static and unmoving sun.

Now we can also appreciate the divine message, that He – God, as it were – is depending upon the Hebrews themselves to effectuate their own freedom. Passover is called by the Bible זמן חרותנו, literally "the time of our freedom," but the Hebrew *ḥerut* is linguistically close to *aḥrayut* (אחריות, responsibility); every child of God must be responsible to the best of his/her ability, to be free before God! So God commands the Hebrews to take a lamb and slaughter it, thereby putting their lives on the line by slaughtering an Egyptian god. The Hebrews' demonstration of their fealty to their God alone was the courageous act of bravery which was the final hammer blow convincing Pharaoh to banish them from Egypt! Under the moon, acts of rebellion against idolatrous authorities can bring about substantial and even revolutionary change!

THE HEBREW NATION IS LIKENED TO THE MOON

The message of the moon teaches us that we live in a world and a time dimension which admits and even encourages change and revolutions. There is a strange but fascinating ritual every month, on Saturday evening at least seventy-two hours after the *molad* (the "birth" or renewal of the new moon) at the time of the departure of the Sabbath, when the congregation leaves the synagogue to look up at the new moon and make a blessing upon its renewal each month, in accordance with the teaching of R. Yoḥanan: "One who blesses the new moon in its proper time is regarded as if he greets the *Shekhina* (Divine Presence)" (Sanhedrin 42a).

This ritual, which concludes with a dance under the renewed moon, is called *Kiddush Levana,* the "Sanctification of the Moon." Ponder the metaphor and message of a darkened sky majestically overseeing a darkened earth, when – on the evening of the first day of the first month of Nisan – a sliver of a golden-yellow disc emerges (is born), enlightening the heavens with its promising rays of splendor and casting its nascent illumination from the sun upon an anxiously expectant night on earth. And the sliver of moonlight changes (or seems to change from our perspective on earth) each evening until it becomes a golden diadem mid-month, flooding the heavens and the earth beneath with its glory. And remember God's mission for Israel to be a light unto the nations of the world, to bring the blessings of Torah to all the families of the earth (Gen. 12:1–3). Now listen to the blessing of the Sanctification of the Moon as it appears in the Talmud (ibid.) and in our prayer books and how it expresses more than our greeting the Divine Presence; it even suggests our partnering with the Divine by renewing and recreating all of humanity by the sacred and redeeming light of Torah:

> Blessed are You, Loving Lord our God, King of the universe, who with His utterance created the heavens and with the breath of His mouth all their legion. A decree and a schedule did He give

> them that they not alter their appointed task. Joyous and glad are they to perform the will of their Owner.... To the moon He said that it should renew *itself* as a crown of splendor for those born from the womb (the Jewish nation, see Isaiah 46:3), those who are destined to renew themselves like the moon, and to glorify their Creator for the sake of the name of His glorious kingdom. Blessed are You, Loving Lord, who renews the months.

God, as it were, the Creator of the heavenly host of sun, moon, and stars, metaphorically sees His "hosts" as agents or messengers serving the Master of the universe in exercising their various functions in the operation of the universe. He gives His heavenly agents a specific path of activity which may not be altered. The moon, however, is different; it has no light of its own, but moves revolving on its axis between the Earth and the sun, reflecting the sunlight upon the earth nights.

The prayer singles out the moon as renewing itself as a crown of glory for Israel – God's chosen people – destined to bring the light of God's Torah to a world darkened by the other nations still blind to God's will of a world enlightened by love, righteousness, and peace, still enmeshed in enslavement, corruption, and wars of aggression.

The promises of God's covenant is that Israel will renew and recreate itself by repentance and bring redemption to the world, just as the renewal of the light of the moon brings illumination to a blackened night– at certain times almost turning it into bright daylight.

And just as the moon seems to recreate itself, change itself, by its own motions and actions, so will Israel renew itself, change itself, by its own acts of repentance, by continually turning in love toward every human being and to the Loving Lord of the universe, by "loving humanity and drawing them near Torah."[7]

Look at the light of the moon amidst a darkened sky and kindle the light of your heart to enlighten a darkened world! Look at the renewal of the month as a result of the activity of the moon and believe that you can renew your life as a result of activating your soul! As free individuals, time and what you do with it depends first and foremost

7. See Mishna Avot 1:12.

upon you. "This moon and its changes – from darkness to light –are in your hands." Look at the reappearance of light as signaling the possibility of a renewed, enlightened, month, the possibility of a sanctified, recreated Israel and humanity.

We are not merely servants waiting for the Messiah; rather we are partners with God actually bringing the Messiah to God, if we but seize the moment! Indeed we, Israel, must become the Messiah bringing all of humanity to compassionate righteousness and universal peace.[8] At that time declares the prophet Isaiah, "the sun will no longer be for you the light of the day and the moon will no longer illuminate for you. The Loving Lord will be an eternal light for you, and your God will be your splendor" (Is. 60:19). Furthermore, "it shall be then that at every new moon and every Sabbath all humanity will come to prostrate themselves before Me, says the Loving Lord" (Is. 66:23).

The biblical commentator Sforno interprets the plain meaning of our verse (Ex. 12:2):

> "This month shall be for you the beginning of the months." From now on, the months (time) shall belong to you (Israel), to do with them (the months) whatever you wish. During the days of your enslavement, your days did not belong to you, but they were dedicated for the work of others in accordance with their (your captors') desire. Therefore (Nisan) is the first month for you of the months of the year. On this month (Nisan) begins the new reality of your freedom of choice!

And the challenge is for you to perfect the world under the majesty of the Almighty God! In the prayer of the renewal of the months, the Jewish nation is compared to the moon; we are both agent-messengers of the Creator, partners of the Divine. There is, however, one crucial

8. Why is the renewal and sanctification of the month the first command God gives to Israel? It is because the first verse of the Bible, "In the beginning God created the heavens and the earth," sets the stage for humans, God's partners, to walk in God's ways: "Just as God created a world – but an imperfect one – we must recreate that world – and perfect it! That is the message of the moon!" as I heard from my teacher and mentor, Rav Soloveitchik.

difference. The heavenly hosts are functional beings, naturally created to do His will. Israel, the chosen people, are volitional, with freedom of choice. Yes, our covenant guarantees that eventually we will comply and repent. But *when* depends on us. From this perspective we understand why Passover is called "the time of our freedom," זמן חרותנו, and the Hebrew *ḥerut* is derived from *aḥrayut* (אחריות, responsibility). Freedom brings with it the responsibility of purposeful freedom, not meaningless free-for-all frivolity and wild abandon. Freedom to follow the ritual and ethical dictates of our Loving God, and ultimately freedom to fulfill our God-given mission of teaching humanity compassionate righteousness, moral justice, and generous loving-kindness.[9] Freedom from serving Pharaoh in order to be free to partner with God.

---

9. We have already seen how God created the universe alone (as it were). In order to activate the potential within the initial acts of creativity, however, the human being was necessary to "develop the world and take responsibility for it" (Gen. 2:5,15). As history developed with concomitant actors – nations playing roles, at times complementary and at times adversarial – roles developed. God chooses Israel – the family of Abraham – to be the source of blessing for all the families of the earth, eventually inspiring all of the nation-states to either accept the Torah from Zion and the word of the Living Lord from Jerusalem (Is. 7) or at least the ethics of turning their swords into plowshares and their spears into pruning knives, with everyone living in peace and security (Mic. 4). As history unfolded, God acted in the world through agents or messengers, the Jewish nation with its prophets and sages, including gentile prophets (like Balaam) and sages (of course the Jewish Sages but also gentiles, like Cyrus King of Persia and physicians). The human agents are volitional. Ultimately the Jews will influence the world and be the major force in its ethical and spiritual development, and along the way God may, but in general will not, step in, and the world will continue in its customary manner (עולם כמנהגו נוהג: Avoda Zara 54b). But God has His emissaries, human beings.

   The story of the Exodus is most instructional in this regard. God is desirous of making Moses His emissary to take the Jews out of Egypt (Ex 3:10), but Moses is reluctant. Finally, Moses agrees, but asks God: "When I go to the Israelites, and say to them, 'The God of your ancestors has sent me to you,' and they ask me for Your name, what shall I say to them ('name' connotes definition)?" (Ex 3:13). And God replies, "I will be what (or whom) I will be…. I will be sent me to you" (Ex 3:14). This, too, is considered a name of God, "I will be what (whom) I will be." (I believe the meaning here is: I am the God of the future, who will ultimately see to it that you – and the world – will be redeemed. The Tetragrammaton, YHVH, may also be taken as a future verb, based on the verb "to be," and it literally may be defined as "He will effectuate, bring about, YehoVah." When or with whom will depend

And so, from an allegorical and mystical perspective, the message of the moon is optimistic and revolutionary. The day under the sun begins in the morning with sunrise, continues on to sunset, and then must endure the ensuing darkness of the night: from light to darkness. The lunar month, on the other hand, begins with the darkness of the night immediately alleviated by the light of the emerging moon, at first a small sliver – a slice of light growing and glowing larger and brighter until it reaches its apex on the fifteenth of the month, when it appears as a magnificent platinum disc, majestically illuminating the blackened skies. And so, thanks to the moon, the darkness of the nights gives way to brighter and brighter evenings for the first two weeks, gently appearing to push away the blackness and lovingly embracing the gentiles on earth still ignorant of Torah and even many Jews who are not yet dedicated to their mission, with the regenerating and redeeming power of God's loving laws. And Passover falls out on the fifteenth day of Nisan, when the moon is at the apex of its illumination!

However, one might question the optimism of the moon message during the second half of the month, when – after the dazzling full moon has illuminated the heavens – there occurs the worrisome and even frightening phenomenon of a slowly disappearing moon, becoming thinner and thinner each evening. Yet, just as the light seems to have been completely extinguished and the night engulfed in total darkness, a silvery delight appears from the depths of the black despair, destined to transform itself – as the new month will near its half-way mark into a magnificent platinum disc of glory enlightening the heavens!

The same process of rebirth will occur to the waning moon the following month, never tiring of a renewal opportunity to repent. That renewed sliver of bright shiny silver enters the darkened skies in the beginning of each month with the same promise, joy, and faith in a brighter future which accompanies a newly born baby emerging from a loving mother's darkened womb. We can now understand why the exact time of the reemergence of the new moon each month is announced

upon the volition of His human emissaries! Who and when will depend on Israel! That is the responsibility of freedom! We are not God's puppets on earth; we are His acting partners!

in the synagogue (on the Sabbath before) as the *molad* – the birth, or rather, the rebirth – of the moon. And for the first two weeks of the newly renewed month, the moon blazes to its fullness, enveloping the enlightened heavens with beams of splendorous rays of hope and glory. And so we, Israel, are compared to the moon, at times in our various exiles almost disappearing, but always reborn to renewed opportunity for repentance.

And herein lies the activism of the moon and the optimism of the moon. If you wish to understand the secret strength of Israel – our ability to have twice suffered the loss of our autonomy in Jerusalem and the destruction of the two Temples, and after having suffered innumerable losses of life and untold suffering at the hands of cruel enemies, having been forced to flee from exile to exile and from persecution to persecution, and scattered to the furthest corners of the earth and to the ends of the heavens for no less than two thousand years, and yet still emerging from all of our tribulations as a faithful remnant, renewing our covenantal commitment – it is because of our understanding that our periods of decline were the result of our turning away from the Divine Presence and our divinely given mission to bring the blessings of peace and redemption to all the families on earth (Gen. 12:1–3). Just remember that God promises that redemption will come, that God has never given up on us, and the sign that God is patiently and lovingly waiting for us again at the beginning of each new month is the continual rebirth of the moon! And so once again at the beginning of each new month, when the light of God's love seems to have completely disappeared from view, we who are compared to the moon must celebrate the renewal of the moon and its promise of renewed opportunity. Indeed, we must find within ourselves the wherewithal to renew and rekindle our souls, hearts, and minds for a renewed relationship with God and our covenantal commitment. We will then be empowered to eventually prevail and recreate a world of love for God, Torah, and humanity. We dare not be dismayed by the mighty powers against us; we must rather be energized and "reborn" by the sacred light without and within us![10]

10. Note that we recite the Psalms of Praise, Hallel, on every new moon, Rosh Ḥodesh, a semi-holiday. We recite Hallel on every supernatural event (like the exodus from

After all, our Israel time is not cyclically repetitive (under the sun) but rather linear and redemptive, moving toward an endgame, as Franz Rosenzweig magnificently explains in his masterful work *The Star of Redemption*, from Creation to Revelation to Redemption. Hence the conclusion of our Sabbath night blessing over the sanctification of the moon, reads as follows:

> May it be Your will, Loving Lord my God and the God of my ancestors, to fill in the flaws of the moon (and in us[11]) so that there be no diminution in the moon. May the light of the moon be like the light of the sun and like the light of the seven days of Creation as it was before it was diminished, as it is said, "the two great luminaries" (Gen. 1:16), and the verse will be fulfilled: "They will turn back and will seek the Eternal their God and David their king" (Hosea 3:5).

And this verse in Hosea refers, of course, to the days of the Messiah. The nation of Israel is destined to renew itself and to sanctify itself, to renew and sanctify the world. Israel is like the moon. כזה ראה וחדש, כזה ראה וקדש.

> Look upon the small sliver of the moon when it is like this (says God) and renew it; look upon the small sliver of moon when it is like this (says God) and sanctify it.

Yes, if time and lifetime is cyclical, doomed to meaningless repetition under the sun; if life is a tale told by an idiot – signifying nothing – then, at best, we must concur that, as we have said:

Egypt on Passover), and we recite Half-Hallel (omitting two Half-Psalms) on the wonders of nature, the recurring new moon!

11. I added that God will then fill in the flaw within us (or help us to remove our flaws) in accordance with the commentary presented in the *Siddur Sukkat David, the Complete ArtScroll Siddur* (p. 617) that the original diminution of the moon was because God knew that humanity would not be worthy, and that Israel would not be worthy. But that would only be a temporary phenomenon, which would be repaired in the Messianic Age!

> *Past* is best-forgotten history,
> *Future* is inconsequential mystery, and
> *Present* is ephemeral and momentary.

But if life is a tale ultimately told by our loving God in accordance with His covenantal partnership with Israel and humanity, then history is lineal, progressing to an endgame – although not without interrupted byways and miraculous highways – toward a world of compassionate righteousness, moral justice, and universal peace. In that case:

> *Past* events, which are significant and memorable moments in history (His, God's, story)
> *Prospectively* can change, revolutionize, and help us realize our cosmic destiny, and
> *Retrospectively* sanctify our present, which is fraught with opportunity.

Exodus Rabba 15:24:

> When one sees the month in its renewal, what blessing ought he make?
>
> Some Rabbis say: Blessed is the renewal of the months, ברוך מחדש חדשים. Other Rabbis say: Blessed is the sanctification of the months, ברוך מקדש חדשים.
>
> Still others say, Blessed is He who sanctifies Israel, ברוך מקדש ישראל.

Because it is after all, Israel that is compared to the moon, who must change and renew the months in preparation for the Messiah!

AFTERWORD

The old (when it is no longer relevant) must be renewed, and the new must be sanctified. In the late 1970s, when still rabbi of Lincoln Square Synagogue, I and my family would spend six weeks every summer in Israel as the summer rabbi of Kibbutz Ein Tzurim, where I would give *shiurim*, study, and look for a full-time position in Israel. I developed a lifelong friendship with one of the founders of the kibbutz, Yehuda Noiman, a fine Talmud scholar, a profound intellectual, and my mentor in modern Religious Zionism. We learned a great deal together and truly became soulmates in the truest sense of the term. The story I shall now recount was one of the deepest lessons I learned from him (taken from *Listening to God*, p. 306):

> And then another one of those special stories "happened" that only intensified my desire to "wait it out" for Efrat. Ein Tzurim was fast becoming our home-away-from-home, our *beit abba* in Israel. There was a kibbutz member (Mivtzari was his name, but everyone called him "Moshavnik") who prayed in the same row as Yehuda Noiman and me in the kibbutz synagogue. His father, who had lived in Kfar Hasidim near Haifa, died, and I joined a whole delegation from the kibbutz to attend the funeral. The funeral cortège was to proceed from the yeshiva in Kfar Hasidim to the cemetery nearby, and the kibbutzniks arrived while the *tahara* – the purification of the body – was taking place inside the yeshiva. Two distinct groups were now waiting for this body to be brought out and for the eulogies to begin: the kibbutzniks, dressed in shorts, colored short-sleeved shirts, and sandals; and the yeshiva students, garbed in black pants and white shirts. It was as if the two groups had an invisible *meḥitza* between them.
>
> The *rosh yeshiva*, Rav Elya Mishkovsky, came out, viewed the assembly from the higher yeshiva portico, and seemed to have noticed my friend Yehuda Noiman. He actually then addressed him in Yiddish, "Yudke? Yudke *iluy*?" (Yudke is a Yiddish affectionate diminutive for Yehuda; *iluy* is Hebrew for "prodigy.") Yehuda, whom I knew as a rather shy and humble individual, turned red, blushed deeply, and responded in Hebrew, "Yes, Reb Elya, that's what they called me in the yeshiva of Rav Shach in Petaḥ Tikva, where we studied together." The *rosh yeshiva*'s eyes narrowed. He asked, in Yiddish, "But what happened to you. I know you left the yeshiva, but how did Rav Shach allow you to leave? You, too, could have been a *rosh yeshiva*." Yehuda answered

in Hebrew, and by this time everyone, from both groups, was listening to the conversation intently. "Rav Shach sent me many letters urging me to stay." Reb Elya, the *rosh yeshiva,* seemed to rise to his full height, literally looking down at my friend, and said strongly (but not harshly) in Yiddish – perhaps more to his students than to my friend: "And those letters of our Rebbe will serve as a prosecuting attorney when you stand before the throne of God after a hundred and twenty years."

I felt very sorry for Yehuda. I didn't think my laid-back, self-effacing friend would give any answer at all. But he responded immediately, decisively, and in Hebrew, "And the kibbutz that I helped build, and the guns that I used in the wars that I fought, and the souls of the many Israeli Jews whose lives I protected – they will be my defense attorneys. And they will win the day and exonerate me before God."

The *rosh yeshiva* took a step backward. He realized that he had lost that first round, and apparently decided not to continue the debate. Again he said in Yiddish, but this time with a smile on his face and in his voice, "*Bist nokh dee zelbe Yudke, dee zelbe iluy,*" "You remained the same Yudke, the same prodigy." My friend didn't let it rest. He responded in Hebrew, "No, Reb Elya, I didn't remain the same Yudke that I was in the yeshiva. I changed. I saw the changes in history. I saw what our generation demanded. I think I even saw what God expected of me. I looked around myself at the ravages of the Holocaust. I understood that our era demanded that the kibbutz, and the battlegrounds of war, had to serve as the infrastructure for the establishment of the Jewish state, the first Jewish state in close to two thousand years. I didn't remain the same because Jewish history didn't remain the same. You remained the same. You didn't change."

The funeral began. But obviously the encounter was very important to me and all I could think of was the first commandment in the Torah, "*Haḥodesh hazeh lakhem Rosh Ḥodashim,*" "This renewal of the moon shall be for you a festival of the Beginning of the Months" (Ex. 12:2). Look at the moon, mark the changes of the moon, praise the God of nature who brings forth

> the bright sliver of the new moon from a blackened, darkened sky, and realize that our God is a God of change and renewal, that our God wants us to change as times change, as needs change, as history changes. "*Binu shenot dor vador*," "Understand the changes in each generation" (Deut. 32:7).

God is the God of history. "I will be what I will be, *YeHoVa*." He will bring about change. "The old must be renewed and the new must be sanctified." That's what Rav Kook taught. That's what Yehuda Noiman was expressing.

Chapter 12

Passover: The Responsibility of Freedom

EVERYONE MUST BE FREE

The festival of Passover begins in the middle of the first month of the Hebrew calendar, the month of Nisan, and marks the birth of our nation. The focus of this festival is the Seder ceremony, celebrated in the Jewish home on the first evening of the holiday. Unlike many nations that proclaim their origins from superhuman beings, or even from the gods, we begin our Seder recitation with the words "We were slaves unto Pharaoh in Egypt." We then immediately recount how God took us out of this slavery "with a strong hand and an outstretched arm." The central message of the Seder – and that of the Passover festival – is a resounding lesson that the Jewish people announces to itself and to the world: The Creator of the universe, the God of the world, does not want human beings to be enslaved; every human being must be free. This seminal idea stems directly from the fact that, as we have learned, all human beings are created in the image of God and are thus supremely equal. Therefore, no human is ever permitted to enslave another human being.

God proclaimed, at the very beginning of the Ten Commandments, "I am the Lord your God who brought you out of the land of

Egypt, out of the house of bondage." With this pronouncement, the Creator of the world was stating unequivocally that the usual order of the world as expressed throughout world history – that the strong are entitled to enslave the weak – is categorically and ethically incorrect. With this proclamation, Passover, with its divine negation of slavery and its celebration of freedom, became the most revolutionary festival ever granted to a nation or a religion. Its message thunders and resonates to our very day, with over half of the population of the world living under totalitarian governments,[1] not to mention the human trafficking, sex slavery, and child labor that still enslave so many around the world.

THE RESPONSIBILITY OF FREEDOM

In Hebrew, there are three different terms for freedom: *ḥofesh, deror,* and *ḥerut. Ḥofesh* is total freedom from responsibility or obligation, as when a slave is set free from working for a master.[2] He no longer has any responsibility toward that particular master. As the Bible says in Exodus 21:2, "If you acquire a Hebrew servant, six years shall he serve, and on the seventh (year) he shall go free without any obligation (*laḥofshi ḥinam*)."[3] *Ḥofesh* certainly does not denote the freedom of Passover; indeed, we begin the Passover Seder by reciting the fourteen specific stages which we must observe during the Seder ceremony – our *responsibility* to God and to our future generations on that special night.

The second word for freedom, *deror,* comes from the Hebrew word *dar,* which means "to dwell," and so this type of freedom signifies

1. The Human Rights Foundation's research says that the world currently has forty competitive authoritarian regimes that rule 1.2 billion people; and fifty-three full-fledged dictatorships that oppress 2.8 billion people or thirty percent of the world's countries. This would mean that fifty-three percent of the world is enslaved to absolute rule. (Human Rights Foundation website, accessed April 1, 2019.)
2. In a usage no longer current, an individual who has decided that he has no responsibilities vis-à-vis God would call himself *ḥofshi,* from the same root. The comparable English term, also no longer current, would be "freethinker."
3. This refers to indigent Jews who sold their work ability to a wealthier Jew with whom the indigent person would live for a six-year period.

that anyone may dwell anywhere he may wish.[4] This type of freedom is exemplified by the verse in Deuteronomy 23:17, "You shall not deliver to his master a slave who has escaped from his master to you. He shall dwell with you, in your midst, in the place that he shall choose, in one of your gates, wherever is good for him; you shall not oppress him."[5] The escaped slave may live wherever he wishes, a sign that he is free. In addition, the Torah states in Leviticus 25:10, "You shall sanctify the fiftieth year and proclaim liberty (*deror*) throughout the land to all its inhabitants; it shall be a Jubilee for you; every person shall return to his possessions and every person to his family." (The "liberty phrase" of this verse is inscribed on the historic American Liberty Bell in Philadelphia.) This Jubilee (fiftieth) Year of which the verse speaks is a foreshadowing of future messianic times when the entire world will be free. Since that is not the case – as yet – regarding Passover, the term *deror* cannot be used, because we have yet to realize complete global freedom.

The third expression for freedom is *ḥerut*, and that is the one that our Sages used to describe the Passover festival – *Zeman Ḥeruteinu*, the "Festival of our Freedom." Extremely instructive is that *ḥerut* is related, certainly by sound and similarity of letters, to the word *aḥrayut*, responsibility.[6] The individual must assume responsibility and even, if need

4. The Talmud (Beitza 24a) asks why the sparrow is called in Hebrew "*deror*." The Talmud answers, "Because it dwells in the house as well as in the field." It lives wherever it chooses.
5. In this case we are dealing with a gentile slave who is actually purchased body and soul by a gentile master. If he is treated badly and runs away to you in Israel for help, you may not return him to his oppressor, but he must live with you. The Rambam (*Hilkhot Avadim* 9:8) emphasizes how Jews must treat gentile servants with great care, never belittling them and certainly not oppressing them physically. It is startling that in 1896, in Plessy vs. Ferguson, a landmark decision by the United States Supreme Court, the court upheld the constitutionality of segregation laws for public facilities as long as the segregated facilities were equal in quality – a doctrine that came to be known as "separate but equal." Only in 1954, in Brown vs. Board of Education, did the court reverse itself by stating that "separate educational facilities are inherently unequal." The Torah, predating these cases by thousands of years, never condoned "separate but equal." The escaped slave was permitted to choose his place of dwelling.
6. Professor Yedidya Stern makes a similar connection in his article "*Ḥerut Hi Aḥrayut*" (Freedom Is Responsibility), Israel Democracy Institute, April 6, 2017, https://www.idi.org.il/articles/14310.

be, lay down his life, to acquire the existential necessity of freedom. Freedom most often must be earned and even fought for. In the most fundamental sense, what happened on Passover was the beginning of our journey toward independent nationhood which is critical in order for the Jewish people to be free.

What happened on Passover was only the first part of that equation. We were not yet in our own land, with defensible borders and an army to protect us. We were like a family freed from the slavery of a foreign ruler, but without a home of our own in which to develop our own culture and to be able to defend our freedom. On Passover we are promised a homeland,[7] but we do not as yet possess it.

In effect, on Passover God wrought miracles to bring about our freedom from slavery, but gave us the responsibility to partner with Him in order for us to become a truly free and independent nation in our own homeland.

As we have seen above (chapter 11), this message is dramatically brought home in the amazing story of the splitting of the Reed Sea, which we celebrate on the seventh and final day of Passover. The Israelites, having just left Egypt, are pursued by the Egyptian army, come to take them back into slavery; the Egyptian hordes are behind them; the Reed Sea, with its huge and threatening waves, is in front of them. They seem to be paralyzed by fear.

At the critical moment, they complain bitterly to Moses: "Because there were no graves in Egypt, have you taken us away to die in the desert? What a terrible thing have you done to us to bring us out of Egypt?" (Ex. 14:11). Moses tries to reassure them, understandably, by invoking the power of the Heavenly Redeemer. "Fear not, stand still and see the salvation of God, which He will do for you today.... God will fight for you; you remain silent" (14:13–14).[8] At this point in the dialogue, Moses calms the panicking Hebrews, guaranteeing them that a miracle

7. In Exodus 6:8 – "And I will bring you into the land which I swore to give to Abraham, to Isaac, and to Jacob, and I will give it to you for a heritage; I am the Lord."

8. It is interesting that the hasidic interpretation of this verse is precisely the opposite of its literal meaning. Using a double play on words (the root letters *lamed-ḥet-mem* form the root of both "fight" and "bread," and the root letters *ḥet-resh-shin* form the root of both "remain silent" and "plow"), this interpretation recasts the verse as

of God will miraculously bring about that freedom. Now, we would rightfully expect a miracle from God, removing the Hebrews from the impossible position of "no exit" in which they found themselves. But that is not what God continued to say: "And God said to Moses, 'Why are you crying out to me? Speak to the children of Israel, that they must move forward!'" (14:15). It is as if God is saying to the Israelites, "I have used My power to get you out of Egypt, but it is not My power that will give you lasting freedom. For true freedom, you must work yourselves."

Rashi understands God's words to Moses as saying: "Speak to the Israelites and let them get going." Let them start acting, let them also take responsibility for their freedom, let them fight against the Egyptians[9] who are threatening to return them to Egypt, or at the very least, let them dive into the Reed Sea and attempt to get to the other side, possibly risking their lives but bringing them much closer to their Promised Land."[10]

---

saying, "If you wish for God to give you bread, first you must plow." In other words, to accomplish what you wish, you must not leave it to God, but rather take action yourself – the very theme we are discussing.

9. Ibn Ezra's commentary on Exodus 14:13 actually suggests that, with six hundred thousand males, indeed they should have fought the Egyptians! The Bible specifically states (Ex. 13:18) that the Israelites came out of Egypt "armed." Under ordinary circumstances, they should have fought. However, Ibn Ezra explains that the Israelites were psychologically unable to do battle against the Egyptians, who had been their masters for so many years, and the relationship with whom comprised only subjugation. But the very least they should have done is to take the initiative to dive into the sea.

10. The great Vilna Gaon notes that in Exodus 14:22 the verse seems to strongly indicate that the Reed Sea only turned to dry land after the Israelites had actually entered the waters: "And the children of Israel went into the sea upon dry land, and the water was for them a wall [of protection], to their right and to their left." However, the story is repeated just a few verses later. Exodus 14:29: "And the children of Israel went onto the dry land, in the midst of the sea, and the water to them was a wall, to their right and to their left." Here, the words are reversed: in the previous verse, they went into the sea which became land; in this verse they went onto dry land, which became the sea. The great rabbi states that this difference indicates that there were actually two groups of Israelites: one who took responsibility for their freedom, and another group who did not want to take responsibility, but rather to wait until God would split the sea. His interesting textual proof is that, in our first quoted verse, the word for "wall," *ḥoma,* is written "full," with the letter *vav.* In the second verse, *ḥoma* is missing the *vav,* which allows for the word to be read as *ḥeima,* anger. For

It is very possible that when Rashi wrote this comment, he had before him an amazing passage from Talmud (Berakhot 3a):

> It has been taught: R. Yosi says: I was once traveling on the road, and I entered into one of the ruins of Jerusalem in order to pray. Elijah the Prophet appeared and waited for me at the door till I finished my prayer.[11] After I finished my prayer, he said to me: "Peace be with you, my master!" And I replied: "Peace be with you, my master and teacher!" And he said to me: "My son, why did you go into this ruin?" I replied: "To pray." He said to me: "You ought to have prayed on the road." I replied: "I feared lest passersby might interrupt or even harm me." He said to me: "You ought to have said an abbreviated prayer."

R. Yossi, a great Rabbi of the Mishna, witnessed the destruction of the Second Temple. It is very likely that he entered this ruined synagogue in Jerusalem to pray for the redemption. But Elijah the Prophet tells him, "You ought to have prayed on the road."

"On the road," in Hebrew *baderekh,* has echoes from the biblical verse Exodus 23:20, "Behold, I send an angel before you, to guard you on the road (*baderekh*), and to bring you into the place which I have prepared" – the Land of Israel. The verse clearly indicates that God will protect the people only after *they initiate their movement on the road* to the Land of Israel. So, too, here in this talmudic quote, Elijah the Prophet is using "on the road" to mean "on the road to Israel and redemption."

Elijah was not merely making a legal point; he was expressing a Jewish worldview: If you wish redemption to come, you must take

---

those Hebrews who took responsibility, the raging waters were a protective wall; for those who did not assume responsibility and relied only upon God, they were "angry waters." Here, at the Reed Sea, God was expecting the Israelites to be His full partners, and to take responsibility for their freedom.

11. Elijah, a great biblical prophet and the harbinger of the King Messiah, rose to heaven on a fiery chariot (II Kings 2:11); his death is not explicitly mentioned. This gave rise to a great deal of rabbinic lore about various appearances of Elijah throughout the ages, often offering important advice to various figures. This talmudic story is such an instance.

responsibility for it and work for it. You must plant, you must build; if need be, you must wage war. You don't bring redemption by praying in a ruin; you bring redemption by beginning to build. Elijah was explaining, "You may say a short prayer, but you must do so only while you are building, while you are planting, while you are battling – while you are 'on the road' toward redemption."

Undoubtedly the era in which we are living is the most fortunate so far for the Jewish people; we live in the blessed era which has seen the restoration of the State of Israel as the homeland for the Jews. Although many righteous Jews prayed *tikkun ḥatzot* (elegies recited at midnight over the destruction of the ancient Temples and the exile from the Land of Israel) for the last two thousand years, ours is the generation that rose up and began to return to Israel, to rebuild Israel, and to fight for Israel. This is to the great credit of modern Zionism. We didn't wait for the Messiah; we paved the road for his coming. This is precisely the message of Passover: the Hebrews assuming responsibility for their national independence, *ḥerut*, freedom, clearly dependent upon *aḥrayut*, responsibility.

A careful reading of the biblical text of the Exodus will even intensify the necessity of the Hebrews' assuming of responsibility. You must bear in mind that in the biblical passage that maps out the precise location in which the Israelites are to encamp, the landmarks mentioned are all places of idolatry. The Bible tells us (Ex. 13:18) that God rerouted the Israelites on their way out of Egypt. In 14:2 we are told that "they turned and encamped in front of Pi HaHirot between Migdol and the sea, in front of Baal Tzephon – opposite these did they encamp near the sea."[12] Pi HaHirot, possibly the idol of the Egyptian god Horus, can also be translated "the mouth (or cusp) of freedom." Baal Tzephon ("Baal of the North") is a well-known Canaanite idol.[13] As we have explained,

12. The significance of these names is emphasized by the fact that this location is mentioned no fewer than three times in the Bible: Exodus 14:2, Exodus 14:9, Numbers 33:7.
13. James K. Hoffmeier, professor of Old Testament and Near Eastern History and Archeology at Trinity Evangelical Divinity School, in his article "The Exodus and Wilderness Narratives," notes that Baal Tzephon is associated with the Canaanite storm god Hadad or Baal. He also refers to the Papyrus Anastasi III which mentions

in idol worship the human being has no real status; all he can do is to propitiate the gods and hope that they remain on his side. Rabbinic commentaries explain that, since the Hebrew letters of Hirot (the idol) and *ḥerut* (freedom) are identical, this means that the Israelites at this point in their journey toward becoming a nation were in between the status of the idolater – who left everything up to the gods and was not expected to take responsibility for his freedom – and the status of the Hebrews whose achievement of freedom and independence was specifically dependent upon their taking personal responsibility.[14] They must be willing to risk their lives in order to achieve their homeland. Yes, God promised them a homeland, but insists that we must be His full partners in achieving freedom and a homeland.

THE FIRST SACRIFICIAL ACT OF ISRAEL: THE PASCHAL SACRIFICE

It is instructive to note how the biblical process of freedom from slavery and the human participation in that freedom actually began. After the first nine of the ten plagues, God issues a commandment to Moses and Aaron: "Speak to the congregation of Israel and say, 'On the tenth of this month (Nisan), you shall take for yourselves a lamb … and on the fourteenth of this month, you shall slaughter it, you, the entire assembly of the congregation of Israel, in the afternoon …. And you shall take the blood and place it upon the doorposts and on the lintel of your houses …. And the blood shall be for you as a sign upon the houses where you are."[15]

---

what seems to be the Reed Sea, and states that this body of water was also called "the waters of Baal" and "the waters of Horus." This supports the idea that the area where the children of Israel were told to encamp "upon the sea" was an area deeply associated with idolatry. (*Ancient Israel's History: An Introduction to Issues and Sources,* edited by Bill T. Arnold and Richard S. Hess [Grand Rapids, MI: Baker Academic, 2014], 78–79.)

14. See Rashi on Exodus 14:2 who states that the Bible calls the place Pi HaHirot because "there they became free people."

15. Ex. 12:3, 5, 7, 13.

The lamb was one of the major gods of Ancient Egypt.[16] By dint of this commandment preceding the exodus from Egypt, the Bible is clearly stating that the slaughter of an Egyptian god as a sacrifice to our Almighty God of the heavens and the earth will be the strongest possible statement against Egyptian idolatry and its belittlement of human action. Indeed, it will require the Hebrews to put their lives on the line; the Egyptians could hardly be sanguine about the Hebrews killing their lamb god. The Bible was unequivocally affirming that true freedom and independence cannot coexist with idolatry.[17]

Hence, the Paschal sacrifice was a "test" by God to ascertain if the Israelites were ready to risk their lives for freedom. This "test" extended beyond the slaughtering of the lamb and the placing of its blood upon the doorposts. God commanded the Israelites to take the lamb on the tenth of the month of Nisan, but to slaughter it only on the fourteenth. For what purpose was the four-day hiatus? According to the Midrash, during this four-day period, the male Israelites circumcised themselves, a commandment that had not been performed during their servitude in Egypt.[18] The symbolism of both acts is clear: Our nation will have to be prepared even to shed blood for our freedom – both in the slaughtering of the god of Egypt in reference to their immediate situation, and circumcision upon the organ of propagation, symbolizing that this same extreme commitment would extend to Jews of every generation, for all time. The cost of human freedom, the overriding message of the festival of Passover, comes at a very high price, even at the cost of shedding our life's blood.[19] This message resonates throughout world

---

16. Rivka Ulmer, "The Egyptian Gods in Midrashic Texts," *The Harvard Theological Review* (Cambridge University Press): vol. 103, no. 2 (April 2010), 189.
17. This point is emphasized by the Midrash, and directed to the Israelites in Egypt who were indulging in idolatrous practices. "This is what is meant by 'Draw out and take your lambs' (Ex. 12:21), that is to say: Draw away your hands from idolatry and take for yourselves lambs, thereby slaying the gods of Egypt and preparing the Passover sacrifice. Only through this will the Lord pass over you" (Exodus Rabba 16:2).
18. *Mekhilta Pisḥa* chapter 5, quoted by Rashi on Exodus 12:6.
19. Rashi, on the verse quoted above, comments on the phrase "and the blood shall be for you." "For you," he explains, "and not for others. That is why the blood was placed on the *inside* of the doorposts." The message of extreme dedication was specifically directed toward the Hebrews.

history. Indeed, after the original American revolutionaries fought their bloody war for independence, it is no wonder that the original suggestion for the Great Seal of the United States, proposed by Thomas Jefferson and Benjamin Franklin, depicted the drowning Egyptians and the victorious Israelites who had sacrificed their lives for their Passover freedom.[20]

It is fascinating to note that we can now understand Passover as the birth of the Jewish nation, when the tribal families began to become a nation and to take responsibility for freedom as they journeyed to their own homeland. The original Abrahamic family consisted of his blood descendants as well as strangers who chose to become members of Abraham's household.[21] In addition, according to midrashic tradition, along with those Abrahamites there were also Egyptians, amazed by the whole drama of the Jewish exodus and the ability of a small group to rise up against the Egyptian empire and actually gain their freedom. Moreover, there were many biological members of the family who had not circumcised themselves during the servitude, because to have done so would most probably have been a capital offence (as it was considered in modern times during the Nazi and Soviet periods).

It is fascinating to note that these very activities of the extended Abrahamic family about to become a nation are precisely the elements later established in Jewish law for a non-Jew to enter the Jewish nation: circumcision, as we have just discussed, which expresses commitment to God even to the point of shedding blood; the offering of a sacrifice to God – the Passover lamb – which was thanksgiving for God's having taken us out of servitude and is a clear statement of the repudiation of idolatry; and the immersion of the Israelites when they actually dived into the sea of flowing waters.[22] I cannot help but draw an association

20. See Lester Olson, *Emblems of American Community in the Revolutionary Era: A Study in Rhetorical Iconology* (Washington, DC: Smithsonian Institution Press, 1991).
21. Harkening back to the verse in Genesis 18:19: "For I [God] have known, loved, and chosen him [Abraham], because he is commanding his children *and his household* after him, that they keep the way of the Lord, doing compassionate righteousness and moral justice."
22. These are the prerequisites for conversion to Judaism to this very day, as noted by the Talmud in Yevamot 46b and the Rambam in *Hilkhot Issurei Bia* 13:1. The

between this act of immersion in the waters of the Reed Sea and the immersion of every prospective convert to Judaism in the *mikve* (the ritual waters of purification) as a necessary prerequisite for conversion. From this perspective, the waters of the Reed Sea are symbolic of the amniotic fluids which accompany every birth; indeed, the immersion represents rebirth into the Abrahamic family.

In other words, the Jewish birth of a nation on Passover was, in effect, a mass conversion! Until this time, we were a family together with disciples of Abraham, who saw themselves as adjuncts to the family; after these requirements of circumcision and *mikve* were fulfilled, we truly demonstrated our willingness to accept the responsibility as an independent people of Israel on the way to entering our national homeland. Therefore, the festival of Passover is truly the festival celebrating the birth of a nation. The remaining element to complete this nationhood is, of course, a land. And, indeed, this newly formed nation is now on its way to its new land, the Land of Israel.

PASSOVER: THE ENGAGEMENT BETWEEN GOD AND ISRAEL

We have just established the freedom of Passover as a sacred partnership between God and Israel. It is true that God wrought many miracles in Egypt in order to force Pharaoh's hand to free the Hebrews from servitude, specifically by means of the ten plagues, which were God's gift to us. However, the true propeller of our free status and the acts in which we expressed our partnership with God and assumed responsibility for freedom were our blood circumcision, our Paschal sacrifice, and our willingness to dive into the Reed Sea. It is especially the blood circumcision upon the organ of propagation – which thereby includes our unborn children into future generations – which enabled us to enter into a loving covenant with the eternal God of all generations.[23]

requirement of a sacrificial offering is, of course, suspended today in the absence of the Temple.

23. Women are clearly included in this concept, even though they do not undergo circumcision. The Talmud in Avoda Zara 27a states: אשה כמאן דמהילא דמיא – that a woman is considered (naturally) circumcised (and therefore included in the

Therefore it becomes beautifully logical that the Hebrew name of the Passover festival is *Pesaḥ*, a word derived from the verb form *upasaḥti*, usually translated as "pass over," describing God's statement that He will "pass over" the Israelite homes during the final plague to be brought upon the Egyptians.[24] However, the authoritative early Aramaic translation of that verb form is *vaaḥus*,[25] "I will show affection, I will love."[26] Hence, the very name of this spring festival is "Love," which expresses the love partnership between God and Israel.

And so it is that Passover is truly the festival of romance: the prenuptial engagement between God and the Jewish people. Passover, more than any of the other Jewish holidays, is the festival of love. We have spoken before about God's love for human beings, and have noted that the Hebrew word *raḥamim*, "compassionate love," derives from the world *reḥem*, "womb," denoting that God's love for the humans He has created is analogous to the love of a mother for the helpless child of her womb. However, the love of which we are now speaking in reference to Passover is a different and more mature kind of love. This love denotes mutuality, a working together. It is a love born of a partnership: the exciting love of prenuptial courtship, the love of mutual giving, a love that assumes responsibility on the part of both partners, a passionate love out of which something new is created – in the human sphere, a child; in our analogy, God and Israel have partnered to create a nation born of their love. Indeed, on the Sabbath of Passover, we read the Megilla Scroll of God's love, the Song of Songs, the love song between the Shepherd (God) and the shepherdess (Israel), a love song of premarriage passion, a love song of engagement, mutuality, and commitment.

In fact, not only does God, in the Bible, speak the word *upasaḥti*, but the biblical text refers to the Paschal sacrifice we have discussed

covenant of circumcision). I believe that this means that since women shed blood and place their lives at risk with every childbirth, they thereby naturally express the necessity of shedding blood for Jewish continuity.

24. Exodus 12:13.
25. *Targum Onkelos* on that verse.
26. The authoritative Aramaic dictionary by Marcus Jastrow offers additional related meanings for this verb: "To protect, to grace, to favor" – all products and expressions of love.

with the same root: *pesaḥ.*[27] Hence, the sacrifice itself is an expression of the love of engagement, in the same way that a bride-to-be's gifts to her fiancé are manifestations of tenderness and affection. The lover always gives of him/herself to her/his beloved; after all, the very word *ahava* – love – is built upon the word *hav* – to give – as we have previously explained.

This loving commitment of the engagement bond between God and Israel is magnificently expressed by the prophet Hosea (2:21–22): "I will betroth you to Me forever; I will betroth you to Me in moral justice, compassionate righteousness, in loving-kindness, and in graciousness; I will betroth you to Me in faithfulness, and you shall know and love God." And so, our festival of responsible freedom, the ultimate expression of which is the moral justice, compassionate righteousness, and loving-kindness which we must display to every human being, is at the same time truly the festival of our engagement to God who is our full partner in His deep and loving relationship with the world.

MATZA: SPIRITUAL AND POLITICAL FREEDOM

Clearly, the whole drama of the exodus from Egypt was the seminal event in establishing the Jewish nation, and therefore needed to be absorbed deeply in the nation's collective memory. As to how this is to happen the Bible states in Exodus 13:3: "Remember this day on which you departed from Egypt, from the house of bondage, by the strength of [His] hand God brought you out from there." This verse, clearly instructing all generations of Jews to internalize the meaning of the Exodus, ends strangely: "And no leavened bread may be eaten." This seems to be a non sequitur; what is the connection between the perpetuation of the national memory of the Exodus and a particular dietary restriction?

In order to comprehend the connection, it is important to understand the nature of the central dietary restriction of Passover, the eating of *ḥametz,* often translated as "leavened bread," but really a technical term

27. Actually, we refer colloquially to the festival of Passover itself as "Pesaḥ," although that name is given by the Bible to the day of the fourteenth of the month of Nisan, the day upon which we offered the Paschal sacrifice in Temple times.

encompassing the Jewish legal (halakhic) definition of leavened foods. The halakhic definition of *ḥametz* is the mixing of any of the five major grains with water, and then leaving the dough untouched for a period of time. That substance will then naturally rise, become higher and fuller, and then constitute *ḥametz*. Matza, which we are commanded to eat on Passover, begins its "life" exactly as does *ḥametz*, as a mixture of flour with water. But, in contradistinction to *ḥametz*, the matza dough is not allowed to be left unattended, and must be baked before it is allowed to rise, swell, and become a fully inflated loaf of bread.

These two different treatments of the dough carry with them profound symbolic meaning.

Ḥametz essentially represents letting nature take its regular course, refraining from acting to interrupt that course. If one leaves the dough alone, it will ferment into *ḥametz*, a sour, fermented, puffed-up, and even swelled leaven, symbolizing crass materialism.

Indeed, the very introduction to Passover, taking place on the evening prior to the beginning of the festival, is the ceremony of *bedikat ḥametz*, the search for leavened foodstuffs throughout one's home, culminating in the ceremonial burning of the *ḥametz* the next morning, before ushering in the festival that night. While this "search and destruction" of leaven has the practical effect of ridding the home from prohibited *ḥametz* during the seven days of the festival, it also carries with it the deep symbolic meaning of ridding oneself from certain instinctive materialistic and animalistic drives which so many individuals explain away as "this is my nature." Even before the Seder evening, in which we tell of our slavery and of our freedom, we state clearly how important our actions are; we search for the fermentation without and within, and we attempt to control and sublimate it.

Many lessons from Passover are based upon the symbolic significance of *ḥametz*. The natural course, throughout history, has been for the strong, animalistic human to enslave the weak and disaffected. Passover proclaims that this natural course is wrong; God stepped in to take the Jews out of Egypt and drew them into a partnership with Him to fight for their freedom, thereby pushing back the "natural process" and universal acceptance of slavery as a proper way of treating the weak. Idolatry, which emphasizes physical prowess above everything else, was the prevailing culture of Egypt and the entire ancient world, and, in many respects, the entire world until this very day. When the Israelites in Egypt were called upon to slaughter the lamb – and, so to speak, the animalistic gods of idolatry, slavery, and self-indulgence – they were really being asked to interrupt that natural fermentation force of the human being's baser animalistic characteristics; instead of the self-indulgence and self-aggrandizement of the puffed-up *ḥametz,* we must eat the more modest and self-effacing matza of self-control and self-sacrifice for the good of the other.

Moreover, society does not naturally love the stranger, the "other." He is seen as an interloper, as someone different from the indigenous population, and therefore threatening to take away from the indigenous population the resources which they consider as belonging to them alone. This is why so many civilizations have gone down the road of xenophobia, enslaving the stranger and taking advantage of the immigrant – if he was allowed to enter their borders in the first place.

However, the Torah commands many times over[28] that we must love the stranger, and certainly not oppress him. It also commands "You shall love your neighbor like yourself"[29] – because he is essentially yourself, because you both have God within you, because all human beings are children of our One Parent in Heaven, and because all human beings are capable of developing the God within them and the good within them. By our obeying and internalizing these commandments, we are, in effect, once again interrupting the natural process, which can, and often does, produce the bitter and sour *ḥametz* of xenophobia and racism.

The symbols of *ḥametz* and matza relate to the life of every human being. Our Bible does not believe in the idea of Rousseau's "noble savage," the notion that every human being is basically good. In fact, the Bible states very clearly (Gen. 8:21): "The inclination of the human heart is evil from his youth." If one looks at history, remembers events such as the Holocaust, and recognizes human egocentricity, one cannot

28. The Torah tells us to love the stranger and not to oppress him thirty-six times. Some examples are Exodus 22:20, Leviticus 19:34, and Deuteronomy 10:19.
29. Lev. 19:18.

escape the conclusion that the human being by nature is not only not good, but is very often bad.

However, at the same time that every human being is based in animal desire and the will to destroy, the human being likewise is created in the image of God, and with the will and need to love and be loved. Freud says it very well in his 1920 book *Beyond the Pleasure Principle,* in which he referred to Eros as the natural life instinct, which includes sexual desires, the drive to live, and the fundamental need to love and be loved. At the same time, there exists in each of us Thanatos, the death instinct, a desire to destroy the other, and sometimes even ourselves. This dichotomy expresses the struggle within the soul of every human being – Eros versus Thanatos. We must work overtime in order to push aside Thanatos, and sublimate Eros to make it part and parcel of the substance of God that is within every human being. We can control our nature, and perfect ourselves. This is the message of matza.

For example, the human being by nature is not necessarily monogamous, but our Torah and Judaism highly value an exclusive, loving husband-wife relationship, in which each must cleave to his/her mate and form themselves into one human entity.[30] Only such a stable and loving family dynamic can provide the vehicle by which generation following generation reexperience the true message of Passover: freedom and responsibility, love and peace. It is, in fact, the festival of Passover, which is the festival of our nationhood, that reminds us that every nation begins with a family, and that familial continuity of specific traditions empowers the individual with a sense that s/he is sharing in eternity.[31]

---

30. This echoes the verse in Genesis 2:24: "Therefore shall a man leave his father and his mother and cleave to his wife, and they shall be as one flesh." Indeed, they become one flesh in their physical and sexual union, and they become one flesh by giving the essence of themselves – their genes – to their children, and on to their children's children.

31. That notion of eternity is referenced eloquently in one of the Seven Blessings recited under the Jewish wedding canopy: "Blessed are you, Lord our God, Sovereign of the universe, who has created the human being in His image, in the image of His likeness, and has prepared for the human – from Himself – a building for eternity. Blessed are you, God, who created the human being." Every human being is a link in the chain of eternity, and our laws and traditions work to imbed this notion in our consciousness.

As the Mishna records (Pesaḥim 10:5): "Every Jew must feel as if they, themselves, came out of Egypt," since every Jew today – even those who are Jews by choice – is, effectively, a descendant and a recipient of the same genome of his familial forebears who left Egypt.

Hence, it is not an accident that the central theme of the Seder – the retelling of the story of our movement from slavery to responsible freedom – is expressed by the Bible as a familial educational initiative, to the extent that the Seder text that we read is called the Haggada, literally "a retelling." "And you shall tell your child on that day, saying, because of this future reexperiencing of the exodus from Egypt from generation to generation that God wrought miracles for me when He took me out of Egypt" (Ex. 13:8).[32]

The Zohar, the sacred ancient mystical interpretation of the Bible, actually translates "matza" as *laḥma dimehemenuta* (in Hebrew: *leḥem emuna*), "the bread of faithfulness,"[33] expressing God's faithfulness to us by taking us out of Egyptian slavery, and our faithfulness to Him by our reaffirmation of God's desire for universal freedom through our observance of the laws of Passover and our celebration of the Passover Seder every year. The very fact that 3,500 years after the Exodus, we eat the matza-bread of freedom – on the very night of the Exodus – links us inextricably to the very first Passover as well as to the future Passover when we shall have communicated to every family of the earth the necessity of human freedom. This linkage establishes the eternality of our message as well as the eternality of our loving partnership with God.

David Ben-Gurion, who would become the first prime minister of the State of Israel, speaking before the Anglo-American Committee of Inquiry, said the following:

> More than three hundred years ago a ship by the name of the Mayflower left Plymouth for the New World. It was a great event

32. Rashi on this verse quotes the *Mekhilta*: "In order that I observe His commandments, such as the Paschal sacrifice, the eating of matza, and the eating of the bitter herbs." These commandments observed at the Seder enable us to reexperience the exodus from Egypt.
33. Zohar II 183b.

> in American and English history. I wonder how many Englishmen or how many Americans know exactly the date when that ship left Plymouth, how many people were on the ship, and what was the kind of bread that people ate when they left Plymouth. Well, more than 3,300 years ago the Jews left Egypt. It was more than 3,000 years ago and every Jew in the world knows exactly the date when we left. It was on the fifteenth of Nisan. The bread they ate was *matzot*. Until today all the Jews throughout the world on the fifteenth of Nisan eat the same *matzot* – in America, in Russia – and tell the story of the Exodus from Egypt. They relate what happened, all the sufferings that happened to the Jews since they went into exile. They finish with these two sentences: "This year we are slaves; next year we will be free. This year we are here; next year we will be in Zion, the land of Israel." Jews are like that.[34]

Yes, we still sit on that Passover night with our families, we still eat that same matza, and we are still awaiting the accomplishment of our mission to teach its message of freedom to all the families of the earth.

THE SEDER: LEARNING HOW TO BE RESPONSIBLY FREE

As we have said often, the mission of the Jewish people is to learn about and achieve freedom for themselves individually and nationally, and ultimately to teach the entire world such freedom. It is very difficult, however, to truly appreciate freedom if one has never been enslaved. Hence, on Passover night, we celebrate by actually reliving and reexperiencing that original period in our national lives when we were enslaved, and then freed, at the very dawn of our history. This magical and mystical night of the fifteenth of Nisan is called the Seder.

The name "Seder" itself presents a perplexing paradox. On the one hand, it is supposed to be our ultimate night of freedom. However, the very word "*seder*" means "order," or "structure," and this very majestic, symbolic, and sumptuous meal, preceded and succeeded by readings

34. "Public Hearings before the Anglo-American Committee of Inquiry" (Jerusalem, Palestine; March 1, 1946), 12.

from a special book called the Haggada, is also the most structured home experience in Judaism, divided into fourteen specific activities, from the beginning of the evening to its end. The solution to the paradox is that the freedom we are discussing and reexperiencing is not the freedom of abandonment of all limitation and structure, but it is rather freedom from serving the Golden Calf of licentiousness and materialism (*ḥametz*) in order to serve the God of human equality and righteousness. It is the freedom from all sorts of human despots and physical addictions in order to serve the God of love and purposeful living.

The Seder is punctuated by four – and, as we shall soon see, I would suggest five – cups of wine, the first cup being the sanctification blessing (Kiddush) that we recite at the beginning of every Sabbath and festival meal.

We then pour a second cup of wine over which we emphasize the period of our servitude in Egypt. As we do the readings, we internalize the suffering of the slaves. This section, called *Maggid* (the "Telling"), begins with questions, because the Haggada really is a handbook for parents, helping them learn to teach their children the most central and important message of the Haggada: the evils of slavery and the importance of freedom for every human being. The wise parent-teacher encourages questions, and learning can only take place between the generations if the younger generation is inspired to ask the older generation, which then attempts to answer by giving a glimpse of the great majesty and sensitivity of our eternal tradition.

The Seder goes on to typologize four types of young adults or questioners. First is the Wise Young Adult, who attempts to understand the rituals and their symbolic meanings. The Rebellious Young Adult is rather sarcastic about the entire proceeding. This young person asks the question, "What is this service-work (*avoda*) to you?" His real question is found in this young person's particular choice of words (in Hebrew). The word *avoda* can mean service, but its basic meaning is "work." This young adult sees all of the ritual, the rules, and the restrictions as "work" – not as the uplifting acts they are meant to be.[35] And so,

35. The version of the Rebellious Young Adult's remarks in the Jerusalem Talmud (Pesaḥim 10:4) adds the words "What is this bother (Hebrew: *toraḥ*) with which

we answer this young person in a completely loving way: the Haggadah says "*hak'heh et shinav*" – "soften his sharpness" – with warmth; speak to him softly and lovingly.[36] We must convey to this young person the beauty and the importance of the Seder in particular, and our way of life in general.[37] We must respond to him/her with warm embrace and loving welcome within the family setting, despite the derisive tone of his/her words. Then there is the Simple Young Adult, with his straightforward question and answer; finally, the Young Adult so far removed from the traditional Jewish world that he does not even know what to ask.[38]

The Haggada goes on to tell of God entering history, bringing plagues upon the Egyptian slave owners, resulting ultimately in the freeing of the Israelites, who fought for their freedom, even to the point of sacrificing their lives, and so were able to leave Egypt as free individuals. We then partake of the festival meal, which is reminiscent of the

---

you are bothering us every year," an even stronger manner of expression by the Rebellious Young Adult.

36. Many Haggadot translate the response to the Rebellious Young Adult as "blunt his teeth." I believe that this is an erroneous translation, perhaps brought about by the similarity of two verbs in Hebrew. The three root letters of the verb used by the Haggada are *kof-heh-heh,* which means "to soften." (This is the first meaning given this root by Avraham Even-Shoshan, *HaMilon HeḤadash.*) That verb should not be confused with the similar sounding (in the imperative form: *hakeh*) but unrelated root *nun-kaf-heh,* which means "to strike" or "to hit." The only way to bring the Rebellious Young Adult back is to be soft and warm with him – certainly not to respond with anger or violence.

37. As noted, many understand our response to the Rebellious Young Adult as spoken in anger, closing with the pronouncement: "If you had been there, you would not have been saved!" I believe that only unconditional love will bring the Rebellious Young Adult back to the community of Israel. There is room at the Seder table even for those who do not believe, and performance of communal mitzvot is the best way to bring people back to faith. My understanding of the response to the Rebellious Young Adult is that it is spoken in sadness, for indeed, had they denied being part of the Jewish people, they would not have merited redemption in the Exodus. It is our job to help show them the beauty of Jewish tradition and have them choose to return to the fold.

38. At my Seder, reading parts are given out in advance, and various family members are asked to play the role of each of the Young Adults. In general, preparation for the Seder involves many playlets in an attempt to make the Seder as "live" an experience as possible.

meal of the very first Seder, and of the Seder during the Temple times, when the focus of the meal was the consuming of the Paschal sacrifice, which has been suspended since the destruction of the Second Temple. After the conclusion of our meal we recite the Grace After Meals, which contains within it many references to the Temple's destruction and the exile of the Jewish people. When we have completed the grace, we drink the third cup of wine. We are left with a certain bittersweet feeling; yes, we have observed the Seder ritual and rejoiced over our freedom from Egypt, but we are still without our Temple and its rituals, and the world is far from being either righteous or free. Therefore, at this juncture, we pour an additional cup of wine, which is not part of the initial four cups. This is the cup of Elijah the biblical prophet, who is pictured as a rather mythical character who spends his time hovering between heaven and earth, frequenting many of the great Sages, and helping Jews in need. His presence is felt at every Seder, since the Bible describes him as the one who will announce the arrival of the King Messiah at a time when the entire world will live in peace. Since Passover is the festival that promises redemption, it makes sense that Jewish folklore maintains that he is present at every Seder and that he will be the one who will ultimately "restore the hearts of the parents to their children and the hearts of the children to their parents" (Mal. 3:24), which is the ultimate expression of the coming together of the generations at the time of redemption.

At this point, the custom is to open the door of our home, to welcome Elijah. It is at this moment that I always think of the Fifth Young Adult, whom we have not at all mentioned, who does not appear in the Haggada, because he or she is not at the Seder, having been completely alienated and removed from Judaism.

This child is even more challenging than the Rebellious Young Adult. It is this Fifth Young Adult who represents the tragedy of so many Jewish families today. Everything – and I mean everything – must be done to ensure that all children – including adult children – no matter what their level of commitment to Judaism, feel part of the Jewish family. We must find the way to welcome this young person into the Seder ceremony, to help him or her to find his or her way back into the history of Israel.

My wife once remarked that if the invisible Elijah the Prophet can be present at everyone's Seder, at the same time and throughout all time zones, then he can certainly find his way into our homes without our opening the door. Therefore, the symbolism of opening the door is not so much that Elijah can enter, but rather is to tell us that we must exit; we must go out and find that Fifth Young Adult and bring them in. The act of opening the door condemns passivity and insists that we must be active in bringing disaffected Jews back to Judaism. At my Seder we sing the Israeli national anthem, *HaTikva,* as a special song welcoming Elijah, who promised that redemption will eventually come, and that Passover freedom will encompass the entire world. We also sing an additional song, the song of Israel's faithfulness to God even in the most difficult of times, even when God seemed silent and absent, *Ani Maamin* ("I believe"). I also, at this time, try to tell the story of Jewish commitment even in Auschwitz, after which we sing *HaTikva*.

At my Seder, the Israeli national anthem leads to the pouring of the fourth cup of wine over which we continue to recite the Hallel, the effusive praise to God for the miracle of freedom and as a testament to God's faithfulness to Elijah's promise of redemption and our appreciation of the restoration of our homeland in our lifetime and in our generation.

These four cups at our Seder correspond to the four expressions of redemption in Exodus 6:6–7: "I will *bring you out* from under the burdens of Egypt, and I will *save you* from their labor, and I will *redeem you* with an outstretched arm and with great judgments. And I will *take you to Me* as a people, and I will be to you a God."

It is very important to note that in the very next verse (v. 8) of the biblical passage we have just cited, there is a fifth expression of redemption, *veheveti* – "I will bring you" into the land. It is true that most Jews still drink only four cups of wine, and conclude the Seder with the drinking of this fourth cup. It is almost as if they have forgotten that now, two millennia after the destruction of the Second Temple, God has once again shown us His love, and we have lived up to the mutuality of our relationship by returning to our homeland, fighting for it, and building it into a magnificently developing new state in the family of nations.

Most Jews of our generation may have forgotten, but our traditional Haggada text, however, did not forget, and includes an addendum to the usual Hallel, a *Hallel HaGadol,* an "extra Hallel," whose refrain is *ki le'olam ḥasdo* ("Whose grace is upon the world") which emphasizes our duty to praise not only the God of Israel, but also the God of the entire world.

The Rambam teaches that it is proper, as we begin to praise the God of all of the families of the earth, to pour the fifth cup and recite this *Hallel HaGadol.*[39] The "headline" of this *Hallel HaGadol* is "Praise God for He is good, and his loving-kindness is *le'olam*" (Ps. 136:1), usually translated as "eternal," but which is literally translated as "for the world." The Haggada continues with further universal praises to God: "The soul of all living beings will bless Your Name" (the *Nishmat* prayer). This testifies to our understanding that, unless the world is free and independent, then we will not be truly free – because all of humanity is one large family.

The Seder helps us understand that the world must be involved in our thanksgiving to God; the world must understand that Israel has the right to be free and independent, and that if the whole world is not free, then we are not truly free – because the entire world is one family. And therefore many scholars throughout Jewish history, in addition to the Rambam, ordained that it is proper to say *Hallel HaGadol* over a fifth cup.[40] When we conclude this section, we drink the fifth cup not just to celebrate our freedom, but to express our prayer and our determination as God's partners to do our share to bring about freedom for the world.

I would like to suggest that the reason the fifth cup is not included in the traditional Seder is the result of Israel's long exile. This lacuna

39. *Mishneh Torah, Hilkhot Ḥametz UMatza* 8:10. He bases this codification on the Talmud's statement in Pesaḥim 118a: "The Rabbis taught: On the fifth cup, one completes the Hallel and recites *Hallel HaGadol;* these are the words of R. Tarfon." (Most manuscripts have the word "fifth." Some have the word "fourth." The Rambam clearly had "fifth," and so makes his suggestion for drinking a fifth cup over *Hallel HaGadol.*)

40. Rabbi Menachem Kasher (1895–1983) presents the case for drinking the fifth cup in great detail with full references to sources in his *Haggada Eretz Yisraelit* (Land of Israel Haggada; Committee for *Torah Shelema* in the United States, 1950), 179–205. Very interestingly, he presents a text from the Maharal of Prague (Rabbi Judah Loew ben Bezalael, 1512?–1609) showing that this great rabbi drank a fifth cup, and noting that "many great figures and righteous individuals followed him."

stems from the travails of exiles that spread the Jewish people throughout the world, weighing us down with trials and tribulations, and tragically, in living memory, a Holocaust. Under those conditions, we can well understand that the best we could hope for as an oppressed people was to aspire to a national redemption – a return home. Longing for full, universal redemption as represented by the fifth cup, was, perhaps, beyond our capabilities and even beyond our imagination. But since the fifth of Iyar 1948 we have returned home. After an almost two-thousand-year exile, our generation has experienced the fulfillment of God's promise to Mother Rachel: "And there is hope for your future, declares the Lord: Your children shall return to their [national] home" (Jer. 31:17). It is now incumbent for us to pray for the realization of God's ultimate promise of universal redemption. Now we can take a fifth cup, declaring our hope for – and faith in – a redemption, not only on behalf of the Jewish people in Israel, but for all people through freedom, independence, and peace.[41]

Just as we have known to respond to the sufferings of past exiles with *kinnot* on Tisha BeAv, it is now incumbent upon us to demonstrate our appreciation of the miracle of our return to Israel with a fifth cup. And having tasted the celebratory cup of national redemption, it would be an act of gross ingratitude were we not to pray for the ultimate, universal redemption of the world by means of a fifth cup and recitation of *Hallel HaGadol*.

41. We close our Seder with a rendition of *Ḥad Gadya*, a song that illustrates the cycle of attack, salvation, and just deserts. One approach suggests that the *gadya* – the kid – represents the people of Israel, "purchased," as it were, by *Abba* – God – with *trei zuzei* – two *zuz*, that is, the two Tablets of the Law. One oppressor follows another, but finally God Himself appears to set all right. That final appearance by God is a vision of ultimate redemption, deliverance for all mankind.

Chapter 13

Passover to Shavuot: Our Journey to Redemption

FREEDOM: THE MARCH FROM HOMELAND PROMISED TO HOMELAND ACHIEVED

The seven-week period between Passover, the Festival of Freedom, and Shavuot, literally the Festival of Weeks, but also described by our Sages as the Festival of the Giving of the Torah, is first and foremost the march from "homeland promised" to "homeland achieved." This period truly reflects and represents the political and spiritual journey of the Jewish people from slavery to our independent homeland, Israel, to God, and to redemption. Indeed, the famous biblical commentary of the Ramban sees this entire period as one mammoth holiday, beginning with Passover and concluding with Shavuot, with the intermediate days marked by a daily count of the intervening days and weeks.[1]

It is important to note that the opening festival of Passover, despite all of its pageantry and luster, is incomplete. Each of our major festivals is marked by the recital of the joyous Hallel prayer, which consists of six biblical chapters (Ps. 113–118), offering thanksgiving to God.

1. Ramban on Leviticus 23:36.

Regarding Passover, the complete version of this prayer is only recited on the first day of the festival. On the remaining six (or seven, in the Diaspora) days of the holiday, a shorter version (sometimes called "Half-Hallel") is said, which expresses a partial, not a complete, festival – a rejoicing, but a limited one.

The reason for this may be obvious to the reader of our previous chapter. Passover represents our birth as a nation, but one may very well argue that we cannot be a nation, in any real sense of the word, without a homeland, without our own land from which we can extract the natural resources, the fruits, grains, and vegetables which will enable us to subsist and develop on that land. Likewise, no national entity can feel safe without fixed and defensible borders that would keep our enemies out and that would provide us with the place and time to develop our own army to protect us. Moreover, the soul of a nation is its culture, the ethos by which it lives, the way it deals with the poor, the weak, and the infirm, how it relates to the strangers within its midst. Likewise, its national days of celebration and its days of mourning speak volumes about the human characteristics that the culture is trying to develop, as well as its national goals, dreams, and the ideals by which its people live, and for which they are willing to die.

Especially in the case of Israel, our cultural message of compassionate righteousness and moral justice – and not only those goals, but, even more importantly, how the members of its society must be taught to achieve those goals in their daily living – is one that we were Heaven-sent to share with all the families of the earth. And so, at the conclusion of Passover we are left with freedom from our slavery, but with only a promise of a homeland; we still have many wanderings, military battles, and desert tribulations to experience before we achieve our own homeland. Interestingly, from a calendrical and agricultural perspective, these are also the days when the grains of the land are ready to be harvested – at first, barley, which is animal food, and seven weeks later wheat, producing bread, regarded as the staff of human life. And so, in subsequent years, after we actually began to live on and work the earth of our land, we spend these days learning how to properly use the produce that we will then begin to harvest.

We begin the count of seven weeks – forty-nine days – from the time of our harvest of the initial produce of the earth, a measure (Omer) of barley, to our conclusion of the count when, in Temple times, we would bring two loaves of bread as the offering to God for the wheat which has been produced upon the earth of our "homeland achieved." Since the most desired, significant, and monumental purpose of our homeland is that it be a beacon for world peace and redemption, the fiftieth day is the festival of Shavuot, when we celebrate our gift of God's Torah – our legal and spiritual constitution – that will teach us how best to live our lives on this land as well as how to bring true blessings to all the families of the earth.

I would suggest that there is a great logic to the bringing of the Omer sacrifice on Passover and the wheat sacrifice at the conclusion of this period, on Shavuot. As we said at the outset, we are moving from Passover to Shavuot, from the promise of land-nation to the achievement of land-nation. We have already stated that the first and most basic aspect of the land is that it provides the nation that lives upon it with food for its subsistence. The Passover-Shavuot festival was created during the period of Jewish history in which the Israelites were an agrarian people, living by means of their agriculture. Shavuot is our harvest festival. We count the days between Passover and Shavuot in terms of the grains and the fruits that we are harvesting, beginning with the first ripened grain – barley – and culminating with the most central grain – the wheat – from which breads are made. Shavuot is also called the Festival of the First Fruits, and we especially bring to the Temple on Shavuot the special unique seven fruits/grains that are specifically indigenous to Israel – wheat, barley, grapes, figs, pomegranates, olives, and dates (Deut. 8:8).

Moreover, the fields of Israel are not only important because of the bounty that they produce; there are special agricultural commandments that are unique to Jewish culture. Every field-owner had to leave a portion of his field – known as *pe'ah*[2] – unattended at harvesttime, leaving it to the indigent to harvest and keep the produce, even though

2. See Leviticus 19:9: "And when you reap the harvest of your land, you shall not completely reap the corners of your field."

they owned no land of their own. Moreover, a certain percentage of the produce had to be tithed and given to the *kohen*-teacher – who also had no land of his own – and who was responsible to teach Torah to the rest of the tribes of Israel. Through the tithes, the *kohen*-educators of Israel were supported. Similarly, tithes were required to be given as well to the Levites, who also served as teachers, and to the poor. These indigents were likewise encouraged to roam about the field and collect fallen grain or leftover grain. All of this demonstrates the concern for the landless and the indigent, in a manner in which they retained their self-respect; they were not given handouts, but were provided with the opportunity of harvesting a field that belonged to others, but whose bounty and leftover produce would go to these "workers."[3]

Thus, the count of the Omer, which begins immediately after the first day of our celebration of the exodus from Egypt, reflects the necessity for a freed nation to have its own land for subsistence as well as for the establishment of the basic rules of giving to the poor, so important for a nation with a mission of teaching righteousness.[4]

DAYS OF THE OMER: FROM JOY TO MOURNING

Since we have already stated that Passover marks the love-engagement between God and Israel, as expressed in our reading on Passover of the Song of Songs, then Shavuot is the marriage between Israel and God, with the *ketuba* marriage contract being our sacred Torah which we received on Shavuot. Despite Hollywood fantasies, it must be recognized that although periods of engagement are usually punctuated with joyous experiences of togetherness, they may also contain times of uncertainty, ambiguity, and even separation. Despite this, the intelligent and sensitive couple (Couple) can utilize these challenges to help them grow into successful and fulfilled marital partners (Marital Partners). So

3. A great challenge nowadays is to transfer the concepts of these agricultural initiatives toward the poor to the post-industrial society in which we now live.
4. The Scroll of Ruth – which is read on Shavuot – portrays these mandated acts of loving-kindness connected with the fields in Israel in a dramatic and absorbing manner.

it is with Israel and God throughout history, a veritable romance, not without unfortunate moments of alienation and pain.

Our Sages – especially the Ramban – have taught us that what occurred to our forefathers in the Bible is a foreshadowing of that which will occur to their descendants in Jewish history. We have already analyzed the Hebrew calendar during the seven-week period between Passover and Shavuot from an agricultural and cultural perspective. Let us now see how our Hebrew calendar and the historical events that it marks teach a great deal about God, Israel, and history.

From this perspective, we can begin to understand the oscillating rollercoaster emotions of the days that follow the Passover holiday. Although we ended Passover with only Half-Hallel, we did, in fact, recite many psalms of praise and even concluded Passover on its last day with the exultant Song of the Jewish People at the Reed Sea. Nevertheless, the early Hebrews would still face a lengthy period of homeless wandering in a desert which often assailed them with its frigid nights and torrid days, a desert which was also hosting unfriendly nations ready to pounce upon our newly freed people devoid of a national homeland. We can certainly see how this period of wandering could very well foreshadow our eventual two-thousand-year-long exile without a homeland, culminating in the horrific European Holocaust.

DAYS OF THE OMER: INITIALLY JOYOUS DAYS OF A NATION SECURE WITH SOVEREIGNTY EARNED, BUT HISTORICALLY TURNED INTO A PERIOD OF MOURNING FOR SOVEREIGNTY LOST

During the biblical and First Temple periods, when, indeed, Joshua had already settled the Land of Israel as a Jewish state, the days of the Omer represented the march from "freedom promised" on Passover on the way to "freedom achieved" on Shavuot, marking the first barley harvest on Passover leading to the grain harvest and the loaves of Shavuot. Then, these were days of happy anticipation, of the completion of the grain harvest and the giving of the Torah, and this period is reflected very well by the statement of the Ramban we have previously cited – that the days between Passover and Shavuot were like one long festival. During the

First Temple period and then until the time just before the destruction of the Second Temple, we were joyously fulfilled by living in freedom on our own land, in our own nation-state.

However, the Hebrew calendar is a concentrated picture of all of Jewish history. As a consequence, the days between Passover and Shavuot took on a melancholy hue when, in later years, these days would become days of semi-mourning.

At the end of the period of the Second Temple, Judea was attacked by the all-powerful Rome; our Temple was destroyed in 70 CE; we no longer had independence; we could not bring our first fruits and grains to the Holy Temple, which was no more, and Jewish sovereignty had come to an end. It was at that time that Rabban Yoḥanan b. Zakkai, the outstanding Jewish leader of that period, asked the about-to-be Roman emperor Vespasian (then the general in charge of the Temple's destruction) to grant the surviving Jews the right to live in Judea, albeit without Jewish sovereignty and so without their capital city of Jerusalem, but under the religious guidance of the Sages of the Sanhedrin, then having been exiled to Yavneh. Rabban Yoḥanan b. Zakkai believed that it would be possible for Israel to live, and perhaps even to flourish, without national independence and sovereignty, as long as we had the protection of the Roman Empire and as long as we could continue our religious way of life with our Great Sanhedrin of seventy-one Sages interpreting halakha and granting us religious independence. Hence, it was for that religious independence that Rabban Yoḥanan requested of Vespasian, "Grant me Yavneh and her Sages."

However, some six decades later, the great Rabbi Akiva took a very different position (according to one citation in the Talmud – Gittin 56b), sharply impugning Rabban Yoḥanan b. Zakkai's decision by quoting a maligning verse from Isaiah 44:25: "(Sometimes) God turns Sages backward and makes of their wisdom foolishness." Rabbi Akiva blatantly held that without a Holy Temple and sovereignty in the Holy Land, the Jewish people could never depend upon the goodwill of the Roman government and would never have true independence and religious freedom without national power and sovereignty. Certainly, under such conditions, with a powerless Jewish people deprived of an independent sovereign state, the Jewish message of compassionate righteousness and moral justice would never be accepted by the rest of the nations of the world. From Rabbi Akiva's perspective, Rabban Yoḥanan asked for too little, too late.

And so, along with his general Bar Kokhba, a religious leader in his own right and whom Rabbi Akiva believed to be the Messiah (the leader of Israel at the time of Redemption), Rabbi Akiva promoted an all-out rebellion against Roman rule. And, indeed, it seemed that Rabbi Akiva was vindicated when Bar Kokhba reestablished Jewish sovereignty and even minted Jewish coins as a medium of exchange. But, alas, after three and a half years of battle, just when it looked as if the Jews might actually prevail, Rome reinforced its legions under a new and powerful general, Gaius Julius Severus, and quelled the rebellion. Bar Kokhba was killed, and Rabbi Akiva and many other Jewish Sages lost their lives during the Hadrianic persecutions that followed the devastating failure of the rebellion (Berakhot 61b).[5]

The Talmud (Yevamot 62b) records that 24,000 of Rabbi Akiva's students died during the Omer period between Passover and Shavuot. Rav Sherira Gaon (906–1006) in his famous *Epistle*, an authoritative history of the composition of the Talmud, states that these students died from *shemada* – religious persecution – presumably during their rebellion against Rome and in the later persecution against the Jews by the Romans.[6] According to the Talmud, their deaths were due to the fact that "they did not accord each other proper respect," which may well refer to the disunity among the Jews themselves as they argued whether or not to pursue rebellion against Rome. Whatever the reasons for this tragedy, these days of the Omer between Passover and Shavuot have become days of semi-mourning for the Jewish people, when it is prohibited to hold weddings and other group celebrations.[7]

---

5. Rabbi Akiva was one of the ten martyrs killed under Hadrian's rule. These ten great Torah scholars are memorialized it two separate liturgical poems, one of which is recited on Yom Kippur and the other on Tisha BeAv.
6. *Epistle of Rabbeinu Sherira Gaon, ḥelek* 1, *perek* 1 (Jerusalem: Keren Ne'emana Publishing, 5727), 23.
7. Chillingly, about a thousand years after these events, and, ironically, during the same period of the year, between Passover and Shavuot, many of the great Ashkenazi Jewish communities along the Rhine were destroyed by the waves of ransacking

The failure of Rabbi Akiva's rebellion can be seen as changing the entire course of Jewish history by offering support to a fascinating passage in the Talmud (Ketubot 111a) which sets forth three oaths that the Almighty presented, two to the Jews, and one to the gentiles of the world. In this dialogue, God adjures the Jewish people "not to storm the ramparts of Israel," that is, not to forcibly take sovereignty in the Land of Israel, and not to rebel against the nations of the world. In turn, God has the nations of the world vow not to oppress the Jews excessively. The theme of this talmudic statement is that we must not try to "rush" redemption; we must not forcefully bring about Jewish sovereignty, but must wait for God to send His Messiah at the proper time.[8]

Christian Crusaders on their way to the Holy Land to "rescue" it from the Moslems. The rabbis of these communities – called the Tosafists, some of the greatest Torah scholars in Jewish history – were very punctilious about Jewish observance, including interpersonal relationships, but they seemed to care very little about Jerusalem and the Land of Israel. Even when the Christians were marching toward Jerusalem to liberate the Holy Land from Saracen rule, these rabbis of the Rhineland remained apathetic about our homeland. Rabbi Yaakov Emden (1697–1776) relates to this in the introduction to his famous *Siddur,* where he emphasizes repeatedly what he sees as the unfortunate failing during this period, because of Jewish apathy regarding the Land of Israel and the possibility of a return to it. The murder and destruction by the Crusaders of European Jewish communities, especially during this period between Passover and Shavuot, is yet another reason for the period of partial mourning during this time of year. Rabbi Jonathan Sacks suggests that these two tragic historical reasons for the mourning of the Omer period explain the two different customs as to when during the Omer the mourning is to be observed: from Passover until Lag BaOmer (the thirty-third day of the Omer), or from Rosh Ḥodesh Iyar until Shavuot. The earlier period of mourning relates to the death of the students of Rabbi Akiva in the Bar Kokhba rebellion and the Hadrianic persecutions, whereas the later period relates to the Rhineland massacres at the time of the Crusades. In the words of Rabbi Sacks, "The Rhineland Massacres took place during the latter weeks of the Omer.… Later, the mourning customs of the Omer were associated with the same period. The Sephardi communities of Spain and Portugal were unaffected by the Crusades, so they continued the earlier custom of mourning for the victims of the Bar Kokhba revolt" (Rabbi Jonathan Sacks, *Ceremony and Celebration: Introduction to the Holidays* [Jerusalem/New York: Maggid Books and The Orthodox Union, 2017], 223).

8. The trauma of the failure of the Bar Kokhba rebellion was probably responsible for the reluctance of the Jewish people to attempt to return to their homeland for the last two millennia. Many rabbinic sages believe that, after the Holocaust, the nations

It is very instructive to study the recounting of Rabbi Akiva's martyrdom within the talmudic text itself (Berakhot 61b):

> When Rabbi Akiva was taken out to be executed, it was the time to recite the *Shema.* As he was being brutally tortured by the Romans with iron combs, he accepted the yoke of the Kingship of Heaven [by reciting the words of the *Shema*: "Hear O Israel, the Lord is our God, the Lord is One"]. His students, observing this, cried out, "Our teacher – even to this point?!" [as if to say, "Does your subservience to God even extend to reciting the *Shema* at the proper time despite the torture to which you are being subjected?"]. To which Rabbi Akiva responded by saying, "All of my life I was troubled by the verse [following the *Shema* verse] 'You shall love the Lord your God... with all of your soul [which is interpreted as] even if He should take your soul.' I would constantly pray, 'When will it come to my hand to observe this command?' And now that it has come to my hand, should I not observe it?!" [He then recited the *Shema* again,] prolonging [the word] *Eḥad* (One) until his soul left him.

A careful reading of this text shows that in the moments before he died, Rabbi Akiva recited the *Shema*, not only once, but a second time. Why? He had already recited the *Shema* at its proper time! I believe that the first time he was reciting the *Shema* in accordance with the command to recite those words each day. The second time, he was giving a critical message to his disciples, for all generations. The meaning of the *Shema* is that the Lord of Love who is presently only our God will ultimately be the God accepted by the entire world – and, indeed, it is our task to convey this ideal to all the families of the earth. Rabbi Akiva, with his dying breath, was teaching his disciples, and, through them the entire nation for all generations, that we must never be satisfied merely by our own religious independence. We must never give up the goal of a national

had certainly disregarded their oath not to oppress the Jews excessively, and once the United Nations granted us our national rights to Israel in 1947, we then had every right to resettle the land and attempt to liberate it.

state and the importance of our teaching a universal acceptance of the one God by all of humanity, the Lord of love, peace, and redemption. In the words of the prophet Zechariah (14:9): "And God shall be sovereign over all the earth; in that day there shall be one God with one name."

We must rather die than transgress this critical precept.

THE HOLOCAUST CHANGES THE ARGUMENT

In a certain sense, the Holocaust declared the difference of opinion between Rabban Yoḥanan b. Zakkai and Rabbi Akiva as moot, and rendered the laissez-faire position of the Jewish leaders during the period of the Crusades – in retrospect – as untenable. With no nation-state, army, police force, or even political representation, European Jewry was doomed. This immense tragedy startled us into understanding the correctness of Rabbi Akiva's view, and stresses the fact that without a sovereign nation we could never depend on maintaining religious independence, and we certainly would never be able to give our message of freedom and redemption to the world.

Another message that arose from the Holocaust was "Never again," inspired in good part by the amazing near-success of the uprising of the Jews in the Warsaw Ghetto which began on April 19, 1943.[9] At the very time that European Jews were in the midst of an Egypt-like experience of servitude imposed by the Nazis, a kind of reversion to life before the

9. There were two initial Jewish resistance groups in the ghetto: The Jewish Fighting Organization (ZOB) and the Jewish Military Union (ZZW), both made up mainly of various Zionist youth movements. The Nazis began the final deportations from the ghetto on April 19, 1943, the eve of Passover. The fighting groups and ghetto inhabitants barricaded themselves in bunkers and hideouts, their demonstrations of resistance taking the Germans by surprise. The ZOB scattered its positions throughout the ghetto; the ZZW did most of its fighting at Muranowska Square, impeding the Germans' attempts to penetrate their defenses. In response, the Germans began to systematically burn down the buildings, turning the ghetto into a firetrap. The Jews fought valiantly for a month until the Germans took over the focal points of resistance. It was the first popular uprising in a city in Nazi-occupied Europe, an amazing feat for the ghetto residents who were horribly food-deprived and were able to secure very limited arms and ammunition. See www.yadvashem.org/holocaust/about/combat-resistance/warsaw-ghetto.html.

Exodus, this brave action – and others like it – was the result of the clear message which arose from the Nazi horror: we Jews must understand that the truest message of the Exodus is our necessity of taking responsibility for our freedom into our own hands, by waging war against the Nazi captors and putting our lives on the line. At this point, and after two thousand years of exile, it became indubitably clear that ultimately, there could never be a free Jewish people without an independent State of Israel. And so it was that the majority of the groups that rebelled in the Warsaw Ghetto were Zionist organizations. It was as if the Jewish people were declaring, echoing American revolutionary patriot Patrick Henry, "Give us liberty, or give us death." We understood that post-Holocaust, we would, once again, as we did when we left Egypt, have to take responsibility to turn our freedom from this latter-day slavery into our becoming an independent nation.

THE THIRD COMMONWEALTH: FROM MOURNING TO NEW FESTIVALS

We have now entered a new phase in Jewish history – the third commonwealth, two thousand years after the second commonwealth was destroyed, and more than eighty years after the Holocaust. So let us now take a deep look at our renewed Hebrew calendar today, and its additions for the first time in the last two millennia.

Yom HaShoah – Holocaust Memorial Day

Let us briefly return to the conclusion of the festival of Passover, our exodus from Egypt, the miracle of the Reed Sea, and the lessons taught by God about responsibility for freedom.

Our first new day of mourning is Yom HaShoah, the day in commemoration of those who perished in the Nazi Holocaust. In 1951, the State of Israel mandated the twenty-seventh of Nisan as the national memorial day for the victims of the Holocaust, known as *Yom HaShoah VeHaGevura* – Holocaust and Heroism Memorial Day – often shortened to Yom HaShoah, Holocaust Day. The Israeli government chose the date for this commemoration because of its proximity to the date of the Warsaw Ghetto Uprising, emphasizing the message we have analyzed deeply, going back to God's words at the Reed Sea, that to gain freedom we must become partners with God, and do our very best to take our destiny into our own hands in expressing the responsibility of freedom. What the Jewish people now understood completely was that the Holocaust was almost an inevitable result of what would happen to them without an independent state. We mourn those who lost their lives in the Holocaust on Yom HaShoah during the memorial days of the Omer-count with the pledge of "Never again" in our minds and in our hearts.

In Israel the day is felt very deeply, with many remembrance ceremonies, elegies, and prayers. At 10:00 am, sirens blare throughout the country, ushering in two minutes of silent reflection. People stand and pause in silence in their homes and on the sidewalks. Cars stop in the road; children in school and adults in the workplace stand at attention and ponder the horrific depths of evil to which human beings are capable of sinking. At the same time, everyone is resolute about the necessity for Israel to be a secure and powerful nation-state from which to teach the world divine morality and the hope for redemption. Although it may be true that power corrupts and that absolute power corrupts absolutely, the greatest corruption comes from powerlessness which enables the world to succumb to the forces of evil.

Yom HaZikaron, Memorial Day for the Fallen Soldiers: The Privilege of Shedding Blood for Our Independence

Just a few days after Yom HaShoah falls the Memorial Day for Israel's Fallen Soldiers, Yom HaZikaron. In our time the Jews have proven that they have learned the lesson of their history, beginning with the Warsaw Ghetto Uprising and continuing with the War of Independence in 1948, in which six thousand Israelis were killed and fifteen thousand wounded, many of them rising from the ashes of the Holocaust to join in the battle against the Arab nations. It is important to note that the Arab countries attacked us, with the intention of destroying the nascent state, immediately after the state was declared by Ben-Gurion on the fifth of Iyar, May 14, 1948, a declaration that was in consonance with the United Nations decision, voted upon and passed on November 29, 1947. In addition, throughout the state's short history, there have been many wars and terrorist attacks in which thousands of Israelis have perished. With great sensitivity, the founders of the state decided that the day prior to Israel Independence Day be declared as the Remembrance Day for Fallen Soldiers, on which bereaved families and friends visit military cemeteries throughout the country, and ceremonies are held in memory of those who died so that the Jewish State of Israel may live.

Once again, the mixture of emotion reigns: The sadness of Yom HaZikaron is expressed in the same way as was done on Yom HaShoah – with remembrance sirens, moments of silence, elegies, and prayers for those lost – and then leads into the heady optimism of Independence Day which follows immediately, as the eternal Jewish story is retold for our day. Memorial tears merge with the Independence Day joy; the lesson of the juxtaposition of these two days is that being a Jew means belonging to a most exalted but dangerous profession. We are taught by our Sages that we must initiate redemption, but that the price will always be high; we will pay with our blood.

Allow me two personal reflections surrounding the most difficult aspect of serving as a rabbi and attempting to bring comfort while informing a beloved congregant that s/he has just lost a child in a war or in a terrorist murder. In carrying out this most difficult pastoral imperative, I have met true Israeli heroes in the most profound sense of the term.

The first is Rav Ohad Taharlev, dean of our Army Torah Program for Women, who lost his son Elhai in a terror attack near Ofra in 2017. He gave the eulogy for his son, which will be seared in my consciousness for as long as I live. Allow me to attempt to present what I remember were his words:

> At times like these we always quote the difficult but magnificent verse from the prophet Ezekiel (16:6), "When I passed by you, and I saw you weltering in your blood, I said to you: 'By your blood you shall live,' and I said to you: 'By your blood you shall live.'" Our Rabbis teach us that the prophet is here speaking of two types of blood: the blood of circumcision and the blood of the Paschal sacrifice. The blood of circumcision represents the fate of the Jew who must suffer and shed blood at the hands of the powerful despots throughout history who have anti-Semitically murdered Jews because we gave the world a morality of compassion and goodness,

> our legacy from the God of Love whom they wished to destroy, a morality which attempted to limit their unbridled animalistic power. That was the blood of Yom HaShoah. But there is also a second blood, the blood of the Paschal sacrifice, the blood that must be shed when we take the responsibility of fighting for our freedom. That is the blood for the sake of Israeli independence and human freedom. With all of my tears, I give great thanks to God that my son was a Paschal sacrifice. That is the blood, not of Jewish fate, but rather of Jewish destiny.[10]

The second hero was one of my closest friends, Mordecai Goodman, of blessed memory, who was a member of my congregation in New York, who taught me how to swim, who came with us to Efrat, and who, with his wife Anne, was blessed with nine children. He was a very popular figure, the owner of what was the very first pizzeria in town. His son Yosef was always a bit mischievous, a master at clever, funny, and always harmless pranks. Yosef was accepted into the elite paratroopers unit of the Israeli Army. It fell to me to tell Mordecai and Anne that their son had fallen to his death during a training exercise. His parachute became entangled with the parachute of his commanding officer. He had only a few seconds to make a most fateful decision: If he did nothing, the greatest chances were that both he and his commander would fall to their deaths. However, if he was able to extricate his parachute from that of his commander, those extra seconds would probably cost him his life, but there was a chance that the commander would live. He chose the second option. Yosef died; his commanding officer lived.

I spent most of the night before the funeral sitting with Mordecai and his family, and I left at two o'clock in the morning. When Mordecai took me to the door, he said, "Rabbi, I have one request. In your eulogy for my son, I don't want you to say – as I've heard you say in many instances – 'This is the price of aliya (moving to Israel).' It isn't the price of aliya; it's the *zekhut* (the privilege) of aliya." In our generation,

10. Rabbi Joseph B. Soloveitchik, in his classic *Kol Dodi Dofek* (The Voice of My Beloved Knocks) makes similar distinctions between what he calls "the Covenant of Destiny" and "the Covenant of Fate."

we have the great privilege of being able to give up our lives, not on the altar of anti-Semitic murderers, but for the sake of a world of Jewish independence on the road to redemption.

Hope Reborn: Israel Independence Day

Immediately following Yom HaZikaron falls Israel Independence Day, or, as it is called in Hebrew, Yom HaAtzma'ut. This day, the fifth of the Jewish month of Iyar, was the date on which Israel was declared as a state in 1948. Leading up to this great moment were the activities of Theodor Herzl, living in Vienna, who published his book *The Jewish State* in 1896. The book argued that only by means of a Jewish state will the Jewish people have true freedom devoid of anti-Semitism, with the ability to express their culture freely, and practice their religion without hindrance. Herzl's book heralded the beginning of modern Zionism, and led, ultimately, to the creation of the state.

As noted, the nations of the world gathered at the United Nations on November 29, 1947, and voted on the partition plan that offered, for the first time in almost two thousand years, a homeland for the Jewish people in the Land of Israel. Perhaps this step was necessary in order to undo one of "three oaths" that were imposed by God at the time of the destruction of the Second Temple – that the Jewish people not "storm the ramparts of Israel," that is, not to forcibly take sovereignty in the Land of Israel. In a moving description of the event, basing himself on a homiletical interpretation of the Beloved seeking His loved one in the Song of Songs, my *rebbe*, Rabbi Soloveitchik, presents that event as follows:

> I do not know who the representatives of the press, with their human eyes, saw to be the chairman in that fateful session of the General Assembly in which the creation of the State of Israel was decided, but he who looked carefully with his spiritual eye saw the true Chairman who conducted the proceedings – the Beloved. He knocked with his gavel on the lectern. Do we not interpret the passage "On that night the *king* could not sleep" (Est. 6:1) as meaning that the *King of the Universe* could not sleep? If Ahasuerus alone had been sleepless, the matter would not have been at all important and salvation would not have arisen on that

> night. If, however, the King, the Master of the Universe, could not sleep, as it were, redemption would be born. If just anyone were to have opened the session of the United Nations, the State of Israel would not have been born. But it was the Beloved who rapped on the Chairman's lectern, and the miracle materialized. Listen! My Beloved knocks![11]

Rabbi Soloveitchik viewed the establishment of the state as an active appearance of God on the world stage, showing, for all to see, His love of the Jewish people. Writing in 1956, he described the loving God's appearance as follows:

> Eight years ago, in the midst of a night of the terrors of Majdanek, Treblinka, and Buchenwald; in a night of gas chambers and crematoria; in a night of total divine self-concealment; in a night ruled by the devil of doubt and destruction who sought to sweep the Lover from her own tent into the Catholic Church; in a night of continuous searching for the Beloved – on that very night the Beloved appeared. The Almighty, who was hiding in His splendid sanctum, suddenly appeared and began to beckon at the tent of the Lover, who tossed and turned on her bed beset by convulsions and the agonies of hell. Because of the beating and knocking at the door of the mournful Lover, the State of Israel was born.[12]

Independence Day is celebrated in Israel – and around the Jewish world – with great joy and thanksgiving. Hallel is sung with great emotion at night as well as during the day, and festive meals, often featuring outdoor barbecues, are held. From virtually all perspectives, the establishment and flourishing of the State of Israel is seen as a miracle, but a miracle brought about through the partnership of God with the Jewish people, determined to take responsibility for their freedom.

---

11. This is the first of Rav Soloveitchik's "Six Knocks." See *Kol Dodi Dofek: Listen, My Beloved Knocks* (KTAV Publishing House, 2006), accessible online at https://www.sefaria.org.il/Kol_Dodi_Dofek%2C_Six_Knocks.
12. Ibid.

Yom Yerushalayim, Jerusalem Day: Even Closer Toward Redemption

The newest of the "new" festivals that fall between Passover and Shavuot is Yom Yerushalayim, Jerusalem Day, celebrated on the twenty-eighth of Iyar, the date during the Six-Day War of 1967 on which the full city of Jerusalem was liberated and united.

The war began as a result of Israel's preemptive attack launched in response to Egypt's expulsion of United Nations peacekeeping forces in the Sinai Peninsula and Arab threat to "push the Jews into the sea." Facing three armies – Syria to the north, Jordan to the east, and Egypt to the south – Israel found herself surrounded by the combined forces of her neighbors. Early news from the Arab countries falsely told of Tel Aviv's destruction and Israel's impending obliteration. The actuality was that Israel won a stunning victory, the marvel of the world, crowned by the liberation and uniting of the full city of Jerusalem. For the first time in two millennia, Jews had control over the Old City of Jerusalem and the very ground upon which both the First and Second Temples stood. After so many years of dreaming and praying, we had regained our full historic and eternal capital, the symbol of our sovereignty over the Land of Israel, and of God's sovereignty. And so, we once again recite the joyous Hallel on that day, for the miraculous victory in the war and the eternal miracle of Jerusalem.

However, our sovereignty over Jerusalem is only a first step; we must see ourselves as the stewards over Jerusalem, until, ultimately, God's sovereignty will reign over the world from Jerusalem, and world redemption will emanate from that holy city.[13] We express both of those ideas in our daily prayers: "Dwell within Jerusalem Your city as You have promised; may the throne of David be quickly established within her; build her with an everlasting building, soon and in our days."[14]

The prophet Isaiah, in presenting his vision of redemption, calls out, "Comfort you, comfort you (*Naḥamu naḥamu*), My people, speak

13. Admittedly, the nations of the world – even nations with which we have good relations – have not yet truly accepted our sovereignty over Jerusalem. In truth, we are, at best, only stewards over the city until God's sovereignty is recognized by all.
14. Daily *Amida* prayer, version of the Oriental Jewish communities, also the version used by Rabbi Joseph B. Soloveitchik. This particular version makes the return to Jerusalem a two-pronged process: the first being the kingship of the dynasty of King

about Heart-Jerusalem (*Lev-Yerushalayim*), and call out unto her; her period [of exile] has been completed, her iniquity has been forgiven" (40:1–2).

Note that the prophet refers to the city as "Heart-Jerusalem," a compound noun; it is "heart" that defines Jerusalem, the love which is the emotion of the heart, the love of God, the love of Israel, and the love of humanity. This is what Rabbi Zvi Yehuda Kook likely referred to when he said of the Western Wall, "There are hearts and there are hearts. There are human hearts and there are hearts of stone. There are stones and there are stones. There are silent stones, and there are stones which are hearts." Such are the heart-stones of the Western Wall; such is Jerusalem – heart-stone.[15]

According to all of our prophets, this message will be conveyed at the end of days from the Holy Temple in Jerusalem, to which all the nations will flock. At that time, they will beat their swords into plowshares, forsake entirely the cultivation of warfare (see Isaiah chapter 2, Micah chapter 4), and "the nations will change to speak a pure language; they will all call upon the name of God and serve Him with a united resolve" (Zeph. 3:9). The love that will emanate from Jerusalem will be a love without cause – *ahavat ḥinam* – for all humanity, repairing the hatred without cause that brought about Jerusalem's demise in the first place. Jerusalem will actually become the embodiment of our mission: it will represent the rule of God over a world at peace – the actual meaning of the name "Jerusalem," being "City of Peace."

It is fitting that this "new" group of festivals between Passover and Shavuot be brought to a climax by Yom Yerushalayim, with its message being the universal message of Judaism itself: love, partnership with God, and world redemption.

David, and the second step being the "everlasting building" of Jerusalem with God as Sovereign over the entire world – *binyan olam* – understood as a building for the entire world.

15. From an article, "Behind our Wall," published in 1939, reprinted in Rav Kook's *LiNetivot Yisrael*, vol. 1, 1967.

Chapter 14

Shavuot: A Festival of Anticipation

Shavuot is a holiday that celebrates anticipation. In that light, I would like to relate to two foundational questions about the holiday.

The first question: Although the Bible instructs us to count fifty days (Lev. 23:16), in truth we only count forty-nine days, and, moreover, the name of this concluding festival is Shavuot, which means "weeks." Every other festival has a name which describes the manner in which it is observed,[1] whereas here the name of this festival is a period of time that seems to end without the last fiftieth day's count.

Secondly, we have noted that we bring two loaves of bread as our Shavuot gift sacrifice. If, indeed, Passover and Shavuot are seen as

1. For example, the festival of Sukkot reflects the main commandment of the festival, dwelling in the temporary structure of the sukka. The festival of Passover colloquially is called Pesaḥ, after the Paschal sacrifice that was offered on the eve of the holiday, and is referred to in the prayers as *Ḥag HaMatzot,* the Festival of Matzot, referring, of course, to the main commandment at the Seder, to eat the matza.

one great festival – at least according to the Ramban – is it not strange that the major gift sacrifice of Shavuot should be that very bread that is forbidden on Passover?

The very name of the holiday – "Weeks" – demonstrates the notion of anticipation. The holiday is not named for itself, so to speak, but rather for the seven weeks of anticipation which led up to it. In a certain sense, Shavuot, with its unique name, is a kind of continuation of the Counting of the Omer period, a time of the achievement of a very significant goal, but still a time of anticipation of even greater things to come.[2]

2. There are two different customs as to the final word of each day's Omer count between Passover and Shavuot. The formula, according to all, is to say: "Today is the such-and-such day, being such-and-such weeks and such-and-such days..." According to some, the final word is *laOmer,* "toward the Omer." According to others, the word is *baOmer,* "within the midst of the Omer." Rabbi Soloveitchik's custom was to count twice – using both variants.

I would suggest that *laOmer* means "toward the anticipated goal of the Omer" and that *baOmer* refers to the preparation necessary if the goal is to be reached. This would mean that anticipation requires preparation if the goal is to be reached, especially this most desirable goal of sovereignty over Jerusalem and the world's acceptance of the Torah's values of universal love and peace. To reach these lofty and crucial goals, we must prepare ourselves ethically and spiritually. Hence, if the goal was to be entering our Promised Land, the way to prepare ourselves was by beginning to till the land and to make certain that we do it in such a way as to leave the gifts for the poor and for the national educators (priests and Levites) in order to demonstrate that we are worthy of the land, that we understand that a landowner must recognize his responsibility for the weaker elements of society.

We have mentioned before, however, that the Jewish message is not merely for *Jewish* freedom and independence in the Land of Israel. Rather, our vision has always been for the entire world to become free, and, indeed, in a global village, it is doubtful that one nation can ever be free unless all nations become free. Thus, the anticipation of the Omer period, culminating in Shavuot, will not be realized when we bring the first fruits from the Land of Israel to the Temple. It will only be realized at a future time when "liberty will be proclaimed throughout the world," and then all nations will be blessed through us with the greatest blessing of all – freedom.

SHAVUOT – OUR ACHIEVEMENT OF INDEPENDENT LIFE IN THE LAND OF ISRAEL

Shavuot demonstrates for us that we are proceeding along the road to redemption. Passover, as we have explained, was just the beginning of our journey. On Passover our sense of incompleteness was profound, since we did not even as yet have our own homeland without which we could never be free, nor did we have at that time an indigenous Jewish culture that would enable us to develop in a unique way our image of God. Although it is true that we had left the bonds of slavery, since we were not yet in our free homeland we recite only "Half-Hallel," and at the Seder we eat matza – the not yet leavened, still unrisen bread – over which we declare: "This is [still] the bread of affliction." It is only on Shavuot, seven weeks later, when we are commanded to bring risen, leavened bread as an offering in the Temple. We bring this bread to symbolize that we are coming closer to "freedom achieved." As if to strengthen this point, our calendar teaches us that after the taste of freedom that we were promised by God with our hasty escape from Egypt, we experience the harbinger of the ultimate redemption with Yom HaAtzma'ut and Yom Yerushalayim that fall out during the period of counting to Shavuot.

With Yom HaAtzma'ut we understood that we must partner with God in establishing our freedom – even as far as initiating the first steps – and with Yom Yerushalayim we understood that our ultimate goal is to enjoy national sovereignty in a world of universal peace.

Partnership with God is magnificently symbolized by bread, still very much the symbol of a formal meal and which initially was the main portion of every meal. Egypt, many millennia ago, actually enabled agriculture to leap ahead of its time with the Gift of the Nile processing the eleven steps in the manufacture of bread.[3] We may very well harvest God's gift of wheat, but only we humans can turn that wheat into bread, and only through the complex process of bread making. All of this demonstrates that we and God must feel ourselves to be true partners in producing the "staff of life."[4] At the Shabbat table, which generally has at its

3. As delineated in Shabbat 73a.
4. To further emphasize the idea of bread symbolizing the partnership between ourselves and God, I heard from my *rebbe* Rav Soloveitchik the following point: Whereas

center the Sabbath candlesticks and two loaves of *ḥalla* bread, there is a time-honored Jewish custom wherein the host of the meal places his/her two hands over the *ḥalla*, reciting the special blessing "Who brings forth bread from the earth." What is the reason for this custom, especially as the blessing states that it was *God* who brought forth the bread from the earth? I believe that this custom emphasizes and declares that God and we, together, bring forth bread from the earth, that God and we are partners. Bread stands as a model of how our national freedom must be achieved: great human endeavor in collaboration with God.[5]

TWO REVELATIONS: THE WRITTEN LAW AND THE ORAL LAW

In order to understand the real significance of Shavuot, we must explore in greater depth the two revelations at Sinai. Yes, the *two* revelations, which are symbolized by the two different sets of tablets. Indeed, the first tablets really did not "work." When Moses witnessed the behavior of the Israelites with the Golden Calf, just forty days after the first revelation at Sinai, he actually smashed the first tablets. It was only on the tenth day of Tishrei, Yom Kippur, that God forgave the Jewish people for their sin of the Golden Calf, and then informed Moses, with the words "Hew out for yourself two tablets of stone," that there was to be a second revelation (Ex. 34:1). What was different about these second tablets that would make them more likely to succeed, given the failure of the first? And why did God command *Moses* to hew them out of stone, as opposed to the first tablets which God Himself hewed?

Midrash Rabba, on the very verse in which God commands Moses to hew out the tablets of stone for the second revelation, explains the specific background for God's request:

---

after consuming any of the seven special fruits/grains by which the Land of Israel is praised, we only recite one blessing (the *Al HaMiḥya/Al HaPerot*), we recite four blessings after eating bread. The Rav stated that this difference demonstrates that "true sanctity comes from human input," i.e., our "partnership of bread."

5. The halakhic commentary *Mishna Berura* states that the ten fingers of the two hands mirror the ten words of the bread blessing.

> [Moses] began to feel pained that he had broken the tablets, but God told him: Do not feel pained about the first tablets, for they only contained the Ten Commandments. But the second tablets that I am giving you [will contain much more material; they] will have halakhot (laws), midrashim (exegetical interpretations), and aggadot (non-legal philosophical and poetic material). (Exodus Rabba 46:1)

This additional material – the halakhot, midrashim, and aggadot – are all part of what is known as the Oral Law, which contains exegetical interpretations and additions to the Torah by the great rabbinical Sages of each generation.

Judaism is our romance with God – our love partnership. Just as we learned from Passover that we are God's partners in bringing about historical events leading to our freedom, so we learn from Shavuot that we must be His partners in the ultimate interpretation of Torah throughout the generations. And, indeed, God's Torah was given four thousand years ago; in order for Torah to be relevant for all generations, it had to deal with new realities in science, medicine, and technology, as well as with societal changes such as issues of gender and our relationship with the gentile world. At the same time, we must make certain that the original ideals of the Torah – the importance of freedom for every individual, compassionate sensitivity for every human being – remain paramount despite the generational changes. Moreover, God believed, as it were, that only if Israel will take a partner's ownership of Torah will Israel truly feel responsibility for Torah and teach it to the world. This would only be possible if it is not only God's Torah, but if it becomes our Torah as well. God's Torah must have human input.

Hence, throughout Jewish history, there were bodies of Jewish Sages – first "the Sages of the Great Assembly" and then "the Great Sanhedrin" – which dealt with Jewish law during both of our original commonwealths. Subsequent to these institutions, we have always had authoritative Jewish rabbinic leadership – courts of Jewish law, learned and even charismatic Torah leaders – who continue to write talmudic interpretations and religio-legal responsa. These are all included in the Oral Law of God's second revelation.

It is fascinating that the biblical discussion of the second revelation is within the context of Moses's heartfelt question to God, "Reveal to me Your glory" (Ex. 33:18), which means "Your attributes." The Hebrew word *kavod* (glory), when applied to God (*kevod Hashem*), refers to the manifestation of God's presence in this world. The source is Isaiah 6:3: "Holy, holy, holy is the Lord of Hosts, the whole earth is filled with His glory (*kavod*)." When Moses asks God, "Show me Your glory," he is asking regarding God's presence in the physical world, which certainly refers to the biblical commandment of how human beings should live their lives by walking in God's ways (Deut. 28:9). Moses is asking: What kind of God are You who leads the world here on earth? Are You a demanding God, or a forgiving God? A God of strict justice, or a God of unconditional love? Who are You – in a way that I may be able to understand You and Your ways, Your attributes in this world; only then can we comprehend and understand how to walk in Your paths.

God responds to Moses that humans will never be able to understand Him completely, to see His face, as it were, but that God will now show him His back, a partial understanding of the Divine which will be possible for humans to understand. This second revelation will take place in the cleft of the rock at Mount Sinai. So ends chapter 33 of Exodus.

Strangely enough, chapter 34, which I would have expected to open with God's revelation of His attributes, instead begins with a commandment to Moses: "Hew out for yourself two tablets." As we have explained, in the first revelation, God Himself gave His Torah, including the fashioning of the tablets and their letters. In answer to the question we posed previously, in the second revelation, it is Moses, representing human rabbinic leadership in every generation, who is to hew out the stones. This is the manner in which God is expressing the necessary human input into a Torah which must be relevant for all generations. The hewing of the stone by Moses is a kind of metaphor for the interpretations of the Jewish sages throughout the generations.

In the fifth verse of this chapter God responds to Moses's earlier request as to the nature of His attributes, calling out that He is the "Lord of Love, Lord of Love, God who is compassionate and gracious, slow to anger, abounding in loving-kindness and truth, guarding loving-kindness for thousands [of generations], bearing sin, transgression, and wrongdoing, and purifying."[6] Indeed, this is an unequivocal statement that these attributes must be the fundamental context from which the human interpretations of the Torah of all generations must be made.

It must be remembered that the fundamental basis for the various interpretations of the biblical law for each generation is the Thirteen Hermeneutical Principles of Rabbi Yishmael, principles of logic and methodology by which new ideas and even laws are extracted from the biblical text by the sages of each generation.[7] The Talmud, in Berakhot 5a, quotes the verse in Exodus 24:12, as God speaks to Moses:

> "I will give you the tablets of stone, and the Torah, and the commandment that I have written, so that you may interpret and derive [halakhic] direction from them."

The Talmud then proceeds to parse the phrases of the verse, and interpret them:

> "The tablets" – these are the Ten Commandments; "the Torah" – this is the text of the first five books of the Bible; "the commandment" – this is the Mishna; "that I have written" – these are the Prophets and the Writings [the rest of the Bible]; "to interpret and derive [halakhic] direction from them" – this is the Gemara.[8] This teaches that all of them were given to Moses from Mount Sinai [from God].

6. The idea that God "bears sin" is important. It follows from God's abundance of love that He is willing to "bear" or "carry" the sins of human beings. The Hebrew *noseh* is often translated as "forgives," but this loses the nuance of God's "bearing" human sin – actually taking responsibility for human sin – because, after all, it was God who created the human being with the propensity to sin.
7. These principles are stated at the very beginning the *Sifra,* the *Midrash Halakha* on the book of Leviticus.
8. The *Gemara* is the voluminous discussion by the Sages of the material in the Mishna, discussion which form the basis of Jewish law. The Mishna and the Gemara together comprise the Talmud.

On this talmudic text (Berakhot 5a) Rabbi Zvi Hirsch Chajes (*Maharatz Ḥayot*) (Galicia [Western Ukraine], 1805–1855) states in his commentary (found in the back of each volume of the Vilna Edition of the Talmud):

> ...the Holy One, Blessed be He, revealed to Moses the seemingly new ideas that diligent Torah students will eventually discover in their future interpretations; that is to say, the Holy One, Blessed be He, transmitted to Moses the hermeneutic principles by which the Torah is interpreted, and Torah scholars will find within these principles various derivatives and extensions from which they extract the hidden from that which is clearly expressed, and all of these derivative ideas originally resided in the primary text.[9]

Essentially, Rabbi Chajes is saying that the new insights, interpretations, and halakhic rulings which were interpreted by the sages throughout the ages and that were originally embedded within the words of the Torah were able to be extracted by the sages of all generations by means of the Thirteen Hermeneutical Principles which were also given at Sinai. It is by means of these interpretive principles that the great sages throughout the ages have rendered their religio-legal decisions. According to this view, everything was embedded in the original Torah, but it takes generation after generation of sages, using the Thirteen Principles, to extract more and more of that original intent of Torah.

Hence, it is no accident or coincidence that there are thirteen principles by which the Torah is interpreted, and that there are thirteen attributes of God's love and compassion that He revealed to Moses. The Oral law is fundamentally derived by way of thirteen *middot* (principles) of biblical exegesis. And I believe that, in reality, these thirteen *middot*

9. He reiterates this important point in Megilla 19b, in his *Mishpat Horaa,* ch. 2, and in his *Introduction to the Talmud,* ch. 3.

must reflect the thirteen *middot* (characteristics) of God and God's love.[10] The same Hebrew word is used for both.[11]

Our understanding of the crucial nature of human input into the Torah for each generation also brings us to answer a question that we posed earlier: Why do we not count the fiftieth day of the Omer, the day on which Shavuot falls, even though the Torah seems to indicate that we should? We now understand that Shavuot is not the end of the

10. A revealing example of this law/compassion melding appears in Rambam, *Mishneh Torah, Hilkhot Avadim* 9:8. The Rambam states the basic law vis-à-vis the non-Jewish slave: "It is permissible to work a non-Jewish slave harshly."

However, very tellingly, the Rambam immediately follows this statement with the following eloquent qualification:

Yet, although this is the law, the way of the pious and the wise is to be compassionate and to pursue justice, not to overburden or oppress a servant, and to provide them from every dish and every drink.... So, too, you should not denigrate a servant, neither physically nor verbally. The Torah made him your servant to do work, not to be disgraced. Do not treat him with constant screaming and anger, rather speak with him pleasantly and listen to his complaints.

The Rambam understood that the ancient world had not yet been ready to accept an across-the-board negation or elimination of slavery. But, by the Rambam's time, things were different. And so, in the passage we have quoted, the Rambam single-handedly changed the law and *made every gentile slave into a Hebrew servant,* conforming to the Torah's sweeping sentiment about the negativity of slavery. Everyone – Jew, non-Jew, slave, master – emerges, as the Rambam quotes from Job, from the same womb, God's womb. Therefore, the Jewish master is existentially equal to the gentile slave, and, therefore, a gentile slave must be treated exactly like a Jewish servant. The Rambam here is forcefully demonstrating what we have explained: The Torah is a partnership between God and Israel, and, in every generation, the great Sages must interpret the Torah according to the compassionate needs and conditions of the times.

11. Avraham Even-Shoshan, *HaMilon HeḤadash*, lists four basic definitions for the Hebrew word *midda*: 1) a measure, 2) the amount of a measurable quantity, 3) an established rule or principle, and 4) a trait or characteristic. So, the very inherent definitions of the word allow for this term to apply "equally" to both the principles of Torah interpretation (definition #3) and the traits or characteristics of God (definition #4). I believe that there are no "accidents" when it comes to the Hebrew language, and so these two definitions of *midda* inextricably link together Rabbi Yishmael's Thirteen Principles of Interpretation with the Thirteen Attributes (or traits or characteristics) of God.

process; the Torah was not "given" in its entirety on Shavuot; the Torah keeps on being "given" – in every generation as human input meets God's words to interpret the Torah for current times and conditions. Just as our freedom is not yet complete and is a work in progress, so the Torah itself, so to speak, is a work in progress; it is never complete – it must constantly be reinterpreted.

SHAVUOT: THE HOLIDAY CELEBRATING RECEIVING THE GIFT OF GOD'S TORAH

We have noted that "Weeks" is a unique name for a festival, since it suggests a work in progress – not, in fact, naming what happened on that day, the giving of the Torah. Perhaps, indeed, "Weeks" was never really meant to be the permanent name of the festival at all, but rather a temporary name, to be supplanted by the "proper" name at some time in the future. We have emphasized throughout this book that, ultimately, our Torah is not just the Torah for the Jewish people, but the Torah for the entire world, and that this was the original intention of God. This goes back to God's original promise to Abraham that "in you shall be blessed all the families of the earth."

I believe that on Shavuot we are not only celebrating the giving of the Torah at Mount Sinai, because it was only the Jewish people who accepted the Torah at that time. Just as we have come to understand that Passover freedom for Israel can only truly be celebrated when the entire world is free, similarly the goal of Torah can only be achieved when at least its ethical teachings are accepted by every nation.

Indeed, the Rabbis of the Midrash queried as to why the Torah was not given on Mount Moriah, in the Land of Israel, where Abraham brought Isaac to be bound, and where the Holy Temple will eventually be rebuilt. Why was the Torah given on Mount Sinai, outside of Israel, in a desert, a no-man's-land? The *Mekhilta DeRabbi Yishmael*[12] makes an amazing statement with regard to this fact:

12. *BaḤodesh* 1:18.

> The Torah was given in an ownerless (public) place, because if it had been given in the Land of Israel, the nations of the world could have said that they had no portion in it. Therefore, it was given in the desert, an ownerless place, so that anyone who wishes may come and accept it.

It seems that the Midrash is stating that the Torah – certainly its ethical and moral code – was not meant just for the Jewish people, but for the whole world, and, in testimony to this, it was given outside the Land of Israel. Only when the entire world will accept the Torah will we truly be able to name a holiday the "Festival of the Giving of the Torah."[13]

FEAST OF WEEKS: AWAITING TORAH FOR THE WORLD

We have noted that Shavuot carries with it a sense of incompleteness. That is because "Weeks" is not the name of a holiday, but rather the name of a process, of a progression. Right now, for most interpretations, it refers to the seven weeks between Passover and the festival of the Giving of the Torah. But perhaps it also refers to another process that is under way: the process of moving the Torah from the exclusivity of the Jewish people and bringing it to the entire world. We see this beginning to happen in our time with the "ingathering of the exiles" in the State of Israel, the deep interest by thousands of individuals and even whole communities around the world to come close to the Jewish people.[14] This interest often results in conversion to Judaism, echoing the prophecy

---

13. As we noted in our chapter on Sukkot, there was a custom on Simḥat Torah during the sixteenth and seventeenth centuries in both European and Oriental Jewish communities to take the Torah scrolls outside of the synagogue and dance with them on the streets, bringing the Torah "out into the world." Also, these communities would invite members of the gentile community to join the celebrations in honor of the Torah, to clearly make the point that it will ultimately be a Torah not just for the Jews, but a Torah for the world (Avraham Ya'ari, *The History of the Festival of Simḥat Torah* [Jerusalem: Mossad Harav Kook, 1964], 255–56).
14. These groups include the tribe of Dan from Ethiopia; the Benei Menashe from India; the descendants of the Marranos from Spain, Portugal, Brazil, and South Italy; the

of Isaiah chapter 2: "And many nations shall go and say: 'Come ye, and let us go up to the mountain of the Lord, and to the house of the God of Jacob; and He will teach us of His ways, and we will walk in His paths'; for out of Zion shall go forth the law, and the word of the Lord from Jerusalem."[15]

This, of course, was exactly Rabbi Akiva's vision, as we learned in the last chapter: that we must have an independent nation-state from which to teach Torah to the world so that we can move this process along.[16] Shavuot moves us toward a perfected world, a world full of justice, a world redeemed. This process will take many "weeks" – perhaps many eons. But when the process is complete, the festival of Shavuot will receive its "permanent" name, with Torah shining forth to illuminate an entire world. As we declare in the *Kedusha* prayer in the Musaf service of Shabbat, "And He will make it known to us, in His compassion, *for the second time, in the presence of all living beings* to be for you a God.... I am the Lord of Love, your God." The "first time," the revelation

descendants of the Jews in Kaifeng, China; the Subbotniks of Russia; descendants of Polish Jews returning to Judaism post-Holocaust; and the Prince of Zambia, Saviour Chishimba, who converted to Judaism and is now Yehuda Ben-David.

15. The Prophet Micah, in his vision of the end of days, also sees the nations of the world flowing to the Temple in Jerusalem and being taught the ways of the Torah, similar to Isaiah's vision quoted above, but adds in 4:5, "For all the nations will walk, each person in the name of his god," seeming to say that, at very least, all of the nations will ultimately accept the ethical and moral principles of Judaism while remaining with the rituals of their own faith – "ritual pluralism and ethical absolutism." The Talmud (Berakhot 57b) quotes R. Shimon b. Elazar, who states that ultimately everyone in the world will convert to Judaism, deriving his opinion from his interpretation of the verse in Zephaniah 3:9 – "For then will I turn to the peoples a pure language, that they may all call upon the name of God, to serve Him with one consent." The Rambam actually codifies this idea as halakha in *Hilkhot Melakhim* 12:1, where he writes that, in the Messianic Era, the wicked of the nations of the world will join the Jewish people.
16. In a number of places the Talmud teaches that Torah should not be taught to gentiles (see, for example, Ḥagiga 13a and Sanhedrin 59a). Given the prophecies of Isaiah and Micah noted above, it is clear that in the period leading to messianic times Torah must be taught to all who seek it. See also Rambam, *Mishneh Torah, Hilkhot Melakhim* 11:8–9 (censored in standard editions).

of Torah was to the Jewish people; the "second time," it will be for all of the inhabitants of the world.

RUTH AS A PARADIGM FOR THE LOVING-KINDNESS OF TORAH

On Shavuot in the synagogue, we read *Megillat Rut,* the Scroll of Ruth. The book presents the fascinating picture of a Jew by choice entering a community of Jews from birth. The book relates directly to the notion of compassion and loving-kindness – *ḥesed* – which, as we have explained, must be the dominant theme of all Torah interpretation throughout the generations.

Ruth, although initially a Moabite "outsider" (gentile), meets the Jewish family of Elimelech from Bethlehem-Judea, who left his homeland in Israel to settle in the plains of Moab because of a famine in Israel. Ruth marries one of Elimelech's sons, becomes widowed and impoverished, acts with profound loving-kindness to her widowed mother-in-law Naomi, now bereft of both her sons, and decides to join her mother-in-law in her return to Israel. She is taken to wife by their Jewish kinsman Boaz, who also demonstrates immense *ḥesed* in showing so much loving-kindness to a woman who was actually a stranger, a Moabite, but who gives birth to a son who will be the forebear of King David, the progenitor of the King Messiah who will eventually bring Judaism and peace to the entire world. The story of Ruth stands as a testimony to the goal of these "weeks" of Shavuot. Our long-term task is to teach Torah to the world – regardless of anyone's race or color. In this sense, we are fully universalists. Hillel teaches in *Pirkei Avot* 1:12: "Be of the disciples of Aaron, loving peace and pursuing peace, loving human beings and bringing them closer to Torah." Note that the expression "human beings" (*haberiot*) is used, and not "Israel" or "Jews," stating unequivocally that our task, as disciples of Aaron, is to bring all of humanity to Torah.

Hence Ruth, a woman born into a gentile nation, is the one who will ultimately, through her descendant the Messiah, give the Torah to the entire world. She declared that the Jewish people will be her people, that the Jewish God will be her God, and thus becomes the mother not only of Jewish continuity, but of Jewish – and, ultimately, global – redemption.

THE MEANING OF SHAVUOT IN CONTEMPORARY REALITY

As we explained in this chapter, Shavuot – the Feast of Weeks – represents our anticipation of a perfected world in which all the nations of the world recognize the true God and the truth of the moral and ethical values of His Torah. Since we have not yet reached that ideal time, I would like to suggest another interpretation of the name "Shavuot," one that, I believe, better represents the significance of the day in contemporary times.

Although the simple meaning of Shavuot as it appears in the Torah is certainly "weeks," the word *shevua* refers to an oath and *shevuot* is the plural form, meaning "oaths." And indeed, the holiday of Shavuot is the anniversary of the most sublime of reciprocal oaths taken by God and His chosen people at Mount Sinai. God committed Himself to us, promising that we would be His eternal people, and we took the oath of *na'aseh venishma* – we will perform His commandments and internalize His teachings, making them the very fabric of our collective beings, allowing us to share them with the entire world.

The Sages (Shabbat 88a) teach:

> The Torah says, "And Moses brought forth the people out of the camp to meet God; and they stood at the lowermost part of the mount" (Ex. 19:17). R. Avdimi bar Ḥama bar Ḥasa said: the Jewish people actually stood beneath the mountain, and the verse teaches that the Holy One, Blessed be He, overturned the mountain above the Jews like a tub, and said to them: If you accept the Torah, excellent, and if not, there will be your burial.

I would like to suggest that far more important than the threat, the overturned mountain served as a *ḥuppa* – a marriage canopy – emphasizing the love relationship between God and the people of Israel that was established and consummated on the day that we received the Torah.

Echoing this idea, the Ramban, in his commentary to the Torah (Deut. 9:17), suggests that the Tablets of the Law served as a kind of *ketuba* – a marriage contract – between the Loving God and the people of Israel,[17] an idea that is expressed in a most beautiful manner by the great liturgical poet and kabbalist Rabbi Yisrael Najara (1555–1625, Ottoman Empire), who wrote hymns on the marriage of God and Israel including a *ketuba* with God as the groom and Israel as the bride.[18]

Up to this point in time, as long as the rest of the world has not yet accepted the truth of the Torah, Shavuot remains a work in progress. Yet it remains a holiday of deep significance and meaning for the Jewish people who celebrate the mutual oaths, reaffirming their commitment to *na'aseh venishma* every year on the anniversary of *Matan Torah*. Our celebration includes the public reading of *Megillat Rut*, with Ruth, the protagonist of that story, serving as a harbinger of universal acceptance of the Torah. Only then will the holiday of Shavuot take its place in the calendar as "the anticipated festival" with the ultimate acceptance of the Torah realized.

---

17. The Ramban is quoting a midrash that suggests that when Moses destroyed the first tablets he was, effectively, tearing up the marriage contract so that the people's sin with the Golden Calf would be judged more leniently: "It is better that you [Israel] be judged like an [unchaste] unmarried woman and not like an [adulterous] wife."
18. It is available in Israel National Library's collection of *piyyutim* at https://bit.ly/IsraelNajara.

Chapter 15

The Ninth of Av: The Unfinished Symphony

"I believe in the sun even when it is not shining; I believe in love even when feeling it not; I believe in God even when He is silent."

– Found in Cologne, Germany, etched on a wall of a prison cell holding Jews later transported to concentration camps.

The festivals of the Hebrew calendar year conclude after Shavuot – some two months later – with the bleak, black, twenty-five-hour fast, the fast of the Ninth Day of Av (Tisha BeAv), commemorating the loss of both of our Temples (in 586 BCE at the hands of Babylon and in 70 CE at the hands of Rome) and concomitantly the loss of our national sovereignty in Israel with the destruction of Jerusalem; this second tragedy resulted in two millennia of Jewish exiles to all corners of the world and persecutions in every place we sought refuge. Hence, we spend the evening and until midday on the morrow as bereft mourners, seated on the floor or on low stools, reading the biblical book of Lamentations with its hauntingly sad melody and reciting dirges (*kinnot*) of travail from our various periods of persecution – from the Christian Crusades to the Spanish Inquisition and expulsion to the Nazi gas chambers of extinction; the fast continues until nightfall.

TISHA BEAV: THE SURPRISE SOURCE OF JEWISH OPTIMISM AND ENDURANCE

You will note that I opened this chapter referring to Tisha BeAv as the concluding "festival" of the Hebrew calendar year – and my language is very precise. The prophet Zechariah (who prophesied after the destruction of the First Temple and during the rebuilding and establishment of the Second Temple) declared: "So says the Lord of Love and hosts … the fast of the fifth month (Tisha BeAv) … shall be for the House of Judah joy and happiness and good festival days" (Zech. 8:19). And indeed, Rabbi Akiva began his optimistic rejoicing even in the midst of destruction. The Talmud, at the end of Tractate Makkot, records that:

> Rabban Gamliel, R. Elazar b. Azarya, R. Yehoshua, and Rabbi Akiva … were walking toward Jerusalem. When they reached Mount Scopus (from where the Temple Mount was visible) they tore their clothing [as a sign of mourning]. When they arrived at the Temple Mount, they saw a fox running from the area where the Holy of Holies had been. They began to cry, but Rabbi Akiva laughed. They said to him, "Why are you laughing?"… He replied: "Isaiah the Prophet said, 'I will bring two reliable witnesses regarding my people, Uriah the Priest (of the First Temple's destruction) and Zechariah (the prophet, of the Second Temple's restoration)' (Is. 8:2) …. Uriah (vindicates Zechariah's prophecy), as it is written, 'Therefore because of you, Zion will be plowed under like a field' (Mic. 3:12). In the case of Zechariah we find, 'Yet again, elderly men and elderly women will once again sit in the streets of Jerusalem … and the streets of the city will be filled with young boys and young girls playing.' Now that I have seen Uriah's prophecy fulfilled in detail with our loss of our homeland,

> I know that Zechariah's prophecy will also be fulfilled." Hearing that, Rabbi Akiva's colleagues said to him, "Akiva, you have comforted us; Akiva, you have comforted us."

Apparently, Rabbi Akiva began to feel the joy of Tisha BeAv redemption even before it occurred, so certain was he of the ultimate prophecy of redemption for that day seen by Zechariah!

The fulfillment of the prophecy of destruction was, in Rabbi Akiva's eyes, a sign that the prophecy of redemption would also come true. This prophecy of redemption is the prophecy of the same Zechariah who prophesied that the fasts of destruction would become times of joy and happiness. It seems that in the depth of the destruction, Rabbi Akiva already felt the happiness and joy that Zechariah predicted for the "fifth fast" in the future.

But the question must still be asked: How can Tisha BeAv ever become a festival day? After all, in the Jewish tradition every festival is declared on the basis of a great event, even a miraculous event of God's saving grace, which occurred on that day. Hence, the Festival of Passover begins on the very same day that the Hebrews exited from Egyptian servitude, Shavuot on the day in which the Jews received the Torah at Mount Sinai. The halakha declaring a day of festivity is dependent upon the miraculous event which occurred on that day, the event which creates the sanctity of the day (*kedushat hayom*). Tisha BeAv will always remain the day of our Holy Temple's destruction! How can it turn into a festival?

I believe the answer may be found in the weekly portion which we read every year on the Sabbath after Tisha BeAv, known as *Shabbat Naḥamu*, the Sabbath of Comfort, when we read from the book of Deuteronomy, the portion of *Va'etḥanan*. Here, too, as in our earlier citation from the Prophet Isaiah, there is a linkage between the tragedy of destruction and the joyousness of redemption, but in *Va'etḥanan* the beginning of the redemption comes on the very heels of the destruction, on the very day of the destruction, from the words of God Himself (as it were).

Let us begin the biblical portion: "When you beget children and grandchildren and will have been long in the land, you will grow corrupt... and do evil in the eyes of the Lord of Love your God to anger Him, I appoint heaven and earth this day to bear witness against you that you will surely be destroyed quickly from the land... you will be utterly destroyed" (Deut. 4:25–26). This means, in effect, that we would be destroyed as a people, certainly as the chosen people of God, to whom He gave the Land of Israel and a mission to bring blessings to all the families of the earth (Gen. 12:3). And, indeed, we had every reason to expect national destruction, since God Himself had previously stated why Abraham's descendants had been initially chosen: "I have loved and chosen (Abraham) because he has commanded his children and his household (students and followers) after him to take responsibility for the pathways of the Lord of Love to do compassionate righteousness and moral justice" (Gen 18:19). And so, once we learn in *Va'etḥanan* that, unfortunately, these descendants would become corrupt, acting evilly in the eyes of God, then the Almighty would declare absolutely: "You shall be utterly destroyed" (Deut. 4:26).

But immediately – so it would seem from the text – God seems to have changed His mind, as it were. After the words of "utter destruction," we read:

> And the Lord of Love will scatter you among the nations, and you will be left few in number among the nations... and there you will serve gods, the handiwork of man.... And from there you will seek the Lord of Love and you will find Him because you will search for Him with all your heart and soul... for the Lord of Love your God is a God of compassion. *He will never abandon you completely nor will He ever destroy you utterly,* since He can never forget the eternal covenant He made with your forebears which He swore to them." (Deut. 4:27–31)

Hence, although the Land of Israel was lost to us as a national homeland with the destruction of the Temple in Jerusalem, the Jewish people remained alive, albeit to be scattered among the nations of the world!

And so, due to His divine omniscience, God knows that the whole of Israel will never forsake His laws completely, that there will always remain a faithful remnant loyal to God, because Israel acceded to the covenant, when the nation assented, "We shall do (the commandments) and internalize them (eternally)" (Ex. 24:7).

Hence, on the basis of this later perspective, taking into account that Israel is God's eternal partner in the covenant, God does not fulfill His earlier statement of complete destruction of the nation, but He rather sends the Hebrews into exile, from whence they will return to God and be returned to the Land of Israel. This is because the compassionate Lord of Love has a covenant with the nation Israel, an eternal contract – one that preceded His statement of destruction – which guarantees that the nation will never be entirely destroyed. It assures us that the Hebrews will eventually return to God's ways and be returned to their eternal homeland, Israel – albeit with periods of separation and alienation. And God continues His love for Israel and belief in Israel's eventual repentance even during the periods of alienation and separation!

And so, when the Rabbis of the Midrash[1] ask how can Tisha BeAv be called a *moed*, a festival day (see Lamentations 1:15), even though it was historically the day of the destruction of our Holy Temple, the rabbinic response is because on Tisha BeAv itself, God vented His anger merely on wood and stones – the Holy Temple – but not on the Jewish people, His covenantal people whom He saved from their deserved destruction! Hence even the original Tisha BeAv must be remembered as the day on which although the Temple may have been destroyed, miraculously the Jewish nation was kept alive, setting the stage for an eventual *moed* on that very day!

We learn a most glorious message of Jewish historiography from these prophetic words of Deuteronomy. As Abraham well understood, God chose Abraham and loved him because Abraham taught his descendants to love and to choose God's ways of compassionate righteousness and moral justice. That mutual love and commitment, that eternal covenant between God and Israel, even an eternal marriage bond between God and Israel, guarantees the existence of Israel as God's beloved people for all historic time. This does not mean, however, that the majority of the nation will always remain true to God's teaching, will not backslide into sin and corruption. When such

1. *Midrash Tehillim, mizmor* 79.

infidelity on the part of Israel occurs, they will go into exile and lose their beloved country. However, there will always be a remnant that will hold Torah dear, and God will always hold Israel dear, knowing in His omniscience that Israel will eventually return to God and His laws, and then to their homeland of Israel.

Dr. Max Nordau (1849–1923) was a prominent physician and diagnostician in Vienna, a very assimilated Jew (married to a Christian woman) with a most tenuous relationship with the Jewish community, who surprisingly became a cofounder with Theodor Herzl of the World Zionist Organization and largely took over the leadership of the modern Zionist movement after Herzl's untimely death. He tells an amazing story of what brought him to the nascent Zionist movement in the first instance:

> When I reached the age of fifteen, I left the Jewish way of life and the study of Torah. Judaism remained a mere memory and since then I have always felt as a German and a German only.
>
> I have a children's clinic in Paris. A woman, an immigrant from Poland, her hair covered with a scarf, came in with a pale boy, eight or ten, sick for three weeks. Someone recommended that she bring him to me. I took out a form for a new patient and tried to speak to him in our local language, but he could hardly understand French. I asked his mother, who was also very poor at French, and she said, "No, he doesn't go to a regular school, he goes to a '*ḥeder*,' a Jewish religious school."
>
> I scolded her harshly. "This only causes anti-Semitism. We have opened the door for you, the gates to the country, to refugees from Poland. Why doesn't your child learn the national language here?"
>
> In anger I asked the child, "In *ḥeder*, what did you learn?" His eyes lit up, and in Yiddish, which I understood because of my German, told me what he had last studied in *ḥeder*.
>
> "Jacob," he said, "was dying and he invited Joseph and commanded him, adjuring him, pleading before him, 'Please, don't bury me in Egypt. There is the Cave of Makhpela in the Land of Israel

– where Abraham, Isaac, Jacob, Sarah, Rebecca are buried – and there I buried Leah. Take me from Egypt and bury me with them. And when I came from Padan, Rachel died in the land of Canaan, on the way to Efrat, and I buried her there, on the way.'

"Jacob felt a necessity to apologize to Joseph and say, 'I bother you like this, to take me from Egypt to Hebron, and I, myself, didn't bother to take your mother Rachel there to have buried her in our ancestral burial place. And despite that I was very close. Next to Bethlehem. Even into the city I didn't take her; I buried her on the road.

'But I am not guilty and didn't act wrongly. God wanted it this way. He knew: The murderer Babylonian Nebuchadnezzar would, in the future, exile the children of Rachel, and the exiles would pass by Rachel's grave and beg her to intercede with God on their behalf. And then she would leave her grave and weep and wail and her voice would be heard: Rachel weeps for her children.

'But the Lord responds to her: "Stop your voice from weeping, and your eyes from tears, because there is a reward for your actions, and a hope for the future, and the children will return to their borders – *Veshavu vanim ligvulam* (Jer. 31:15–16)."'"

And I, I didn't know what to do with myself. I turned to the window so that the mother and child wouldn't see the tears rolling down my cheeks, and I said to myself, "Max, aren't you ashamed of yourself? You are an educated man, known as an intellectual, with a doctor's degree, but you don't know anything about the history of your people. From all of the holy Scriptures, nothing! And here, this sick child, weak, an immigrant, a refugee. And he speaks of Jacob and Joseph and Jeremiah and Rachel, as if it was yesterday; it all lives in front of his eyes!"

I wiped the tears from my cheeks and turned to them and said, in my heart, "A people, with children like this, who actually live their past, they will have a sparkling future."

In the weekend newspaper I saw an advertisement, "Whoever believes that the fate of the Jewish people is important to

> them, please call to help find an answer. Dr. Theodor Herzl." I called immediately.
>
> When we founded the Zionist Congress, at the first one, when I was honored to speak, the figure of that little boy, whose name I don't even remember, stood in front of my eyes. But those words I will never forget, because they are the foundation of Zionism, they are the pillars of Judaism: *Veshavu vanim ligvulam* – "And the children will return to their borders."[2]

If you want to understand how the Jews remained faithful to God and His laws during their two thousand years of exile, it was because they still felt God's promise of His covenant, God's eternal love and commitment that the Jews would live eternally and ultimately return to Israel and redeem the world. They were empowered and enabled by God's love and covenantal promise!

THE CHALLENGE OF TISHA BEAV TODAY

The prophet Zechariah received a question from a delegation of Diaspora Jews at the time when Emperor Darius I (Persia, reigned at about 520 BCE, midrashically identified as the son of Queen Esther and Ahasuerus) gave permission for the Jews to rebuild a Second Temple – and indeed the Temple was being rebuilt. They had been fasting and mourning on Tisha BeAv since the destruction of the First Temple in 586 BCE (see Zechariah chapter 7): "Must we (still) weep (mourn) on the fifth month (the month of Av, when counting the months from Nisan as the first month), separating ourselves (from pleasures like food and drink) as we have done these several years (since the destruction of the First Temple – now that the Temple is being rebuilt)?"

The prophet's response, in God's name, begins with a question directed at the Diaspora delegation:

> When you fasted and mourned in the fifth (month)… for these seventy years, were you fasting for Me? Did I benefit from your

2. A. S. Yahuda, *Ever VaArav* (New York, 1946), 257.

> fast (asked God)? And when you eat and when you drink it is you who are eating, and you who are drinking!

What was the prophet telling the delegation from the Diaspora (at a time when the Diaspora delegation was apparently reasonably comfortable as Jews in their diaspora)? And what is the prophet telling us in our generation, when we can even ask a better question? Why must we still weep and mourn over the destruction of the first and second commonwealths if we are now happily living in the third commonwealth, with our nation-state, *Medinat Yisrael*, and a liberated Jerusalem as our capital, expanding borders, a comparatively high standard of living, an admirable Israel Defense Force, amazing scientific discoveries and medical cures emerging from our universities, and more people – both men and women – learning Torah on an advanced level than ever before in our history?

Nevertheless, and despite the magnificent divinely granted and Jewishly earned gift of our independent State of Israel and our liberated city of Jerusalem which we are privileged to enjoy in our generation, we still lack and are in desperate need of our Holy Temple, to which representatives of all nations will flock and accept upon themselves at least the ethical and moral imperatives of our Torah: compassionate righteousness, moral justice, and world peace. Until then, the land, nation, and people will never truly be secure, as we know tragically from the daily news reportage about terrorism.

To be sure, there must be changes in our manner of mourning, especially in our Tisha BeAv afternoon (Minḥa) Prayer for Comfort, *Naḥem*. We dare not speak to God about the obsolete and falsely depicted "desolate, disgraced, destroyed, and mournful city of Jerusalem, swallowed up by the (Roman) legionnaires and inherited by the idolaters." We dare not lie to God about our present reality and we dare not be so ungrateful for the miracles of our generation! (See Yoma 69b, where such personalities as Jeremiah and Daniel did not recite prayers that did not conform to their realities.) I would recommend using the text suggested for *Naḥem* by the much-revered halakhist Rav Nachum Eliezer Rabinovitch, *rosh hayeshiva* of Maaleh Adumim, which speaks not of the desolation of our holy city of Jerusalem which has been restored, but rather of the desolation of the sacred Mount Moriah, the

Temple Mount, whose status bereft of our Holy Temple does conform with the adjectives of desolation in our traditional text.[3] Moreover, I would also suggest adding – after the *kinnot* (dirges) on Tisha BeAv evening and on Tisha BeAv morning – Psalm 126 ("A Song of Ascents; when the Lord of Love will return the captivity of Zion, we shall be as dreamers") and the *HaTikva*, both in heartfelt gratitude for our free and independent State of Israel after our two-thousand-year-long exile.

But certainly we must continue to mourn and fast on Tisha BeAv because, as we have pointed out, mourning and remembering past glory keeps the past and the present very much alive; this will enable and empower us to hopefully cure past mistakes and prevent another destruction, God forbid! It is crucial, therefore, especially now, to relive and reexperience the mourning and the destruction and, at the same time, remember what it was that Zechariah told the delegation in answer to their question about still needing to fast on Tisha BeAv, a message that powerfully applies to our situation today:

"When you fasted and mourned, were you fasting for Me?" asked God. Do you think I benefit from your fasting, do you think it is for Me that you do the ritual, do you think I really care if you fast or not? The purpose of your fast is to lead you to repentance, and so what I really care about is that you repent and change your unethical ways, that you love others who, like yourself, are created in God's image, because all humankind are My children and your siblings, because I love you and all of humanity. And as for the Jews, I chose you as My beloved partners to teach the message of love and Torah ethics to all of humanity because you chose to take responsibility for the ways of the Lord of Love, to suffuse the world with compassionate righteousness and moral justice (see Genesis 18:18, 19; Micah 4:1–5). Then, after you begin the process, it will be upon Me to complete it. But it must begin with you.

3. Rabbi Rabinovitch's version of *Naḥem* reads, in part:
נחם ה׳ א-להינו את אבלי ציון ואת אבלי ירושלים. רחם ברחמיך הרבים ובחסדיך הנאמנים עלינו ועל עמך ישראל ועל ירושלים עירך ועל ציון משכן כבודך ועל ההר האבל והחרב וההרוס והשומם הנתון ביד זרים הרמוס ביד עריצים ויירשוהו לגיונות ויחללוהו עובדי פסילים ויתנו נבלת עבדיך מאכל לעוף השמים ולבהמת הארץ.
The full version in Hebrew can be found online. See, for example, https://bit.ly/nahem.

Therefore, after the prophet makes the point that it is not God who benefits from the fasting, but rather that it is we as Jews who must learn from the fasting to repent, God will then, through the mouth of the prophet, teach us very clearly what kind of repentance we must do:

> Judge with truthful justice and perform kindness and mercy toward one another. Do not oppress the widow and the orphan, the stranger and the poor, and do not think in your hearts of wronging one another.... So does the Lord of Love say, "I have returned to Zion and I am dwelling in the midst of Jerusalem; Jerusalem will be called the City of Truth and the Mountain of the Lord of Love and Hosts will be called the Holy Mountain. So says the Lord of Love and Hosts: Elderly men and elderly women will once again sit in the streets of Jerusalem...and the streets of the city will be filled with young boys and girls playing in the streets.... So says the Lord of Love and Hosts: Just as this will be wondrous in the eyes of the remnants of this nation in those days, so will it be wondrous in My eyes, says the Lord of Love and Hosts. And I shall bring them and they shall dwell in the midst of Jerusalem, and they shall be for Me as a nation and I shall be for them as a God, [but only if you return to Me] *in truth* and *in righteousness*. (Zech. 7:9–10; 8:3–8)

The Jewish people are not only My partners, says God. They are my covenant children, initially responsible together with Me to perfect the world. Hence this, our miraculous return to Israel our state, is not the final movement of our symphony! You will remember that God initially told Abraham, "I shall make you a great nation and through you shall be blessed all the families of the earth." Israel has a special mission, not only to follow God's laws by themselves, but Israel must be the examples and teachers to the rest of the world, each person created in God's image and each person loved by God. And so, even after God's return of Israel to Zion, the prophet Zechariah continues:

> Thus says the Lord of Love and Hosts, it shall yet come to pass that there shall come people, and the inhabitants of many cities,

> and the inhabitants of one city shall go to another, saying, "Let us go quickly to entreat the favor of the Lord of Love, and to seek the Lord of Love and Hosts; I will also go." And many peoples and strong nations shall come to seek the Lord of Love and Hosts in Jerusalem, and to pray before the Lord of Love. Thus, says the Lord of Love and Hosts, in those days it shall come to pass that ten people out of all the languages of the nations shall take hold, and shall seize the corner of the garment of a Jew and say: "We will go with you, for we have heard that God is with you."

What we must learn from Tisha BeAv is our special historiography. Yes, God has created us together with the entire world in His own divine image, but because we have committed ourselves to His laws, He made us His beloved partners to redeem the world by means of our ethical teachings. Just as He is a God of loving-kindness and righteousness, we must be people of loving-kindness and righteousness. He has given us the Land of Israel, upon which to develop our unique culture of love, compassion, universal freedom, and peace.

When we backslide, we lose our ancestral homeland and must wander throughout the world. But our covenant, and God's love for us as a faithful remnant of our chosen people who love God and remain true to God's pathways, will remain strong eternally. Eventually Israel entire will return to the Land of Israel and the God of Israel, as is happening in our generation, and *mirabile dictu* – remnants of the lost tribes (of Dan from Ethiopia and Menashe from India) as well as many sincere converts are entering our portals. This is the message we must give the world through the medium of our nation-state and hopefully our Holy Temple –may it soon be rebuilt in Jerusalem – newly reestablished as our capital city as a "house of prayer for all nations" (Is. 56:7).[4] In these blessed times we must love every human being and dedicate ourselves to teach compassionate righteousness, justice, and universal peace. Then will the world truly be redeemed; only then will our mission and destiny truly be fulfilled.

---

4. Indeed, at the inauguration of the First Temple, King Solomon declared clearly that the House of God in Jerusalem was meant to welcome all nations that came in search of Him (see I Kings 8:41–43).

Chapter 16

Tu BeAv: From Destruction to Renewal

A further indication of the truth of the interpretation that Tisha BeAv is a holiday that calls out for redemption is the fact that just a few days later we celebrate Tu BeAv, the fifteenth day of Av, the talmudic "Sadie Hawkins Day." Indeed, at the end of Tractate Taanit, we have a fascinating description of this very strange celebration (Mishna Taanit 4:8), in which the women would court the men, against the traditional manner of men pursuing the women (Kiddushin 2b), and a veritable festival of marriages so close to Tisha BeAv!

> Says Rabban Shimon b. Gamliel: There were no festivals in Israel like the fifteenth day of Av and Yom HaKippurim, that on these days the daughters of Jerusalem would go out in borrowed white dresses so as not to embarrass those who did not have such dresses, and they would go out dancing in the vineyards. What would they say? "Young man, lift up your eyes and see whom you wish to choose for yourself. Do not look for beauty, rather look for the right family." (As it is written in Proverbs 31:30) "Grace

> is false and beauty is vain, a woman who is in awe of God, she is deserving of praise," and as it further says, "Give her of the fruit of her hands and may her good deeds praise her in the gates" (Prov. 31:31).

The Gemara then asks (30b): Such joyous activity is understandable on Yom Kippur because that is a day of pardon and forgiveness, the day in which the second tablets of stone were given, but of what significance is the fifteenth day of Av?

The Talmud lists no fewer than eight reasons for this day's significance, which would seem to indicate that there was no one specific reason. Within the list of eight is the reason given by Rav Matana (Taanit 31b), explaining that on the fifteenth of Av the dead of Beitar (the last stronghold which maintained itself during the abortive Bar Kokhba rebellion) were finally permitted burial.

In line with this idea, permit me to suggest another reason for Tu BeAv. Josephus records that apparently a great number of Jews – especially the priests – came from their Diaspora communities and from wherever they were living in Israel to join their brethren fighting against the Roman General Vespasian in a last-ditch abortive attempt to protect the Temple from destruction. He reports that on Tisha BeAv there was hardly a home without the loss of a family member; just about everyone was in mourning.[1] Seven days after Tisha BeAv is Tu BeAv – when the mourners would have risen up from their *shiva*, which had begun on Tisha BeAv.[2]

I would suggest that another reason for Tu BeAv, and perhaps the real reason for its festivities, is that the rabbinical halakhic authorities told their constituent mourners to end their mourning by getting married on that day – because of God's promise to us on Tisha BeAv that the Jewish nation will never be destroyed – since our religious leaders

1. Josephus writes, "Not one spot in the whole city [of Jerusalem] was empty: every single one had its corpse" (*The Jewish War* [Penguin Books, 1974], 355).
2. On the last day of *shiva*, we apply the halakhic rule of *miktzat hayom kekulo*, that even a small portion of the day is considered like a full day. Therefore, the Beitar mourners could arise on the morning of their seventh day, after having mourned for about an hour.

were anxious to instill and inspire the Jews with continued faith in the God of redemption, the God of our covenant.[3]

Yes, the Temple was destroyed – but the Jewish nation lives and the Parent in Heaven of the Jewish nation lives, the Lord of Love and Compassion. He has not forgotten the nation to which He is covenanted never to forsake completely. Our mourning on Tisha BeAv preserves the memory of the loss of our beloved Temple, just as a mourner's remembrance of a loved one brings back the very presence of the loved one in a very palpable way. Mourning a significant deceased person or a significant past experience enables the person and experience to continue to live with us in our present, and if we learn from them, we can then even enable them to live in our future as well. And so, on Tisha BeAv we not only mourn the loss of the Temple; we likewise remember at the same time that the Jewish nation was preserved, that Israel is still God's beloved nation, that the covenant with God is indestructible, and that the Jewish people will once again experience the return of sovereignty to Israel and the rebuilding of the Temple as a magnet for all the nations of the world to return to the God of Love: compassionate righteousness, moral justice, and peace for all humanity.

As I have already indicated, the best way to express this faith in future redemption is with the marriage ceremony and the future family it engenders. This is especially true in light of our earlier explanation of the Blessing of Engagement recited under the wedding canopy: "Blessed are You, Lord of Love, who sanctifies His people Israel by means of the marriage canopy and the covenantal engagement of sanctity."[4] As we invoke this blessing, we understand that it also refers to the eternal relationship between God and His people; God sanctifies (weds) Israel to Himself as His covenantal nation.

Of the explanations offered in the Gemara, Rav Matana came closest to this idea when he said that on Tu BeAv we celebrate our

3. As an example of this phenomenon of faith in the face of destruction, DP camps in Europe after the *Shoah* saw hundreds of weddings and in the years 1946–1948, the birth rate in those camps was the highest in the world. See https://www.yadvashem.org/exhibitions/dp-camps/family.html.
4. The true meaning of *kiddushin* is "sanctity."

ability to bury our dead killed in the rebellion. His explanation for the joy of Tu BeAv is that even after the destruction of the Temple, there were still living Jews to ritually bury their dead, who were still concerned with the proper religious ritual for burial. This served as proof that God's covenant with the Jewish people remained in force and that the exiles would return to the Torah of Israel and the Land of Israel.

But I would argue that celebrating marriages at the conclusion of the *shiva* period following Tisha BeAv is an even more powerful statement about the Jewish belief in our covenant with God and our partnership with Him in redemption.

As part of the symbolism of the Jewish wedding, we understand from the prophet Jeremiah that whereas in the first redemption from Egypt it was God who played the dominant role with the ten plagues and splitting of the Reed Sea, in the ultimate redemption it will be *Kenesset Yisrael* – God's true partner in history and redemption – who, God insists, must play the initiating and therefore dominant role. In Jeremiah's words (31:20–21):

> Erect markers, set up signposts;
> Keep in mind the highway, the road that you traveled.
> Return, Maiden Israel!
> Return to these towns of yours!
> How long will you waver, O rebellious daughter?
> For the Lord of Love has created something new on earth:
> A woman courts a man.

"Maiden Israel" is called to return, and a world tradition will change: "A woman courts a man." In order for redemption to occur, it is the bride who must make the first move. In the spirit of Jeremiah's prophecy, it is customary in Ashkenazi Jewish communities for the bride to circle the groom seven times, and as noted above, in the Tu BeAv celebration of the Mishna, the women are the ones who take the initiative. On Tu BeAv we look forward to the complete redemption in which Israel, the "bride," is expected to be the initiating party. God, the "bridegroom," will respond to her to bring about the return of the entire people to Israel.[5]

"Return to Me and I will return to you, says the Lord of Love and Hosts," in the words of the prophet Malachi (3:7).[6] This process is already foretold in Deuteronomy (30:2–6), where God predicts that the people of Israel, mired in their places of exile, will return with all their hearts to God – and then God will complete the work:

> ...and you return to your God, the Lord of Love, and you and your children heed God's command with all your heart and soul, just as I enjoin upon you this day, then your God, the Lord of Love, will restore your fortunes and take you back in love. [God] will bring you together again from all the peoples where your God, the Lord of Love, has scattered you.
>
> Even if your outcasts are at the ends of the world, from there your God, the Lord of Love, will gather you, from there [God] will fetch you. And your God, the Lord of Love, will bring you to the land that your fathers possessed, and you shall possess it; and [God] will make you more prosperous and more numerous than your ancestors.
>
> Then your God, the Lord of Love, will open up your heart and the hearts of your offspring – to love your God, the Lord of Love, with all your heart and soul, in order that you may live.

God will purify our hearts and will return to the Land of Israel even those exiled to the farthest corners of the earth. Here, in the Land of Israel, we will live in peace and security, values that we will pass on to the whole world. And, *mirabile dictu*, if you ask why we are the blessed generation of return to the land of Israel after two thousand

5. The *Geula* (Redemption) blessing recited before the *Amida* in the daily Shaḥarit service reflects this idea with the words "Rock of Israel, arise *with the help of Israel* (*be'ezrat Yisrael*)." While the ultimate redemption will be carried out by God, the initiative must come from us.
6. See Sanhedrin 97b.

years of prayer and fasting, perhaps it is because we are the first generation since the destruction of the Second Temple to actually begin to settle, plant, build up, and fight for the land – because we initiated, and so God responded!

Epilogue

In this book I have laid out an optimistic – some would say, utopian – vision for the Jewish people's relationship with God and with the world. Still, I do not make any promises that the path to the idyllic world that I present here is a straight and simple one. I am certain of God's love for the Jewish people and for the world that He created, but I am under no illusions about the difficulties that we must face as we endeavor to live lives full of holiness and love and spread those values and beliefs to the world. Even as we struggle through those setbacks and occasionally lose sight of God's love for us, the belief and knowledge that that love is always there has given the Jewish people the power to survive through the ages and the support to believe in a future reconciliation with Him, even at times when His face appears to be hidden.

Our Composer is God. Our music is our Bible and its loving-kindness. Our conductors are the Jewish people. The musicians are all of humanity. The promise of a world of peace and redemption is deeply inscribed within our eternal Torah and, indeed, the prophecy has truly begun to come to pass in our generation with our return to our homeland Israel together with the scattered exiles and a proliferation of seeking converts from Africa and South America. As of yet, the symphony is unfinished: it still awaits many more conductors and many more musicians gathering in the reestablished Davidic Temple of Jerusalem – literally City of Peace – when God's House (*Sukkat David*) will become a house of prayer for all nations, and when the streets of the world will be filled with songs of praise and joy for a universal Torah of peace and compassion. At that time, the entirety of humanity will be blessed with entry into God's covenantal marriage; at that time, the present world of being will be united with the messianic World to Come, redeemed by human love and the spirit of the Divine. Inspired by Israel and God's response to the Holocaust in our generation, what each of us must do is play our instrument as actively and lovingly as possible and prepare for a world redeemed.

Let us each attempt to play our instrument properly and lovingly.

Other works by Shlomo Riskin
available from Maggid Books

Bereshit: Confronting Life, Love & Family

Shemot: Defining a Nation

Vayikra: Sacrifice, Sanctity & Silence

Bemidbar: Trials and Tribulations in Times of Transition

Devarim: Moses Bequeaths Legacy, History and Covenant

Brushes with the Bible: The Book of Genesis

Listening to God: Inspirational Stories for My Grandchildren

Siaḥ Shulḥan (Around the Family Table)

Yad LaIsha (Women and Jewish Divorce)

Maggid Books
The best of contemporary Jewish thought from
Koren Publishers Jerusalem Ltd.